Shugo Chara!

5

PEACH-PIT

Translated by
Satsuki Yamashita

Adapted by
Nunzio DeFilippis and Christina Weir

Lettered by
North Market Street Graphics

KC
**KODANSHA
COMICS**

Shugo Chara! volume 5 is a work of fiction. Names, characters, places, and incidents are the products of the author's imagination or are used fictitiously. Any resemblance to actual events, locales, or persons, living or dead, is entirely coincidental.

A Kodansha Comics Trade Paperback Original.

Published in the United States by Kodansha Comics, an imprint of Kodansha USA Publishing, LLC., New York.

Publication rights for this English edition arranged through Kodansha Ltd., Tokyo.

First published in Japan in 2007 by Kodansha Ltd., Tokyo.

ISBN 978-1-61262-344-3

Original cover design by Akiko Omo.

Printed in the United States of America.

www.kodanshacomics.com

9 8 7 6 5 4 3

Translator: Satsuki Yamashita
Adapter: Nunzio DeFilippis and Christina Weir.
Lettering: North Market Street Graphics

Contents

Honorifics Explained

Throughout the Kodansha Comics books, you will find Japanese honorifics left intact in the translations. For those not familiar with how the Japanese use honorifics and, more important, how they differ from American honorifics, we present this brief overview.

Politeness has always been a critical facet of Japanese culture. Ever since the feudal era, when Japan was a highly stratified society, use of honorifics—which can be defined as polite speech that indicates relationship or status—has played an essential role in the Japanese language. When addressing someone in Japanese, an honorific usually takes the form of a suffix attached to one's name (example: "Asuna-san"), is used as a title at the end of one's name, or appears in place of the name itself (example: "Negi-sensei," or simply "Sensei!").

Honorifics can be expressions of respect or endearment. In the context of manga and anime, honorifics give insight into the nature of the relationship between characters. Many English translations leave out these important honorifics and therefore distort the feel of the original Japanese. Because Japanese honorifics contain nuances that English honorifics lack, it is our policy at Kodansha Comics not to translate them. Here, instead, is a guide to some of the honorifics you may encounter in Kodansha Comics books.

-san: This is the most common honorific and is equivalent to Mr., Miss, Ms., Mrs. It is the all-purpose honorific and can be used in any situation where politeness is required.

-sama: This is one level higher than "-san" and is used to confer great respect.

-dono: This comes from the word "tono," which means "lord." It is an even higher level than "-sama" and confers utmost respect.

-kun: This suffix is used at the end of boys' names to express familiarity or endearment. It is also sometimes used by men among friends, or when addressing someone younger or of a lower station.

-chan: This is used to express endearment, mostly toward girls. It is also used for little boys, pets, and even among lovers. It gives a sense of childish cuteness.

Bozu: This is an informal way to refer to a boy, similar to the English terms "kid" and "squirt."

Sempai/
Senpai: This title suggests that the addressee is one's senior in a group or organization. It is most often used in a school setting, where underclassmen refer to their upperclassmen as "sempai." It can also be used in the workplace, such as when a newer employee addresses an employee who has seniority in the company.

Kohai: This is the opposite of "sempai" and is used toward underclassmen in school or newcomers in the workplace. It connotes that the addressee is of a lower station.

Sensei: Literally meaning "one who has come before," this title is used for teachers, doctors, or masters of any profession or art.

-[blank]:   This is usually forgotten in these lists, but it is perhaps the most significant difference between Japanese and English. The lack of honorific means that the speaker has permission to address the person in a very intimate way. Usually, only family, spouses, or very close friends have this kind of permission. Known as *yobisute,* it can be gratifying when someone who has earned the intimacy starts to call one by one's name without an honorific. But when that intimacy hasn't been earned, it can be very insulting.

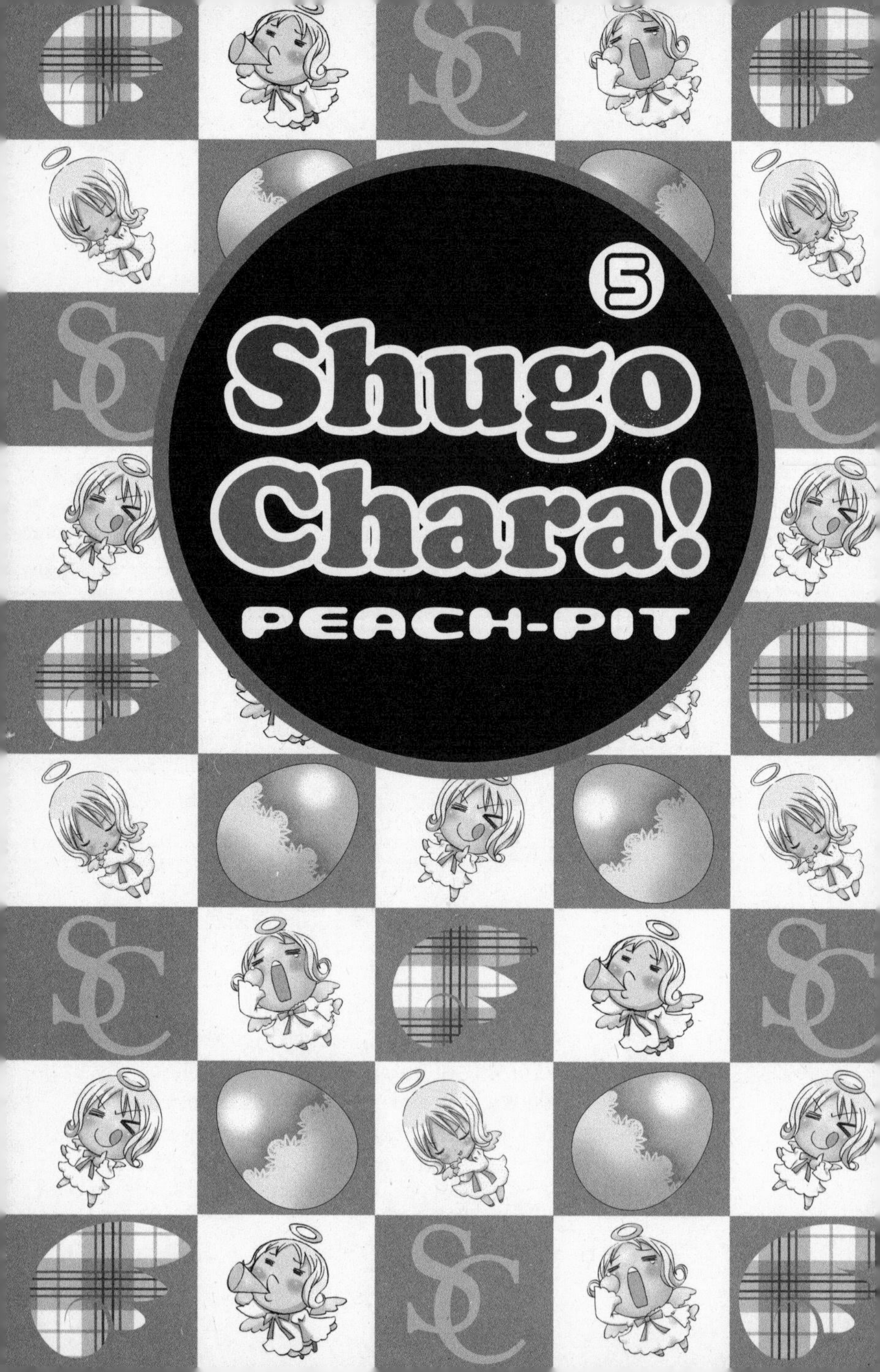
5
Shugo Chara!
PEACH-PIT

Character Introductions

Shugo Chara!

Ran
The first Guardian Character to be born. She is very athletic.

Miki
A Guardian Character with artistic abilities. She has a levelheaded personality.

Su
The third Guardian Character to be born. She loves to cook.

Diamond
The fourth Guardian Character to be born. She had an X on her.

El
Utau's Guardian Character. She's staying with Amu for the time being.

Amu Hinamori
A 6th grader at Seiyo Academy. She worries that the personality everybody sees does not match her true character. One day she found three eggs, and afterward, she was selected to be the Joker of the Seiyo Academy Guardians.

Kiseki
Tadase's Guardian Character.

Yoru
Ikuto's Guardian Character.

Tadase Hotori
He holds the King Chair among the Guardians. Amu has a crush on him. The students call him Prince.

Ikuto Tsukiyomi
He seems to be involved with the Easter Corporation, a company looking for an egg called the Embryo.

Musashi
Kairi's Guardian Character.

Pepe
Yaya's Guardian Character.

Kusukusu
Rima's Guardian Character.

Yaya Yuiki
The Ace Chair of the Guardians. She's a little immature for a fifth grader.

Kairi Sanjo
The new Jack Chair of the Guardians. This fourth grader is cool and intellectual, and he's also Sanjo-san's little brother!

Rima Mashiro
The new Queen Chair of the Guardians. A sixth grader, she's cute but a little devious.

Yukari Sanjo
Utau's manager. She's an Easter Corporation employee and she is after the Embryo.

Utau Hoshina
A pop singer and idol. She's Ikuto's little sister. She may be being used by the Easter Corporation.

II
Utau's Guardian Character.

The Story So Far

● Everyone thinks Amu is the coolest. But that's not who she really is: Deep inside, she's shy and a little cynical. One day, she wished she could be more true to herself, and the next day she found three eggs in her bed!

● Ran, Miki, and Su hatched from the eggs. As Amu's "Guardian Characters," they claim to be Amu's "true selves." When Amu undergoes a "Character Change" with them, she can become good at sports, art, or cooking! Soon after they hatched, Amu found herself recruited to become one of the Guardians of Seiyo Academy. Ever since, she's become good friends with the other students who have Guardian Characters, including the boy she has a crush on, Tadase-kun. But in the spring, Kukai graduated and Nadeshiko went abroad to study.

● Rima and Kairi replaced them, but they're both a little weird. And to make things worse, Amu's fourth Guardian Egg has a mysterious X on it!!

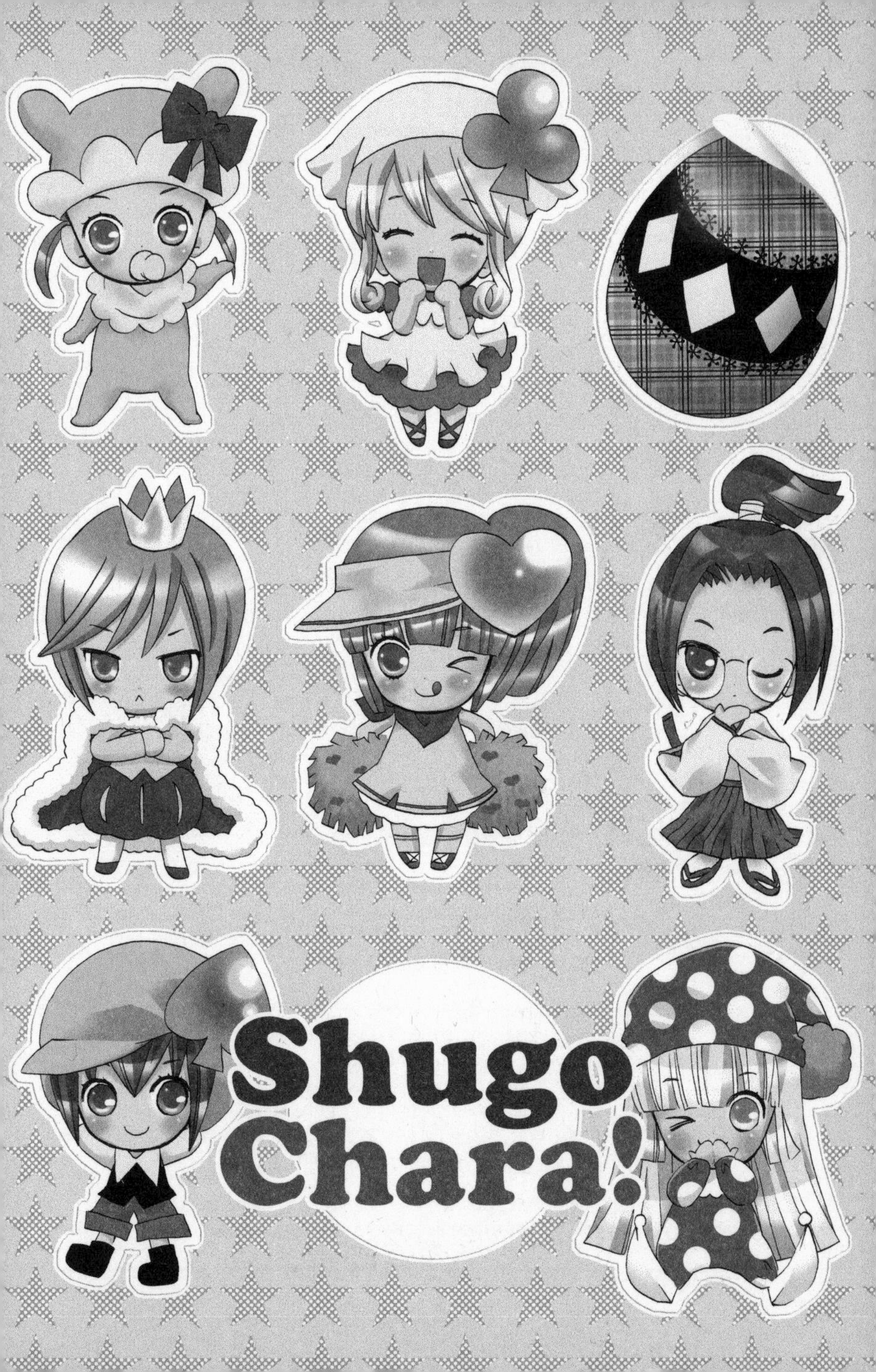
Shugo
Chara!

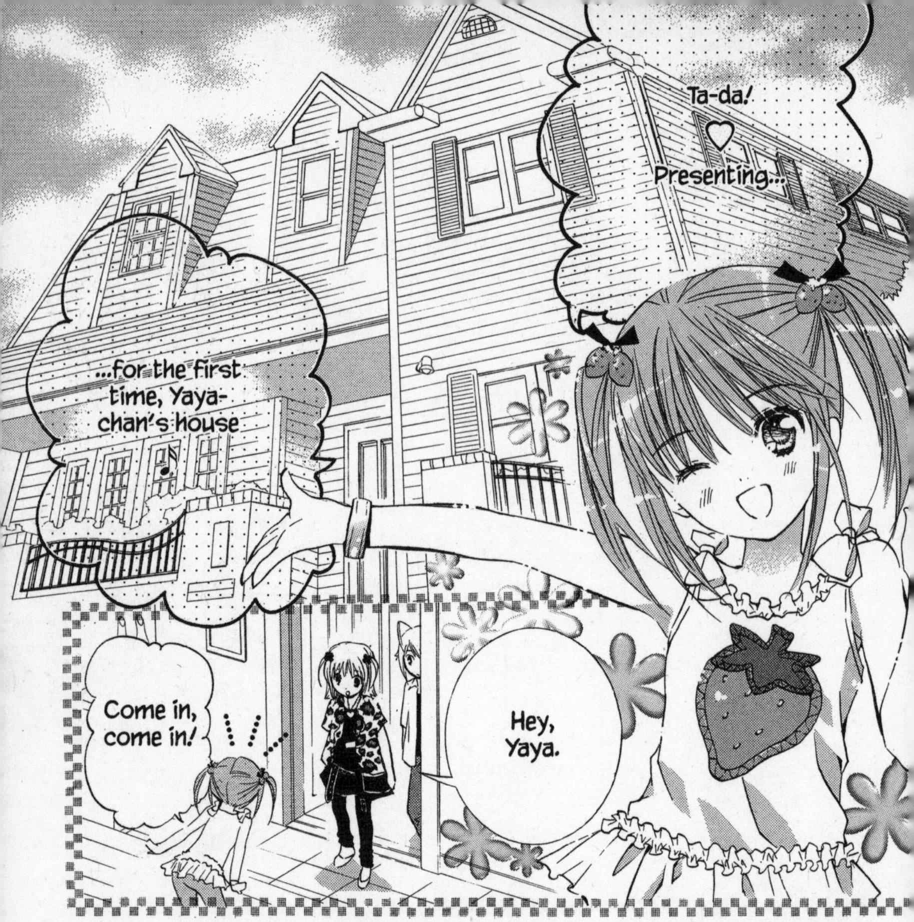
Ta-da! ♡ Presenting...
...for the first time, Yaya-chan's house
Hey, Yaya.
Come in, come in!

Hello! It's Shibuko Ebara of PEACH-PIT ♡ Thanks to all the readers, *Shugo Chara!* has reached its fifth volume! Woo hoo! Clap, clap! And even better, the anime for *Shugo Chara!* has premiered, too ♡ I look forward to it every week ♪ I hope everyone else does, too! So let's go on to the Q&A!

Q1: Did you ever want to grow up to be anything else besides manga artists?

A1: Let's see... I wanted to be an elementary school teacher, and Sendo wanted to work at a corporation! Maybe we can Character Change... (laugh)

character profile

Rima Mashiro

Birthday: 2/6
Blood Type: B
Sign: Aquarius
Guardian Character:
    Kusukusu

Babies are so lucky.

They're just cute. They can't eat or go to the bathroom on their own.

But they can still hog Mom and Dad.

Really?

It's not that great.

Sigh... I wanted to be an only child.

SMACK

Is that why her Guardian Character is a baby? Is that who she wants to be?

Tsubasa-kun wants something.

What?

Oh. Mashiro-san is an only child.

Joker! Joker!

No, it's not. I think...

UGG

Could it be his diapers?

There's hot water in the pot.

No, it has to be boiled and then cooled.

GASP

Let's go boil some water.

Oops, I forgot to give him milk!

He's hungry.

Did you disinfect the bottle?

Huh?

Huh?

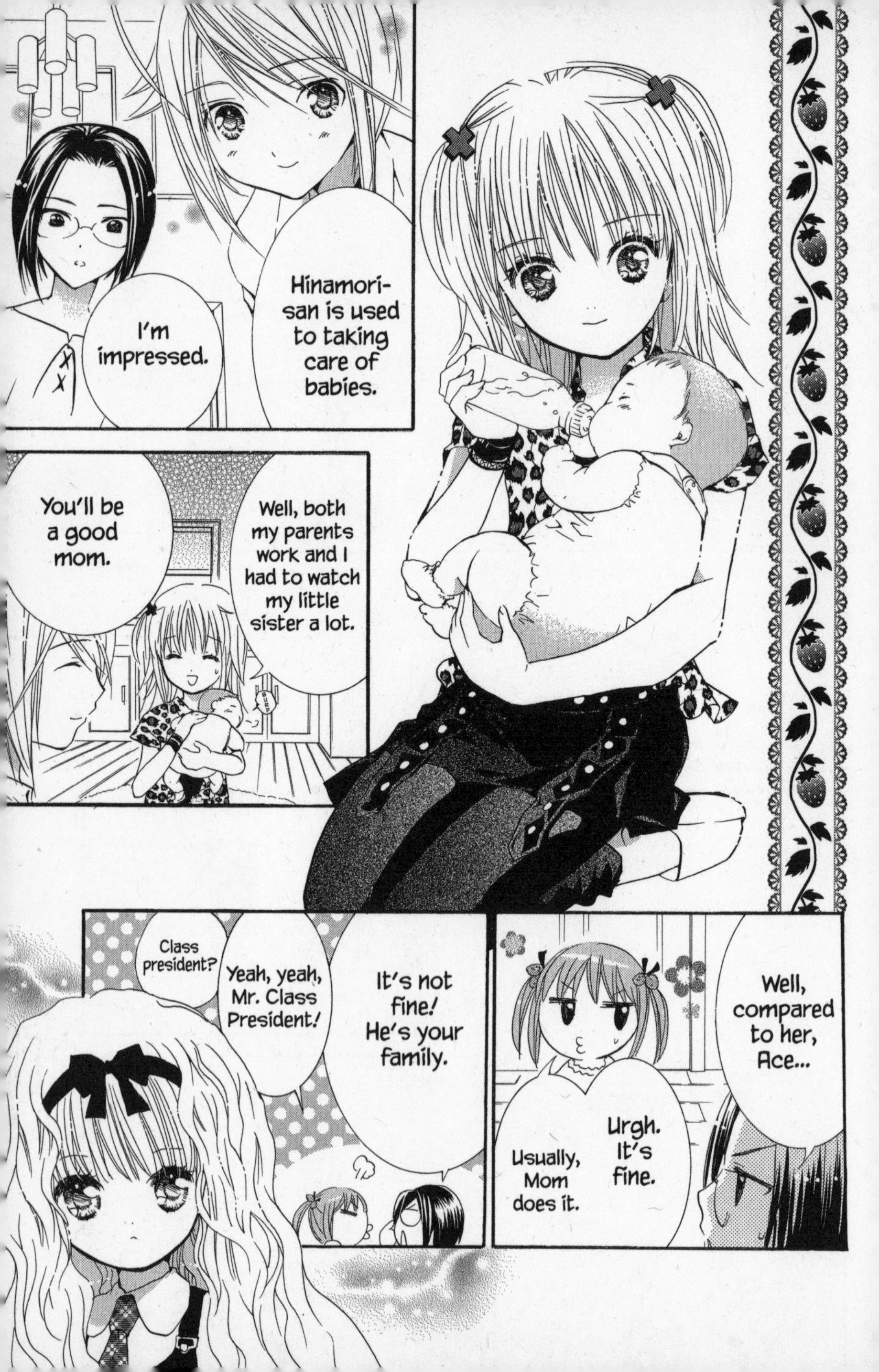
Hinamori-san is used to taking care of babies.
I'm impressed.
Well, both my parents work and I had to watch my little sister a lot.
BURP
You'll be a good mom.
Well, compared to her, Ace...
Urgh. It's fine.
Usually, Mom does it.
It's not fine! He's your family.
Yeah, yeah, Mr. Class President!
Class president?

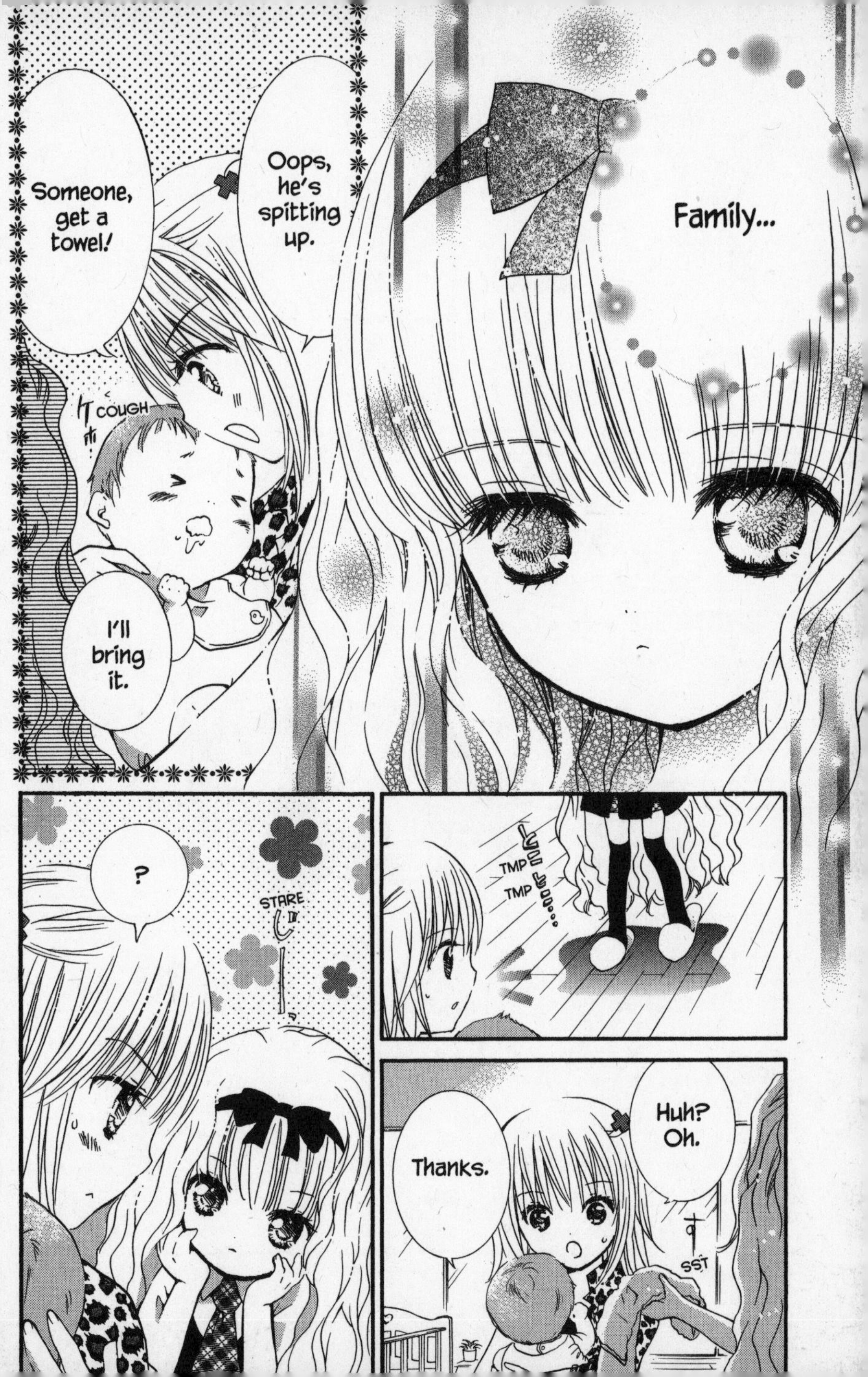
Family...
Oops, he's spitting up.
Someone, get a towel!
COUGH
I'll bring it.
TMP
TMP
Huh? Oh.
Thanks.
SST
?
STARE

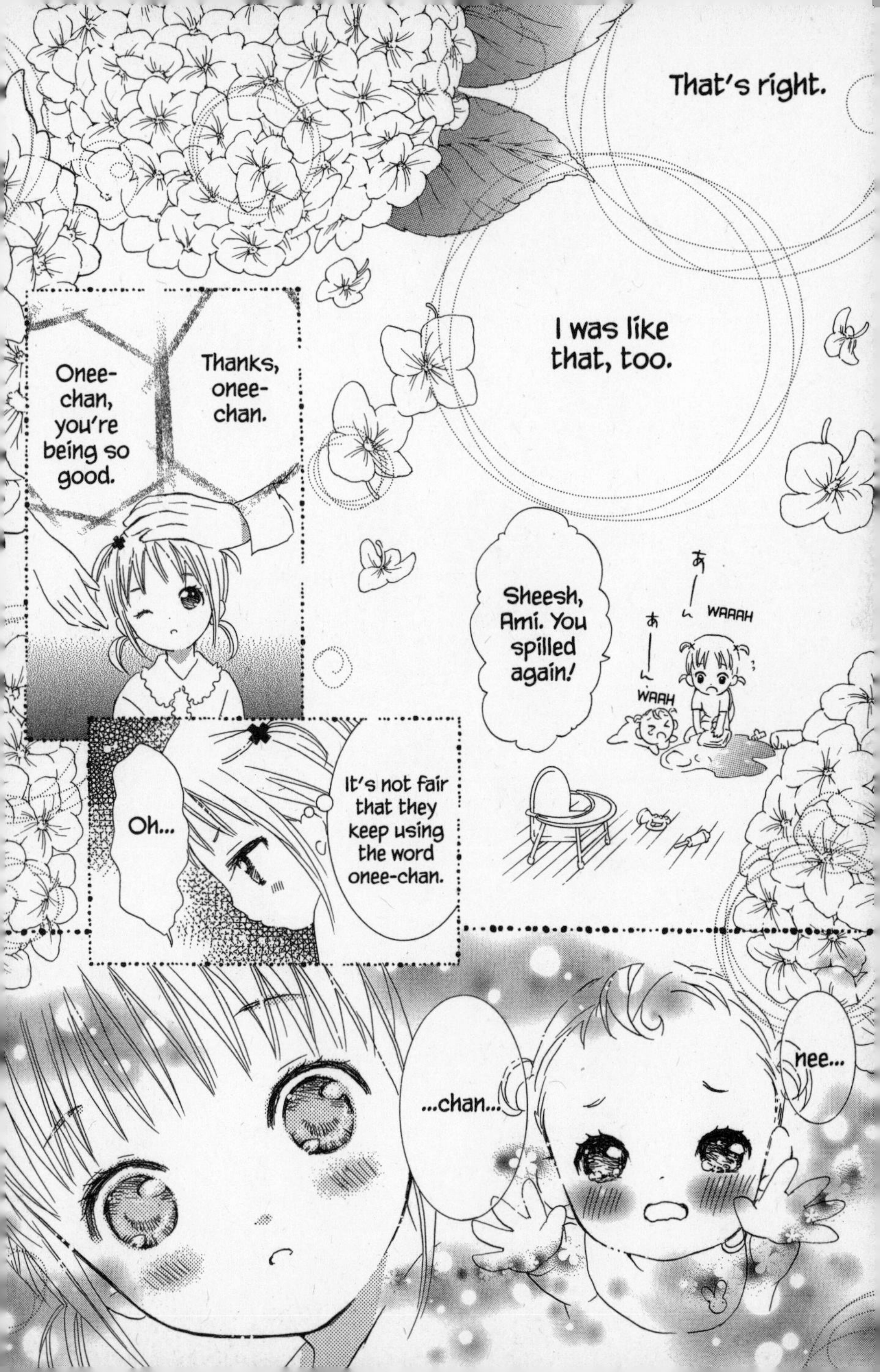
That's right.
I was like that, too.
Sheesh, Ami. You spilled again!
あーん WAAAH
あーん WAAH
Thanks, onee-chan.
Onee-chan, you're being so good.
It's not fair that they keep using the word onee-chan.
Oh...
nee...
...chan...

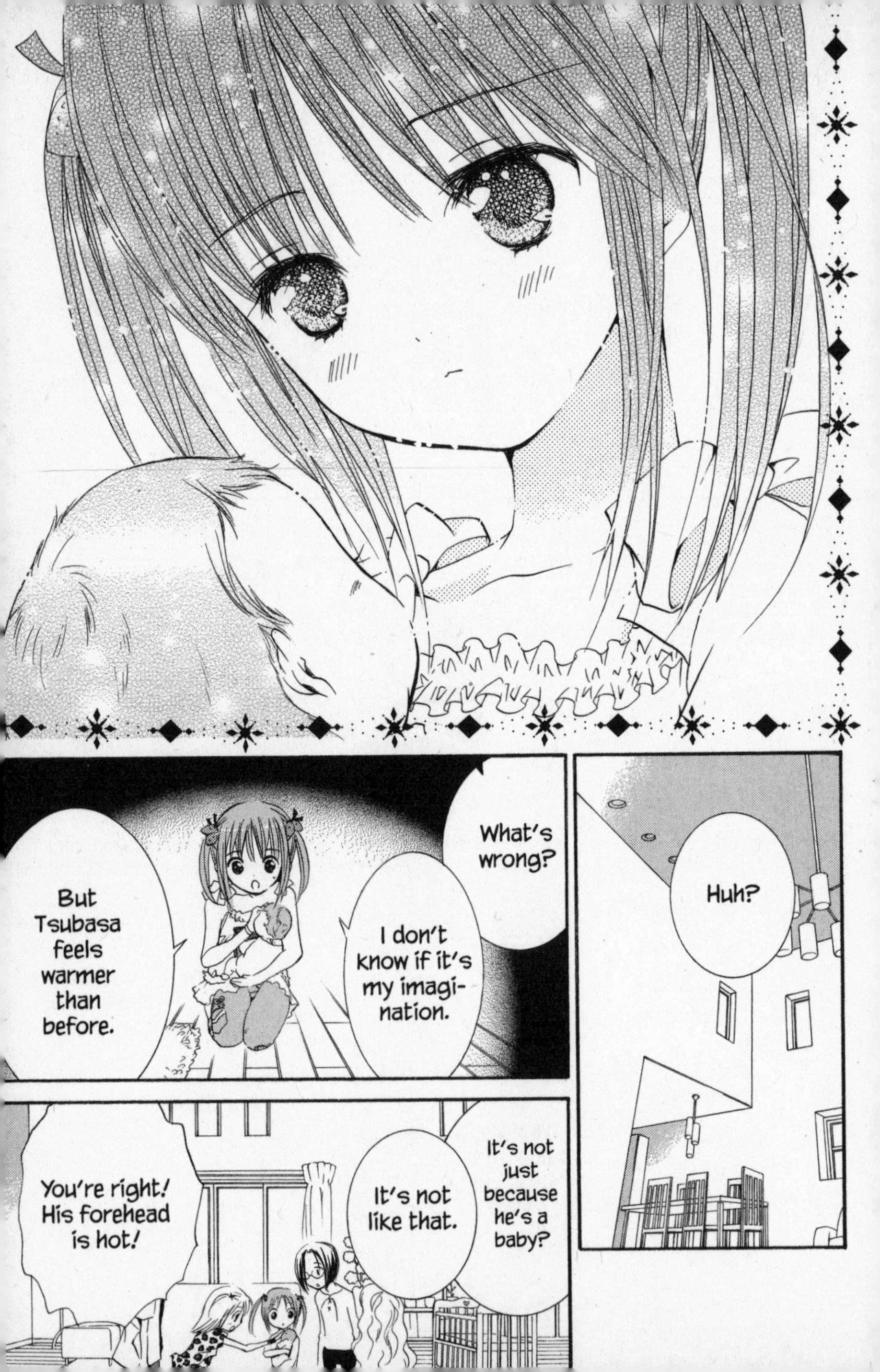
Huh?
What's wrong?
I don't know if it's my imagination.
But Tsubasa feels warmer than before.
It's not just because he's a baby?
It's not like that.
You're right! His forehead is hot!

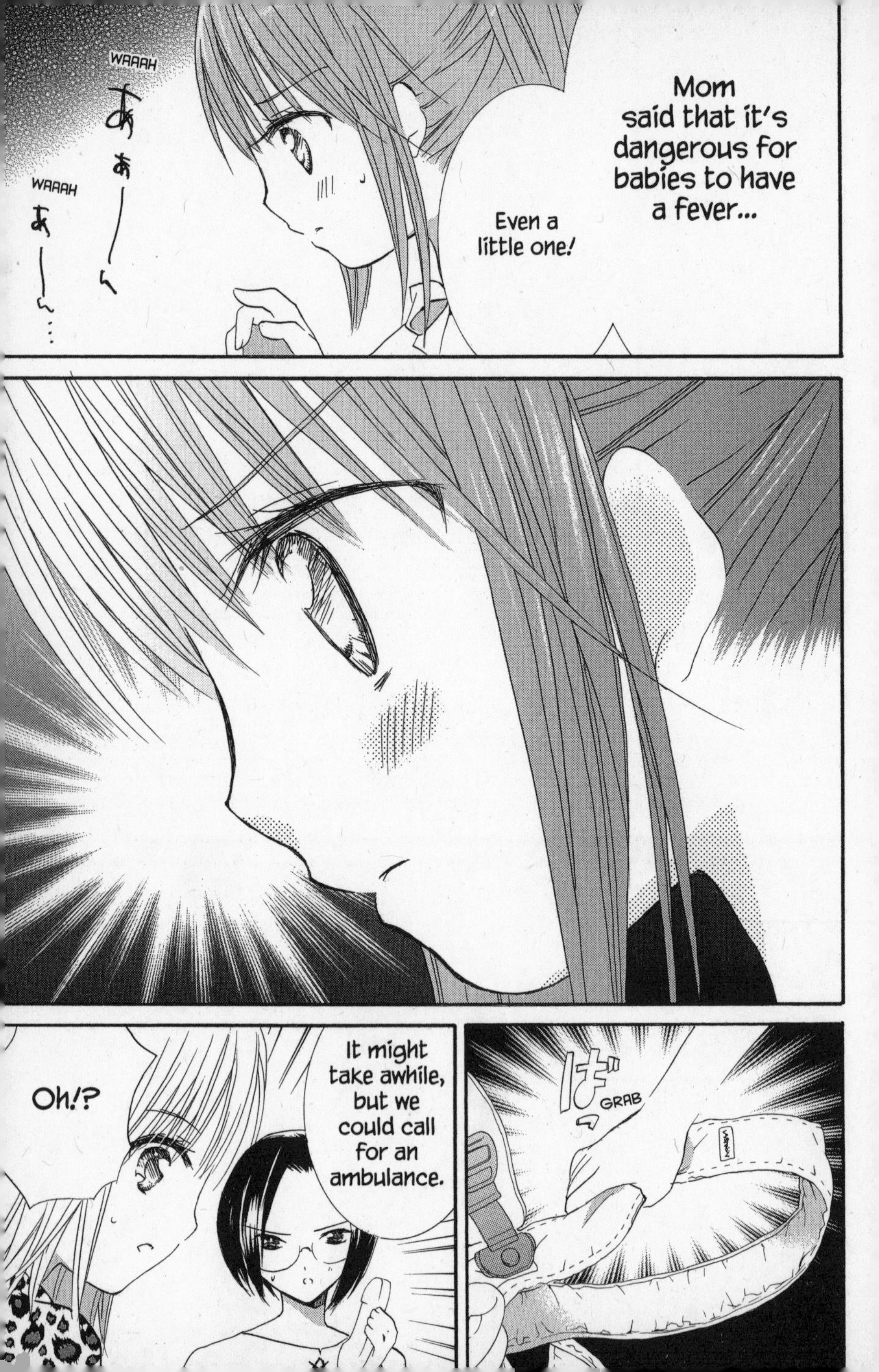
Mom said that it's dangerous for babies to have a fever...
Even a little one!
WAAAH
あぁーん
WAAAH
あーん…
ばっ
GRAB
It might take awhile, but we could call for an ambulance.
Oh!?

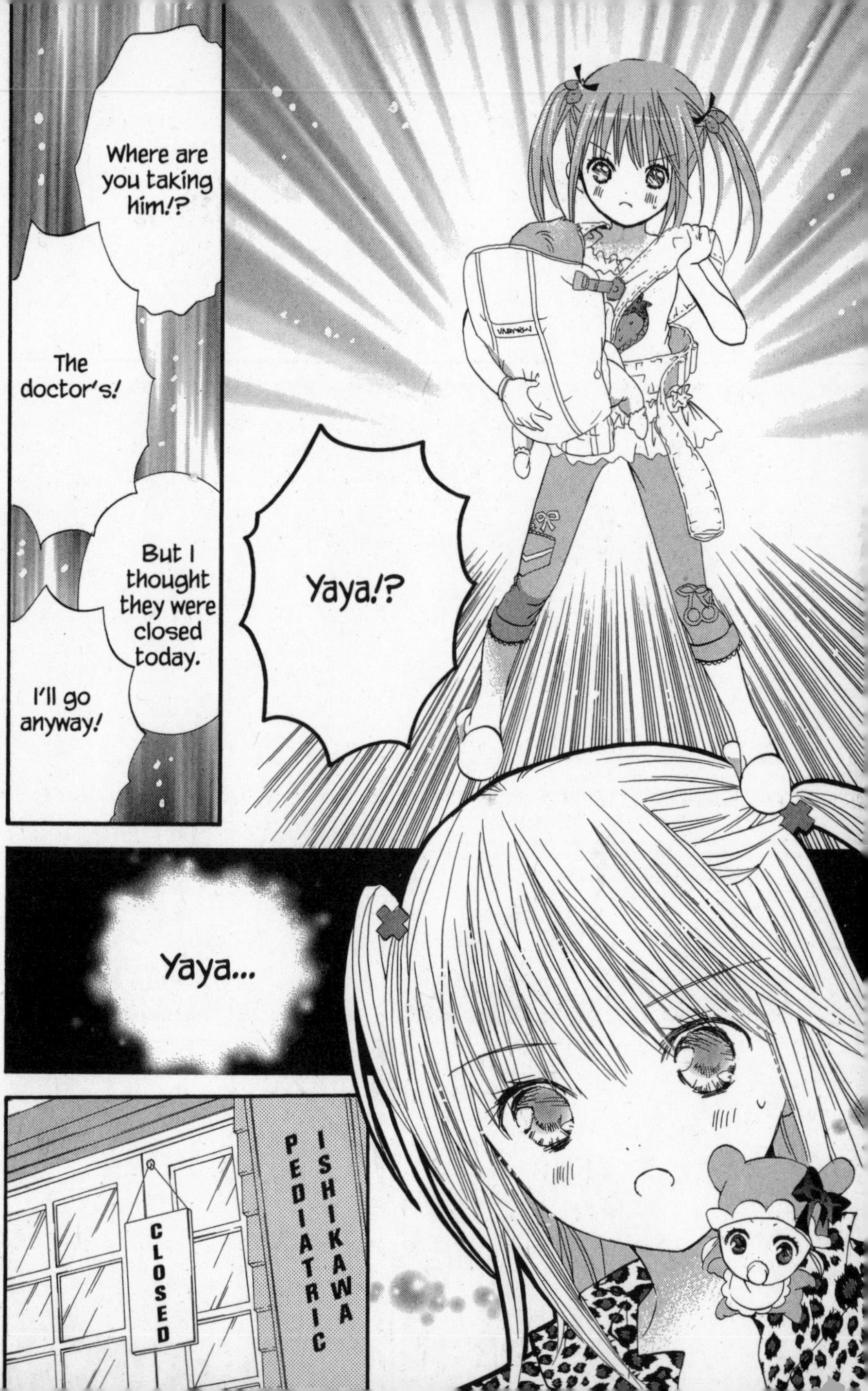
Yaya!?
Where are you taking him!?
The doctor's!
But I thought they were closed today.
I'll go anyway!
Yaya...
ISHIKAWA PEDIATRIC
CLOSED

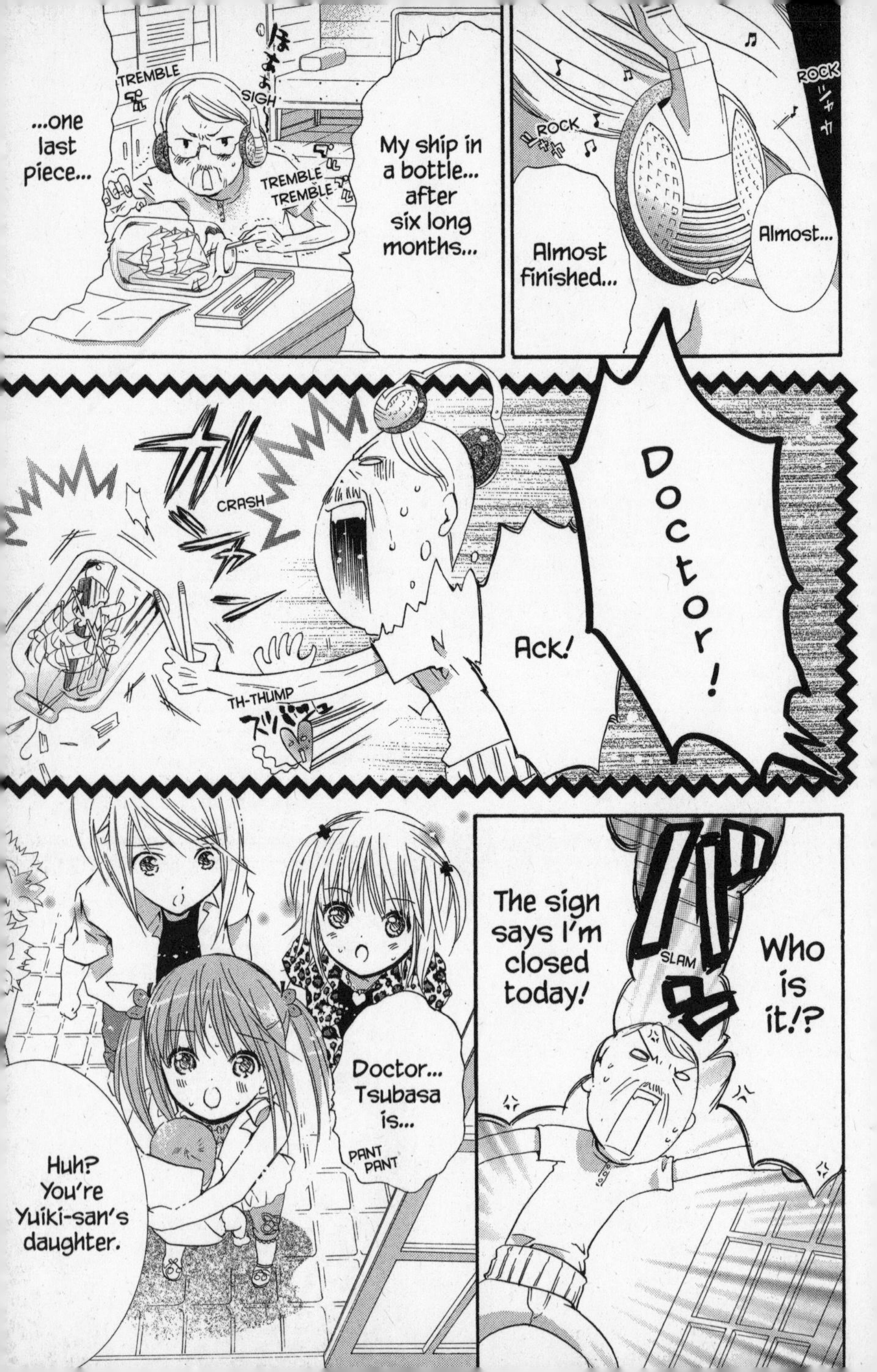
ROCK
Almost...
ROCK
Almost finished...
My ship in a bottle... after six long months...
SIGH
TREMBLE
TREMBLE TREMBLE
...one last piece...
Doctor!
Ack!
CRASH
TH-THUMP
Who is it!?
SLAM
The sign says I'm closed today!
Doctor... Tsubasa is...
PANT PANT
Huh? You're Yuiki-san's daughter.

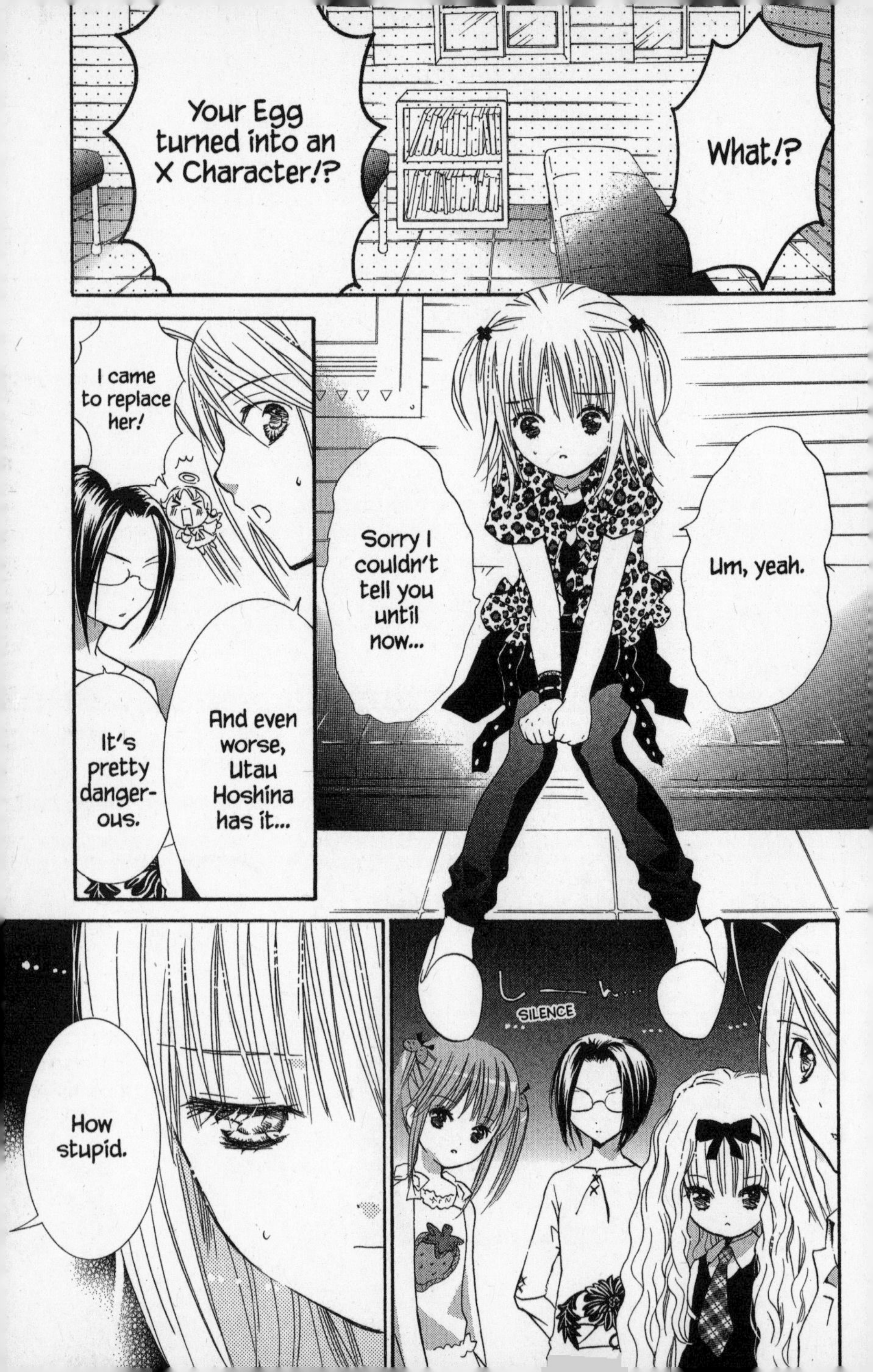

What!?
Your Egg turned into an X Character!?
Um, yeah.
Sorry I couldn't tell you until now...
I came to replace her!
And even worse, Utau Hoshina has it...
It's pretty danger-ous.
SILENCE
How stupid.

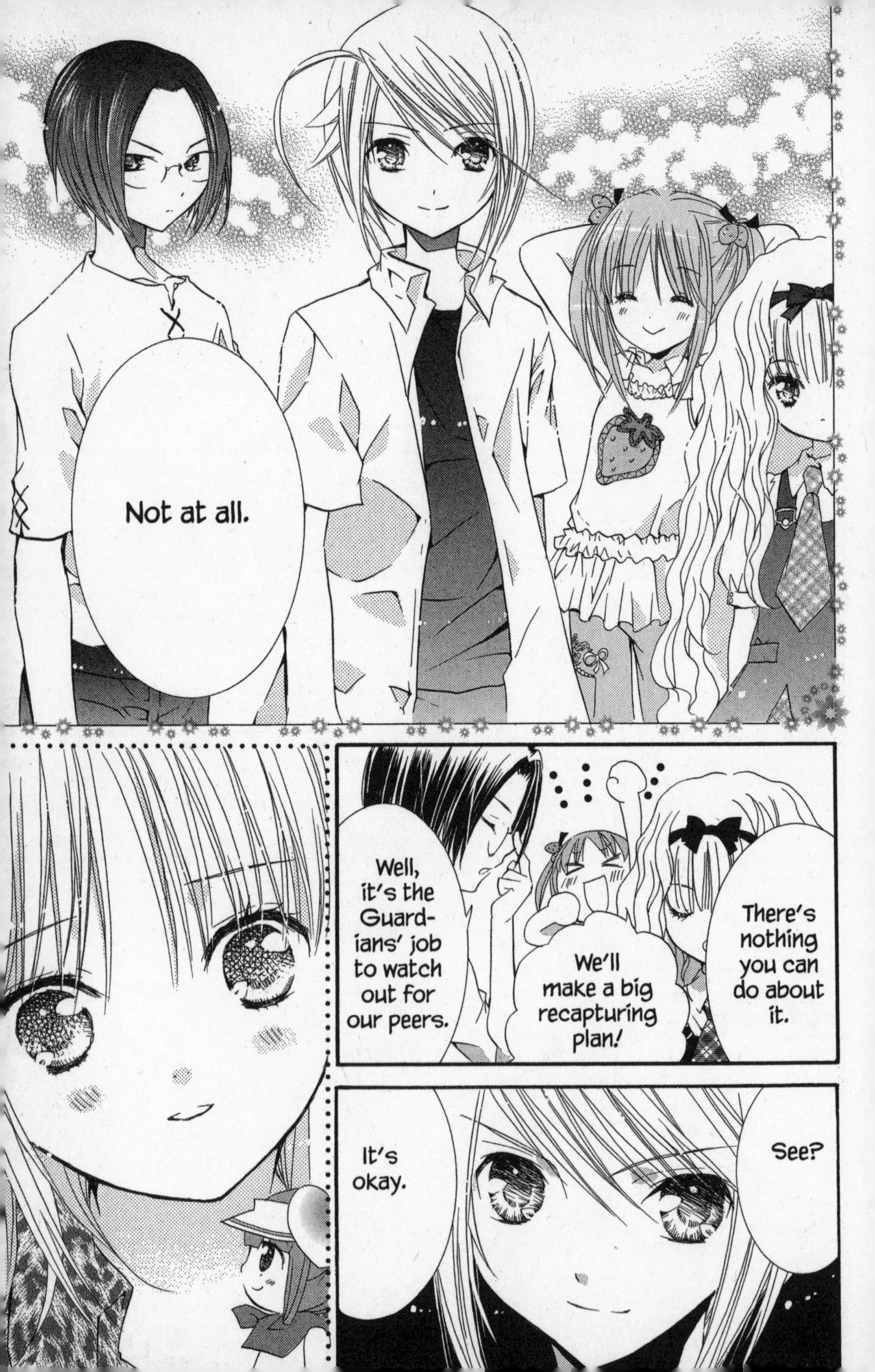
Not at all.
There's nothing you can do about it.
We'll make a big recapturing plan!
Well, it's the Guardians' job to watch out for our peers.
See?
It's okay.

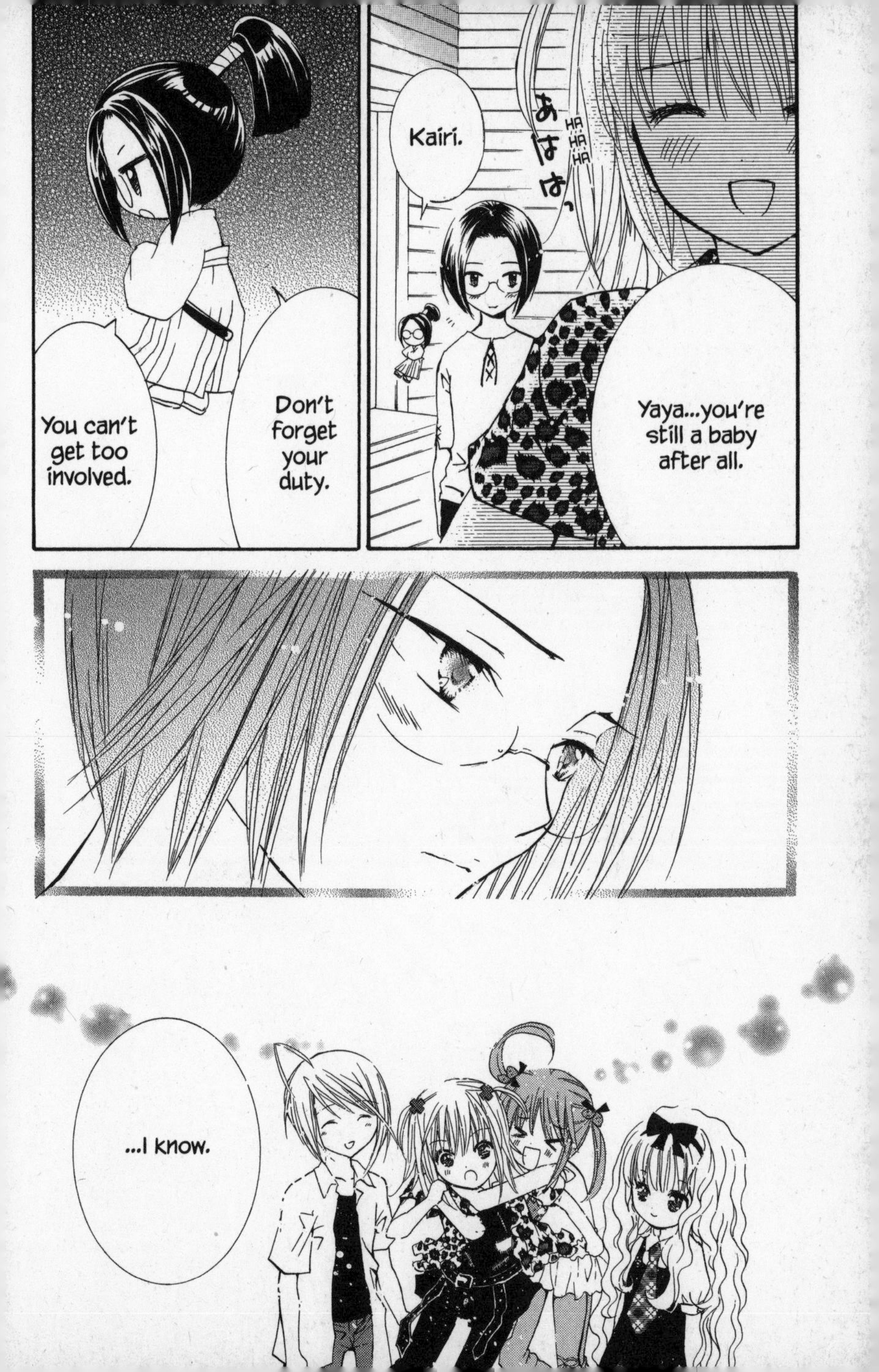
あはは
HA HA HA
Yaya...you're still a baby after all.
Kairi.
Don't forget your duty.
You can't get too involved.
...I know.

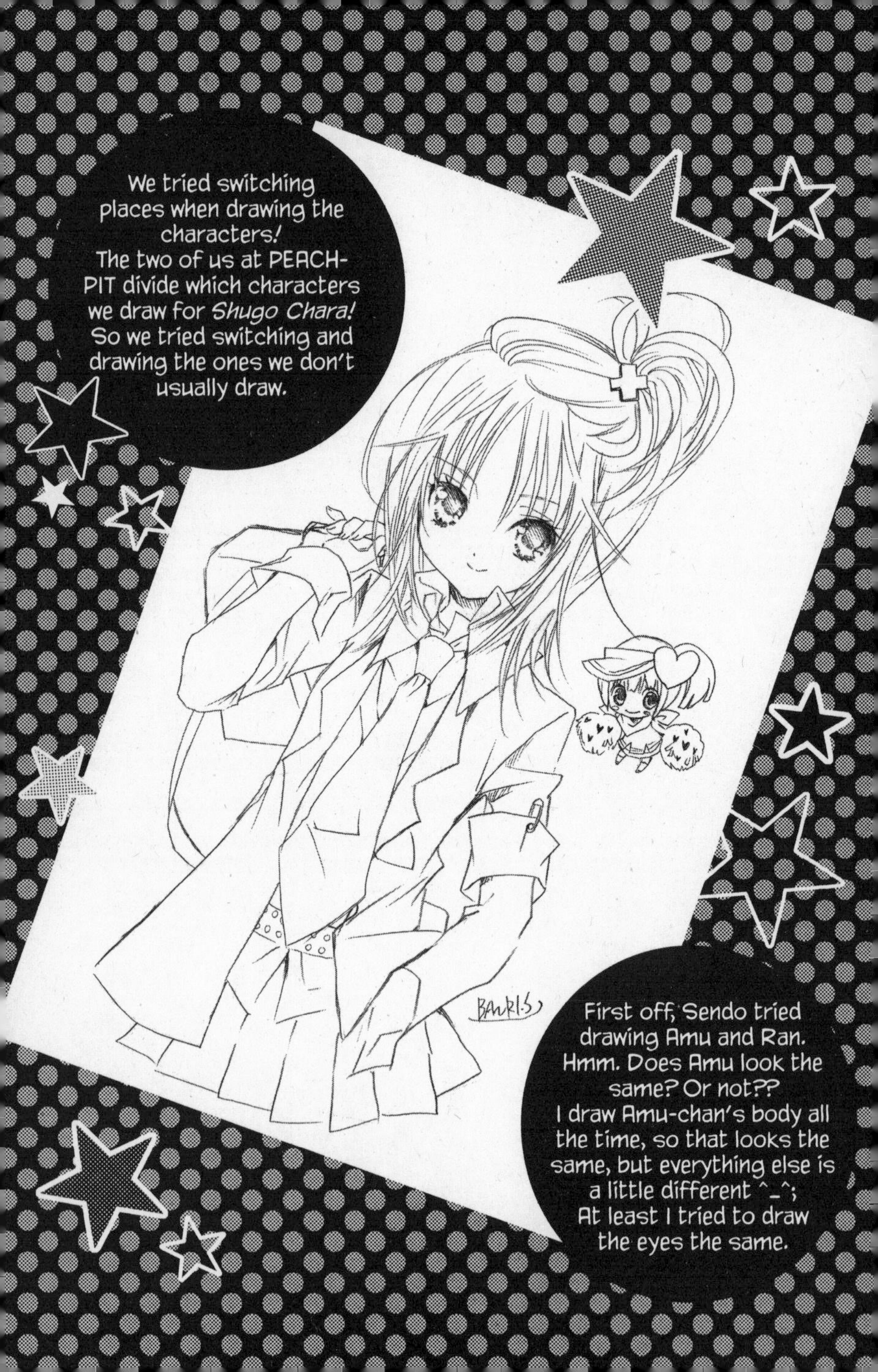
We tried switching places when drawing the characters! The two of us at PEACH-PIT divide which characters we draw for *Shugo Chara!* So we tried switching and drawing the ones we don't usually draw.
First off, Sendo tried drawing Amu and Ran. Hmm. Does Amu look the same? Or not?? I draw Amu-chan's body all the time, so that looks the same, but everything else is a little different ^_^; At least I tried to draw the eyes the same.

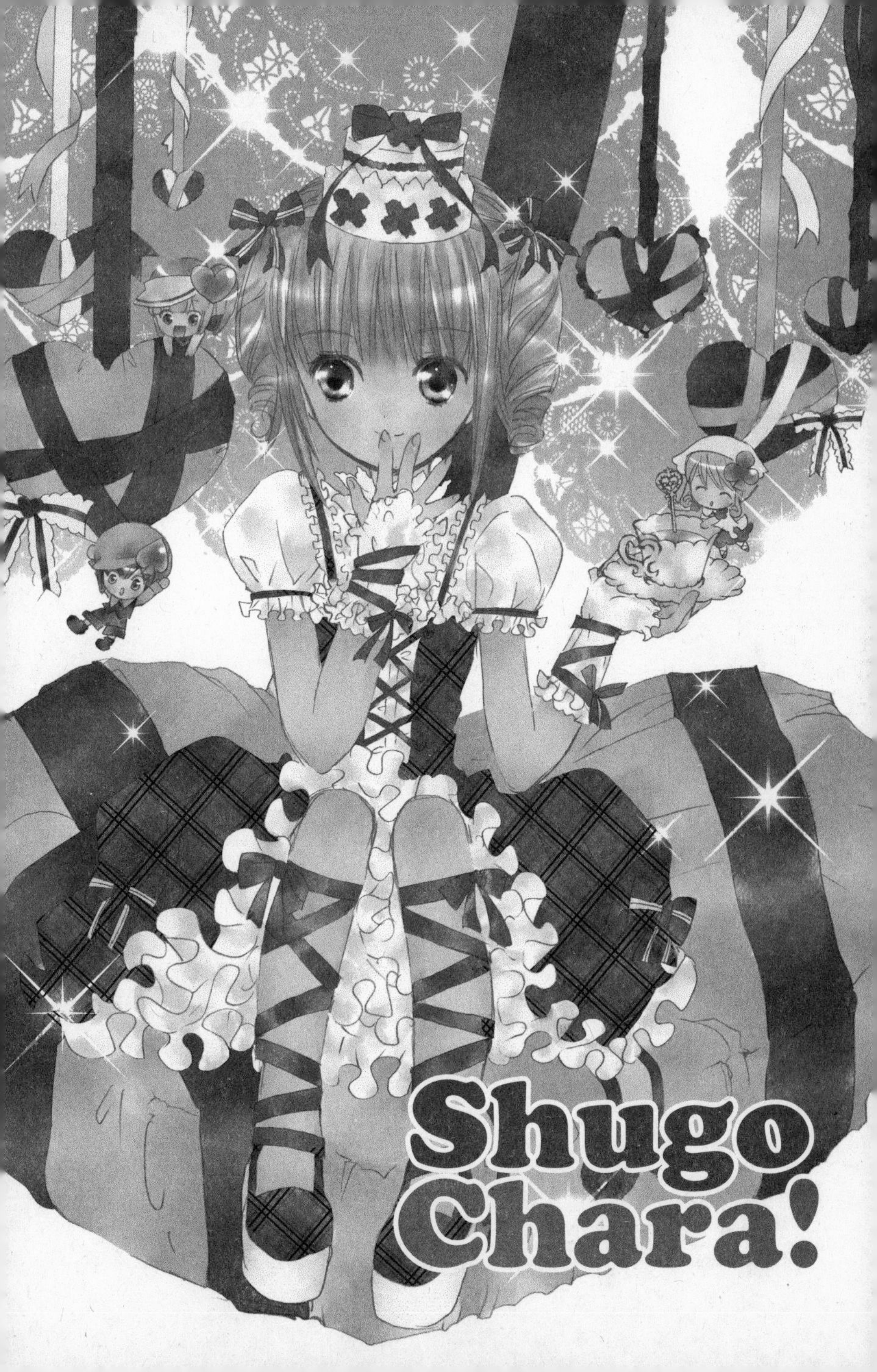
Shugo
Chara!

Okay, we've chosen which flowers to plant in the garden, so that's it for today.

And there's no Guardian business for tomorrow.

Thanks, everyone.

Hee hee hee.

CREAK

Q2: Can I call you "Pitocchi"?

A2: Go ahead ♡ We also got other unique nicknames such as "Pitton" and "Pipicchi" in the mail! You can call us whatever you want! Even "Piccolo"!

Q3: Aren't Ran, Su, and Miki the names of the members of an idol group from a long time ago?

A3: Oh, we're amazed you knew that! You're right ♡ They're a pop idol group called "Candies." But they're not idols from our generation—they're from our mothers' generation. We saw some old footage of them, and their names were so cute, we used them ♡ Can you guess what the fourth name is?

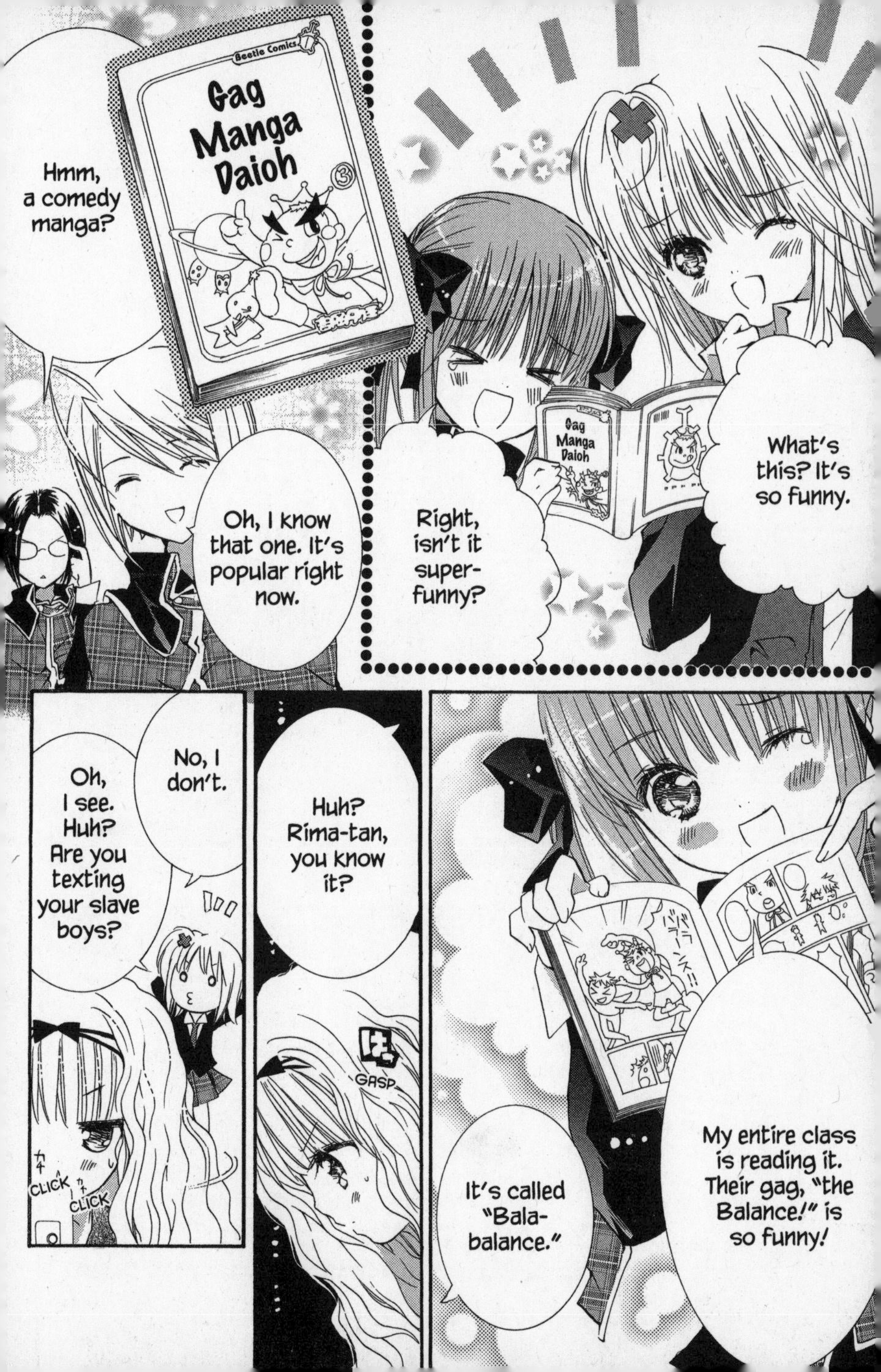
What's this? It's so funny.
Right, isn't it super-funny?
Gag Manga Daioh
Beetle Comics
Gag Manga Daioh
Hmm, a comedy manga?
Oh, I know that one. It's popular right now.
My entire class is reading it. Their gag, "the Balance!" is so funny!
It's called "Bala-balance."
Huh? Rima-tan, you know it?
は、
GASP
No, I don't.
Oh, I see. Huh? Are you texting your slave boys?
CLICK
CLICK

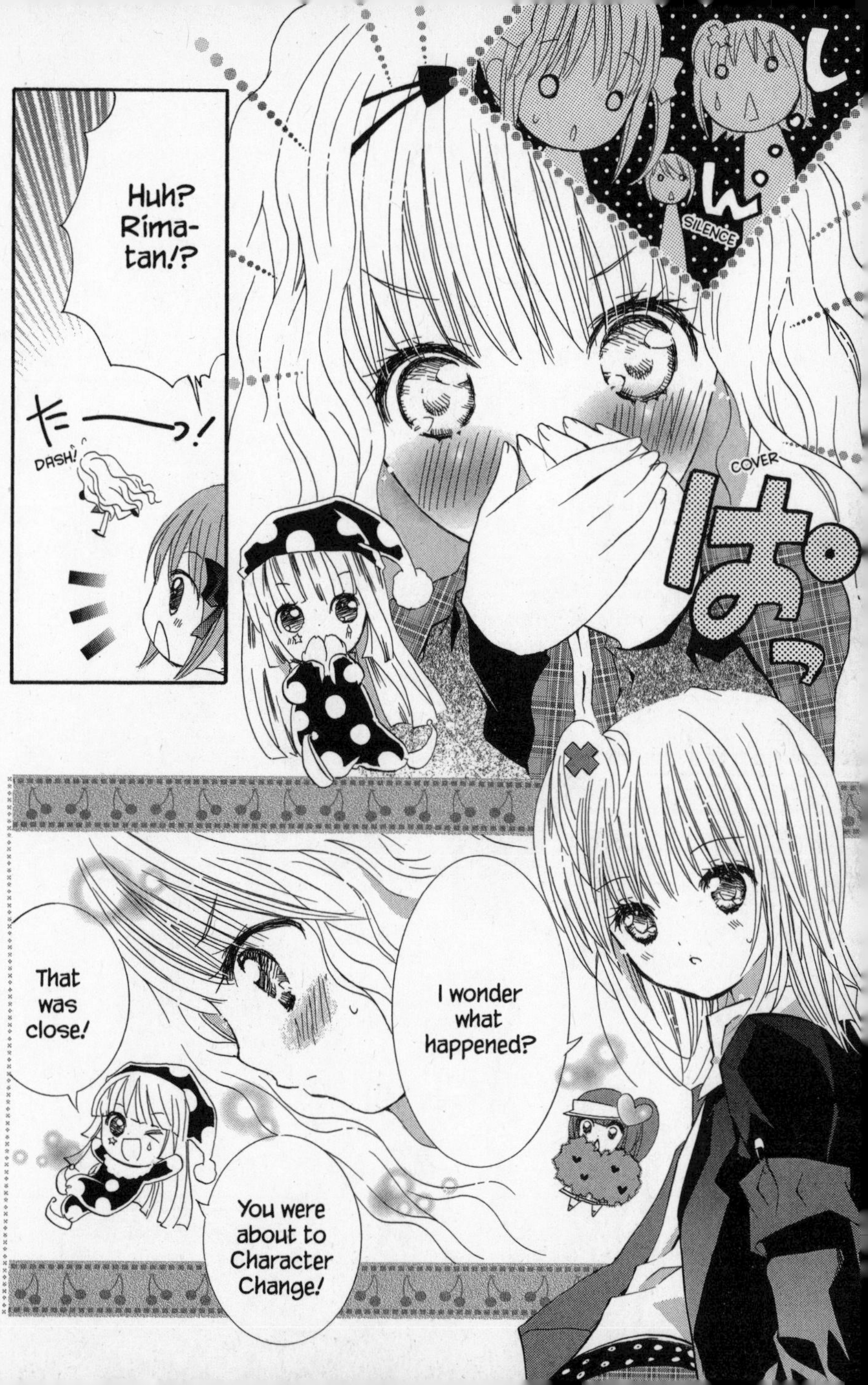
しーん
SILENCE
ぱっ
COVER
Huh? Rima-tan!?
だーっ!
DASH!
I wonder what happened?
You were about to Character Change!
That was close!

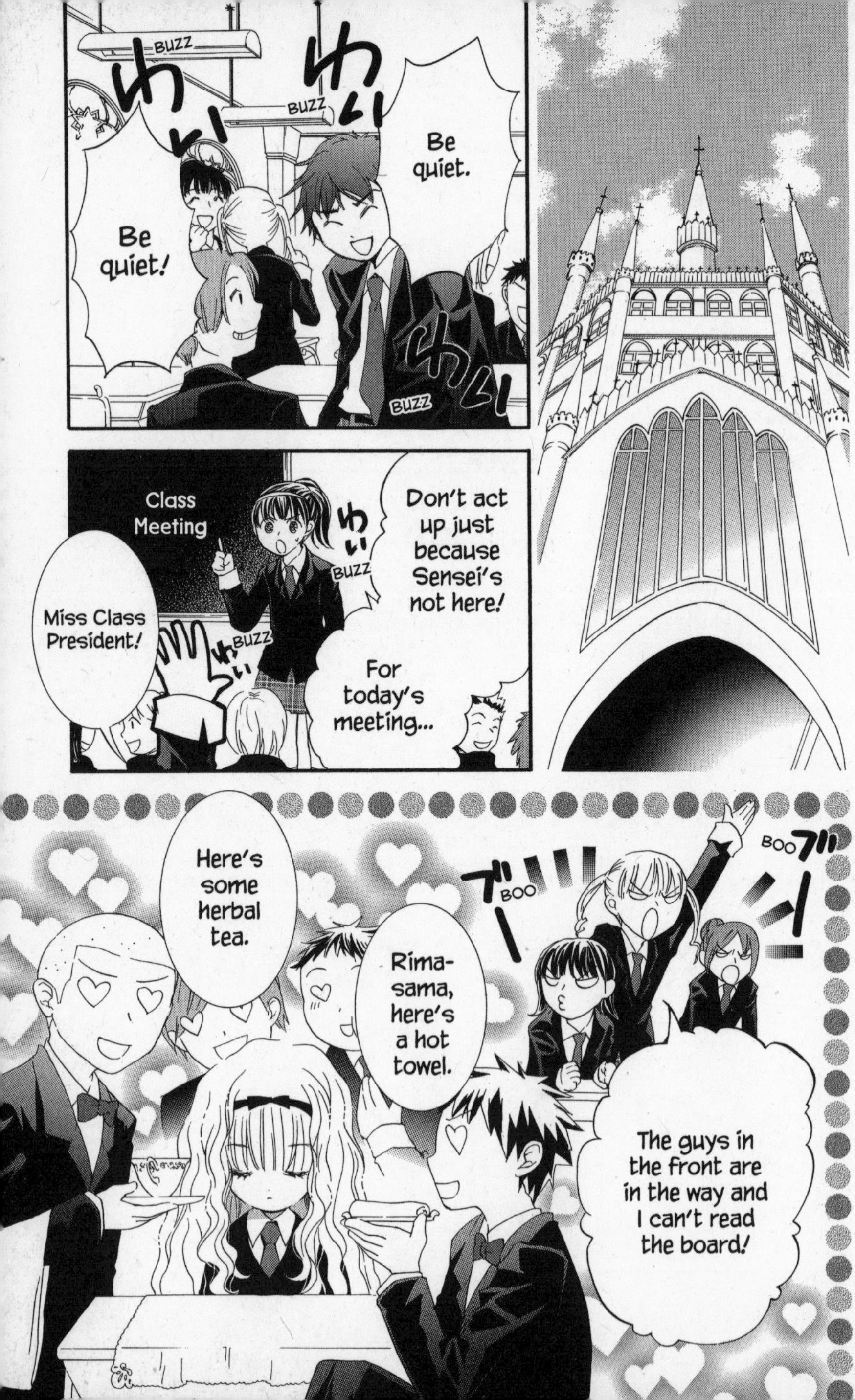
BUZZ
わい
BUZZ
わい
Be quiet.
Be quiet!
わい
BUZZ
Don't act up just because Sensei's not here!
わい
BUZZ
For today's meeting...
Class Meeting
わい
BUZZ
Miss Class President!
ブー
BOO
ブー
BOO
The guys in the front are in the way and I can't read the board!
Rima-sama, here's a hot towel.
Here's some herbal tea.

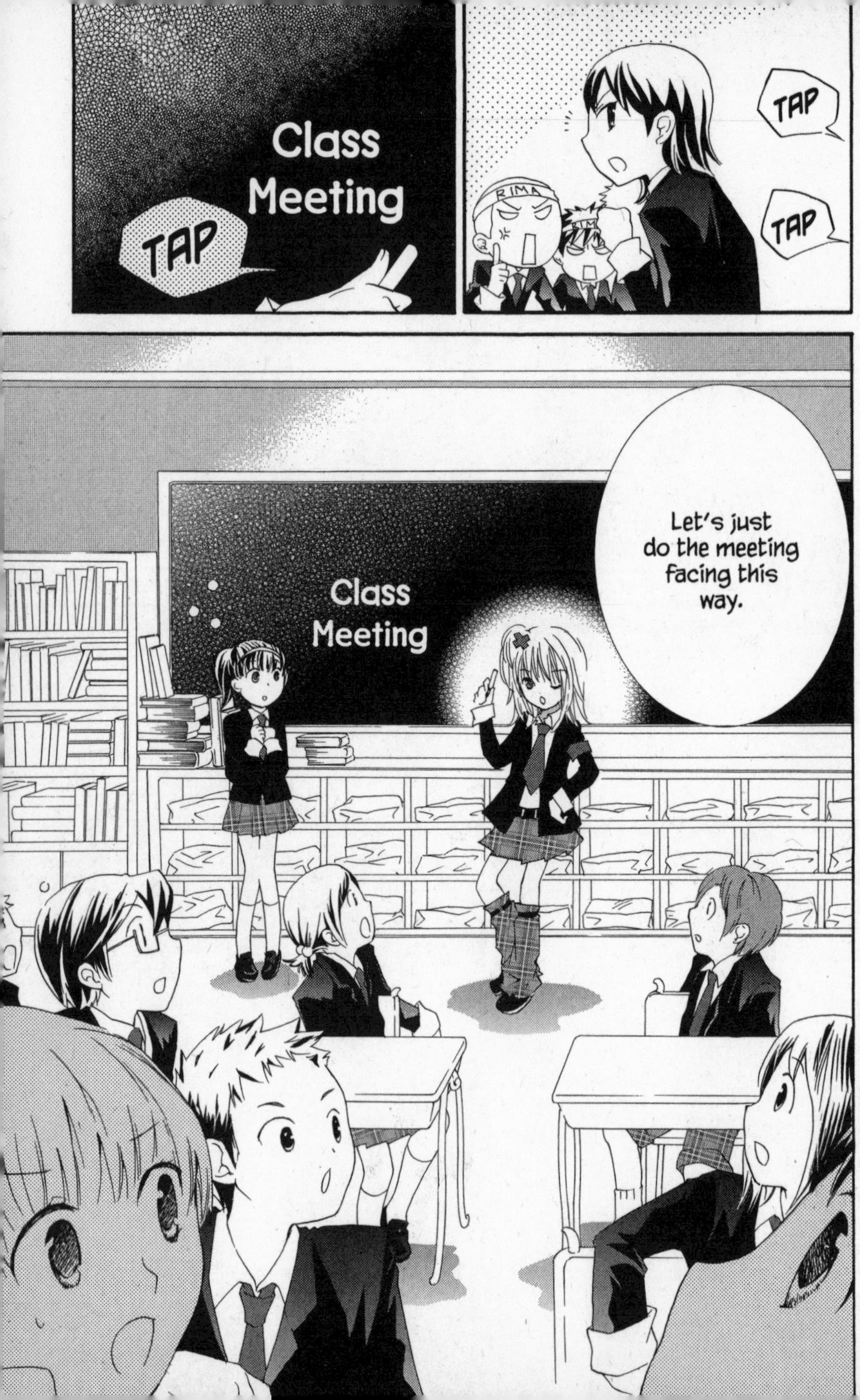
TAP
TAP
RIMA
Class
Meeting
TAP
Let's just
do the meeting
facing this
way.
Class
Meeting

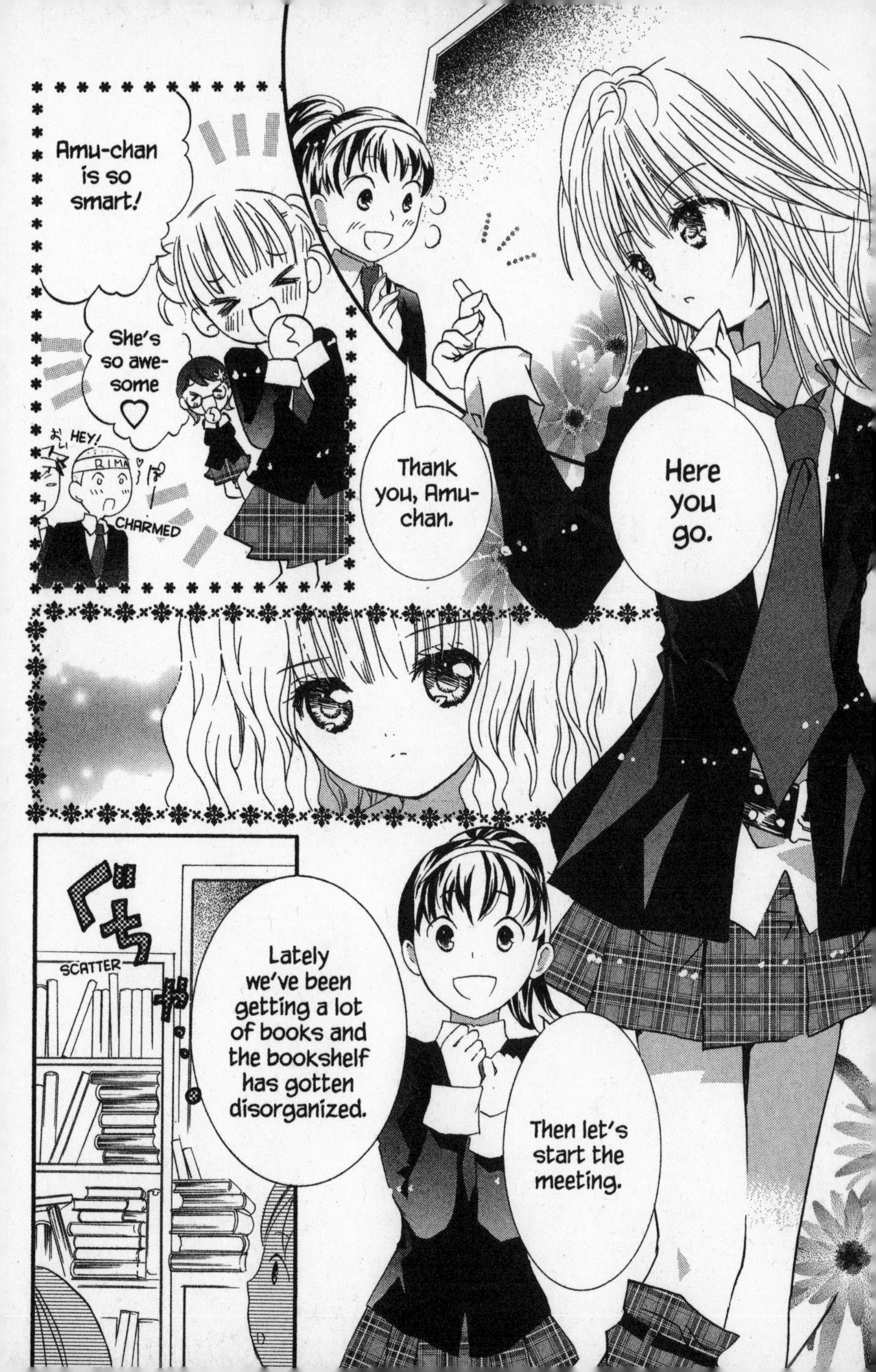
Here you go.
Thank you, Amu-chan.
Amu-chan is so smart!
She's so awe-some ♥
HEY!
RIMA
CHARMED
Then let's start the meeting.
Lately we've been getting a lot of books and the bookshelf has gotten disorganized.
SCATTER

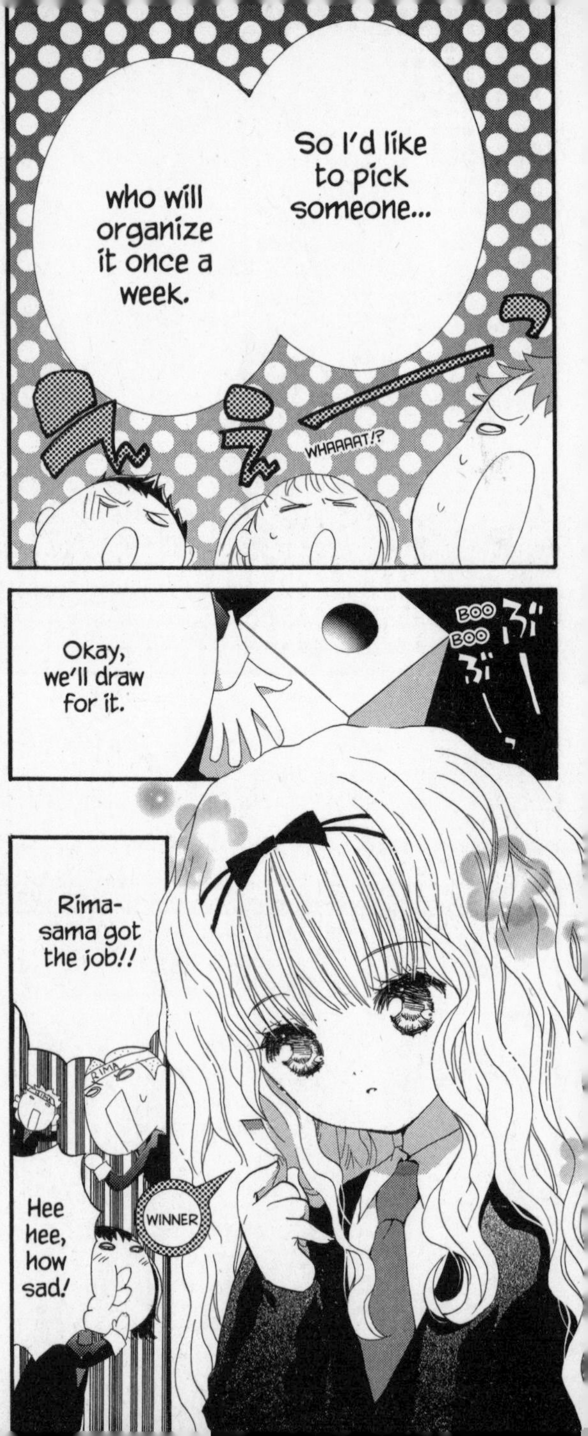
So I'd like to pick someone...
who will organize it once a week.
WHAAAAT!?
BOO
BOO
Okay, we'll draw for it.
Rima-sama got the job!!
RIMA
WINNER
Hee hee, how sad!

character profile

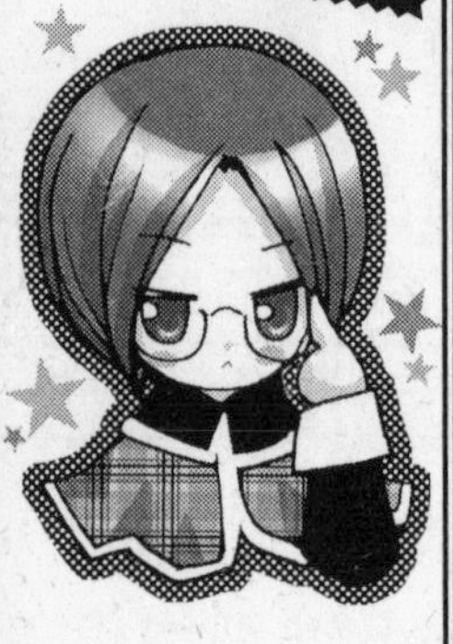

Kairi Sanjo

Birthday: 6/12
Blood Type: A
Sign: Gemini
Guardian Character: Musashi

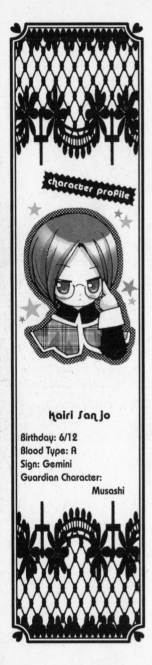

You don't have Guardian activities today, right? You should be able to do it.

The class has decided, so you better do it!

...can't stay that late after school.

But I...

She looks worried.

I would help, but my club is meeting.

Well, good luck, Mashiro-san.

I have prep classes.

BR-RING

ry,
na-
na.

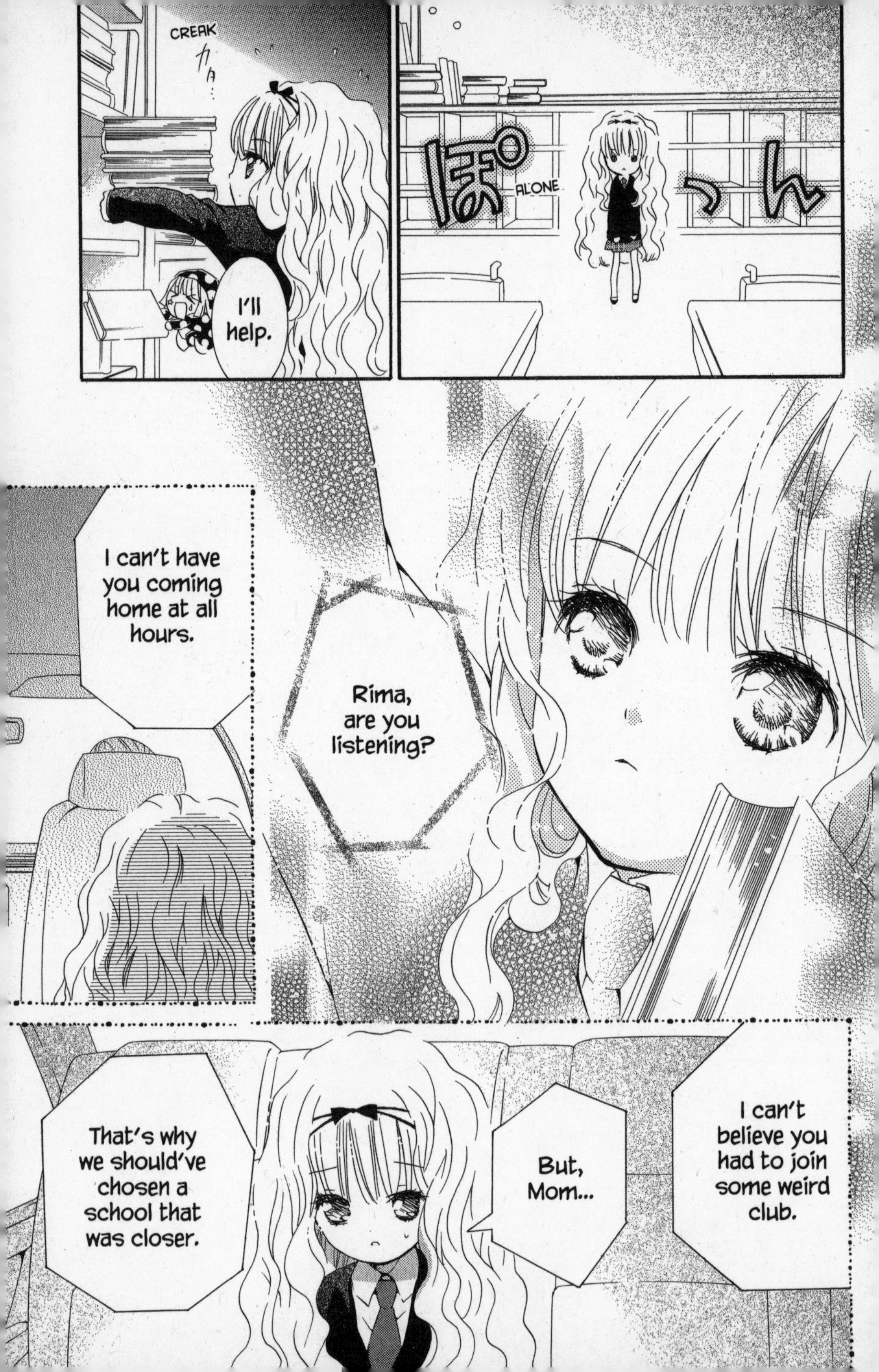
ぽつん
ALONE
CREAK
カタ
I'll help.
Rima, are you listening?
I can't have you coming home at all hours.
I can't believe you had to join some weird club.
But, Mom...
That's why we should've chosen a school that was closer.

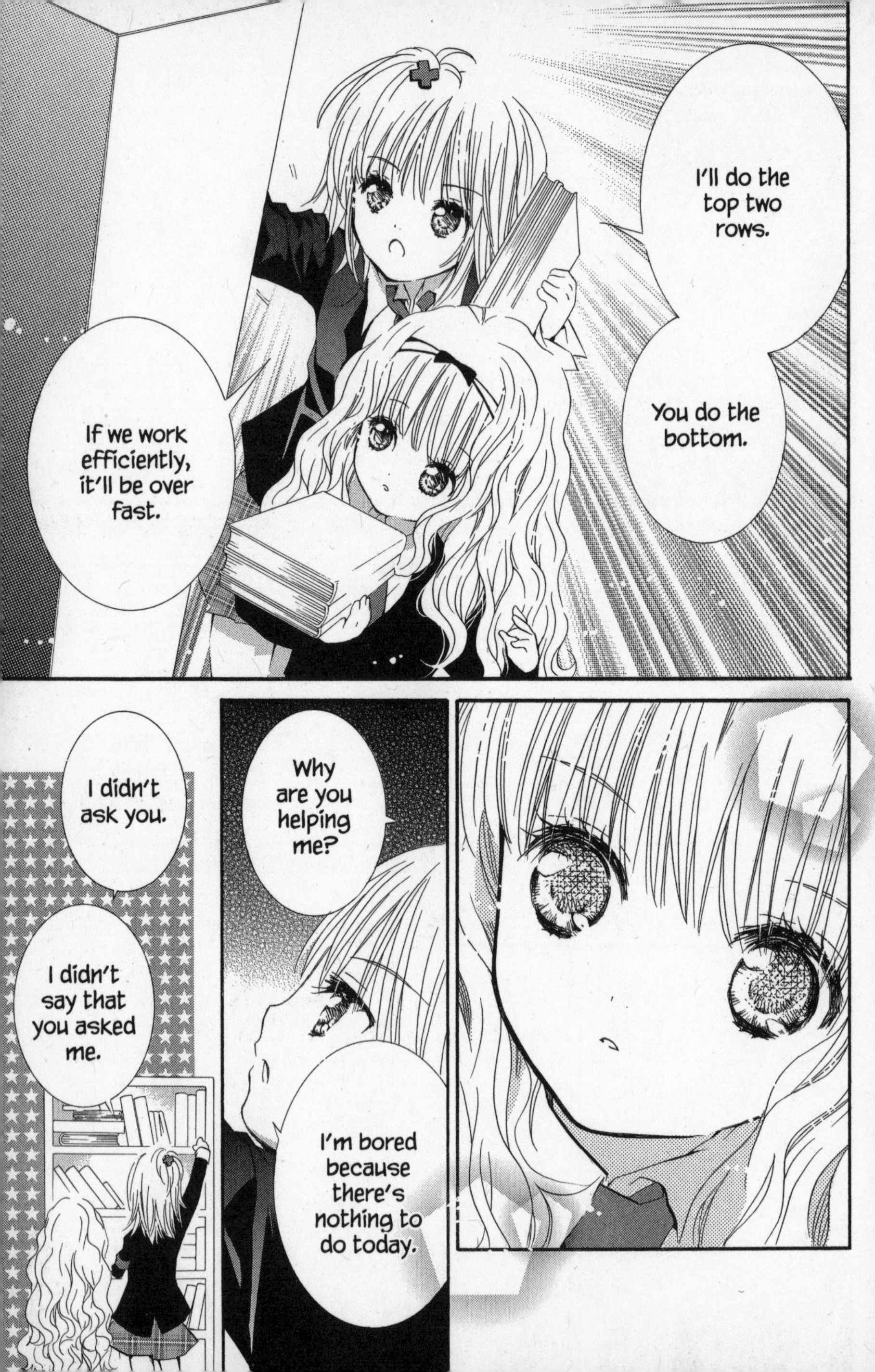
I'll do the top two rows.
You do the bottom.
If we work efficiently, it'll be over fast.
Why are you helping me?
I'm bored because there's nothing to do today.
I didn't ask you.
I didn't say that you asked me.

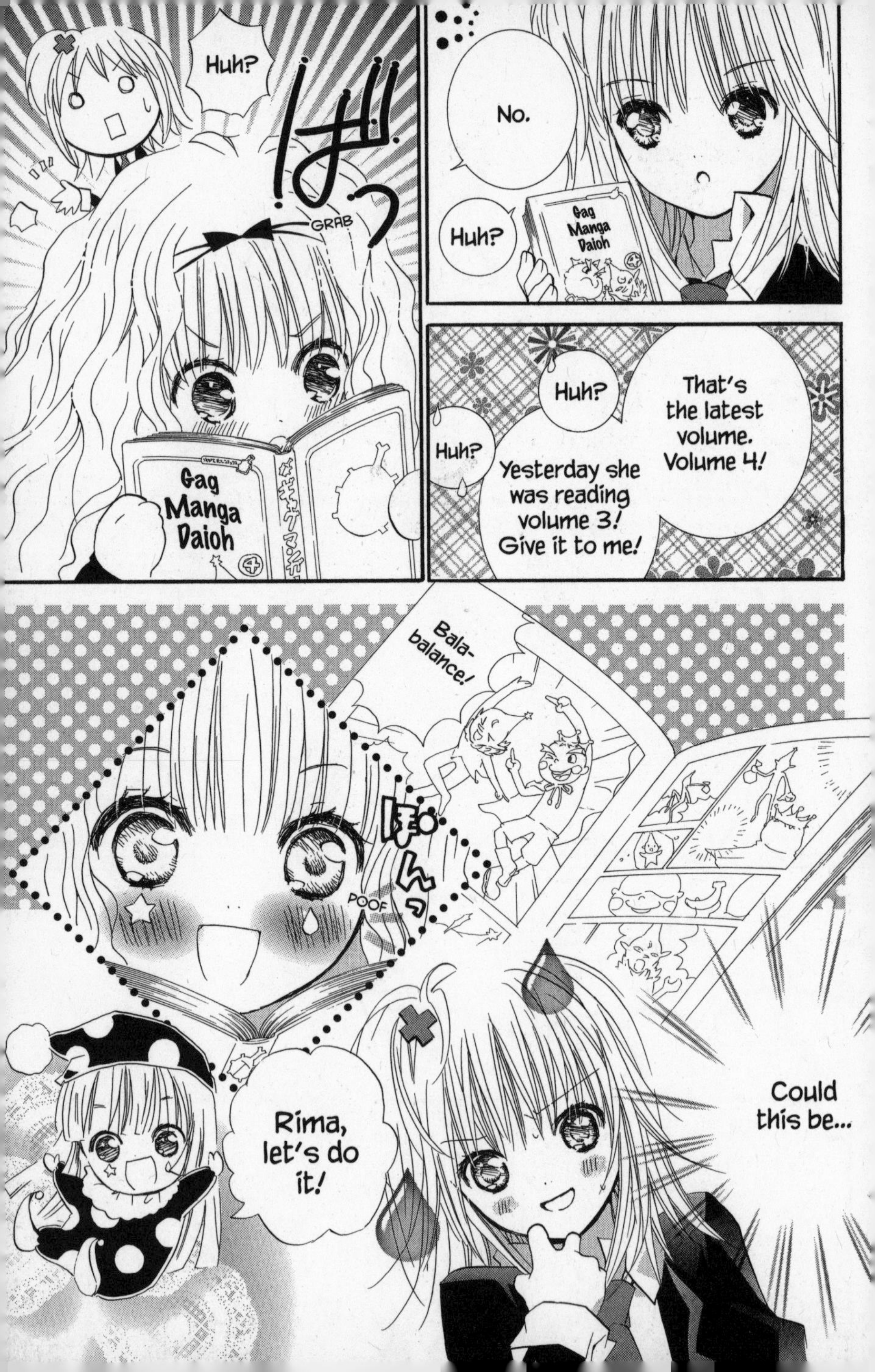
No.
Huh?
Gag Manga Daioh
That's the latest volume. Volume 4!
Huh?
Yesterday she was reading volume 3! Give it to me!
Huh?
Huh?
GRAB
Gag Manga Daioh
Bala-balance!
POOF
Could this be...
Rima, let's do it!

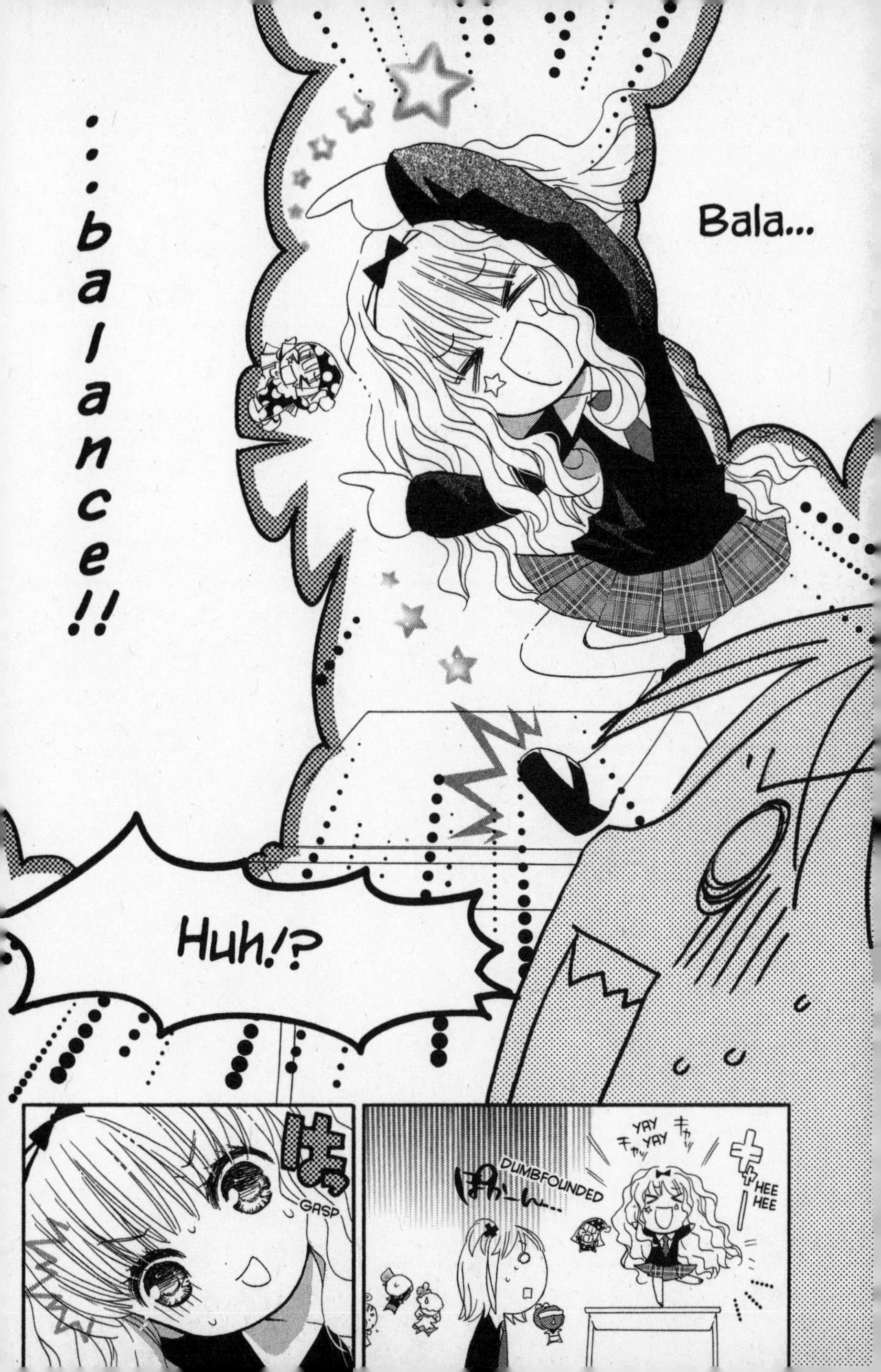

Bala...
...balance!!
Huh!?
YAY YAY
HEE HEE
DUMBFOUNDED
GASP

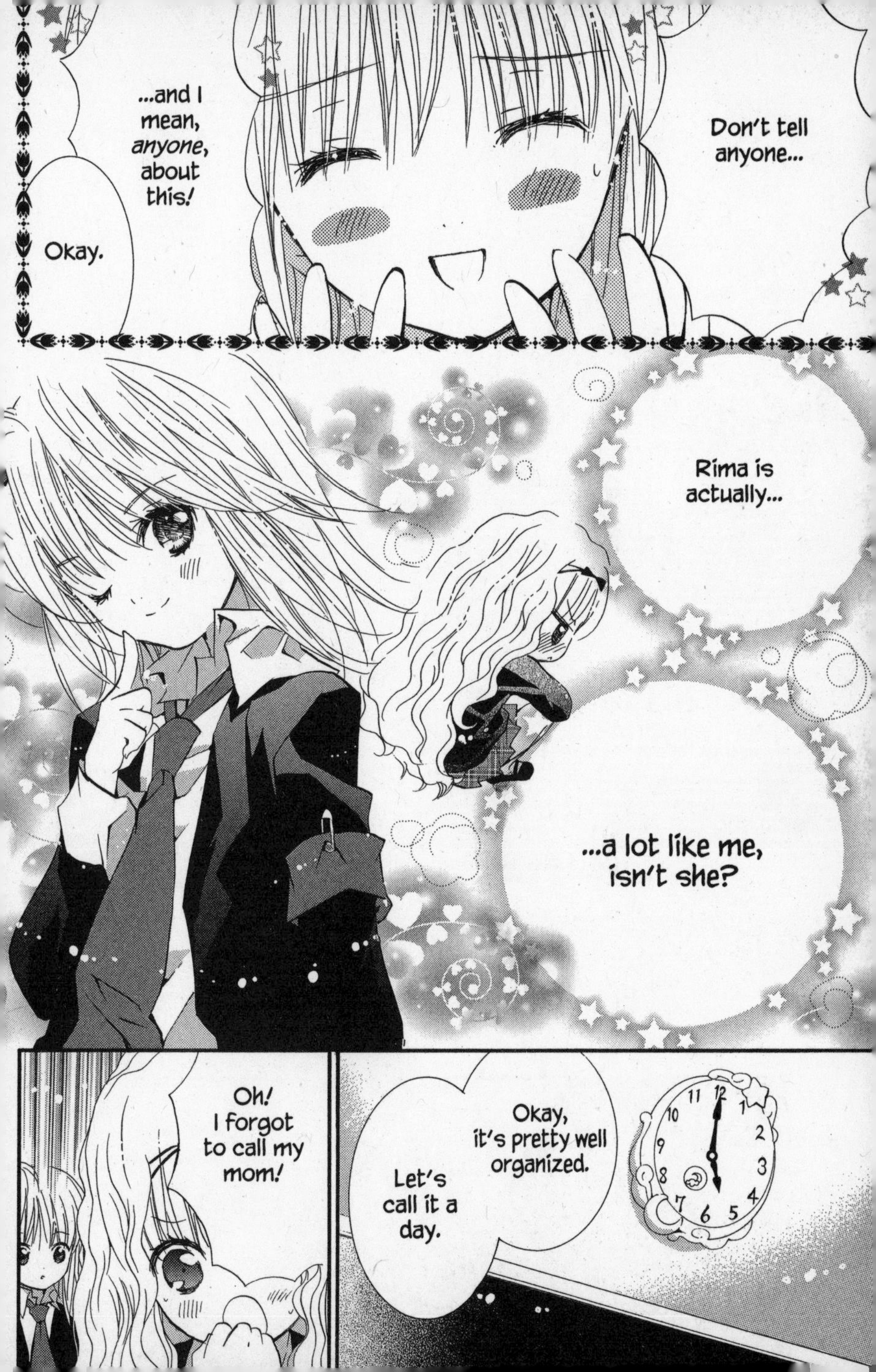
Don't tell anyone...
...and I mean, *anyone*, about this!
Okay.
Rima is actually...
...a lot like me, isn't she?
Okay, it's pretty well organized.
Let's call it a day.
Oh! I forgot to call my mom!

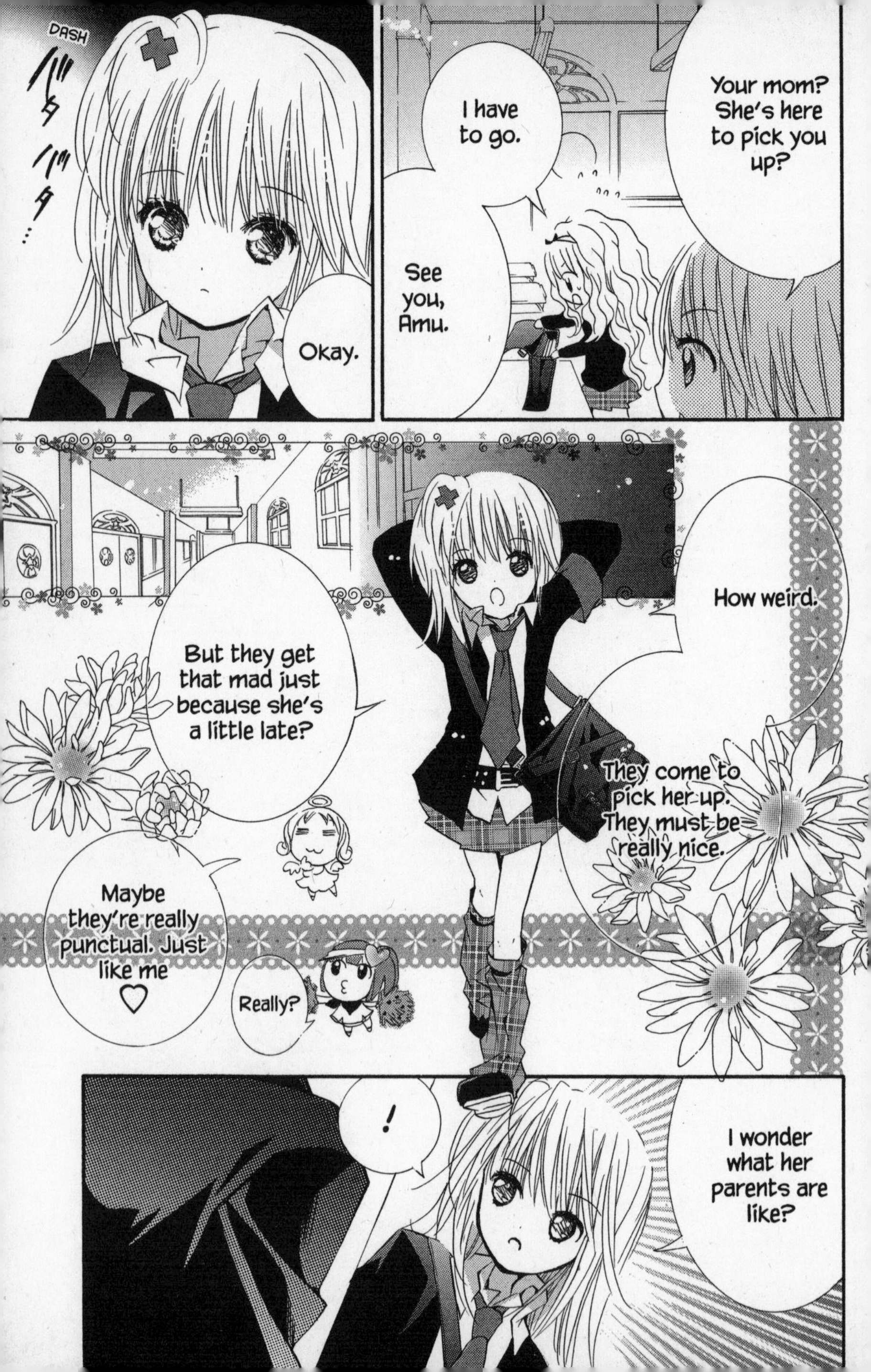
Your mom? She's here to pick you up?
I have to go.
See you, Amu.
DASH
Okay.
How weird.
They come to pick her up. They must be really nice.
But they get that mad just because she's a little late?
Maybe they're really punctual. Just like me ♡
Really?
I wonder what her parents are like?
!

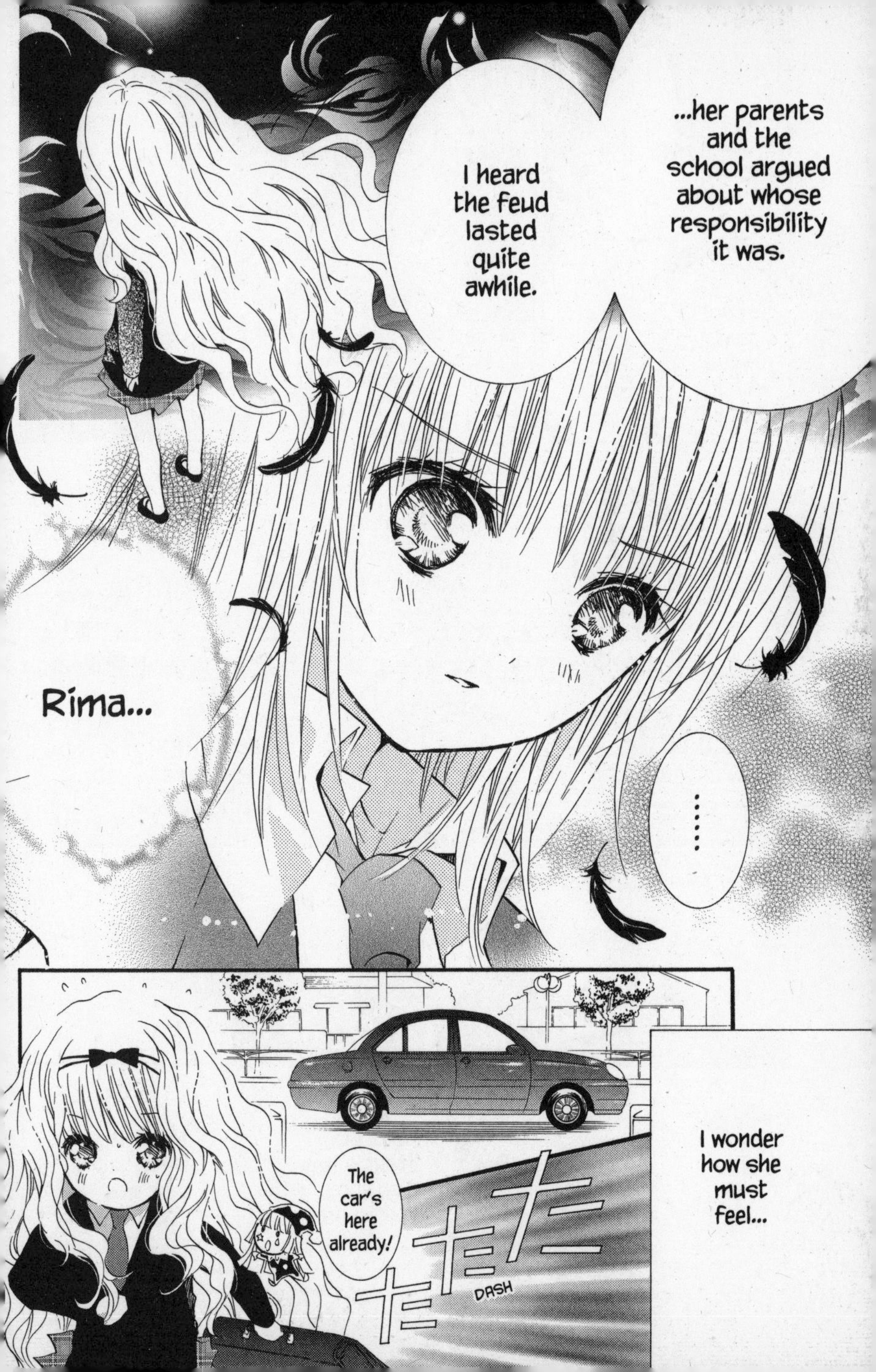
...her parents and the school argued about whose responsibility it was.
I heard the feud lasted quite awhile.
Rima...
......
I wonder how she must feel...
The car's here already!
DASH

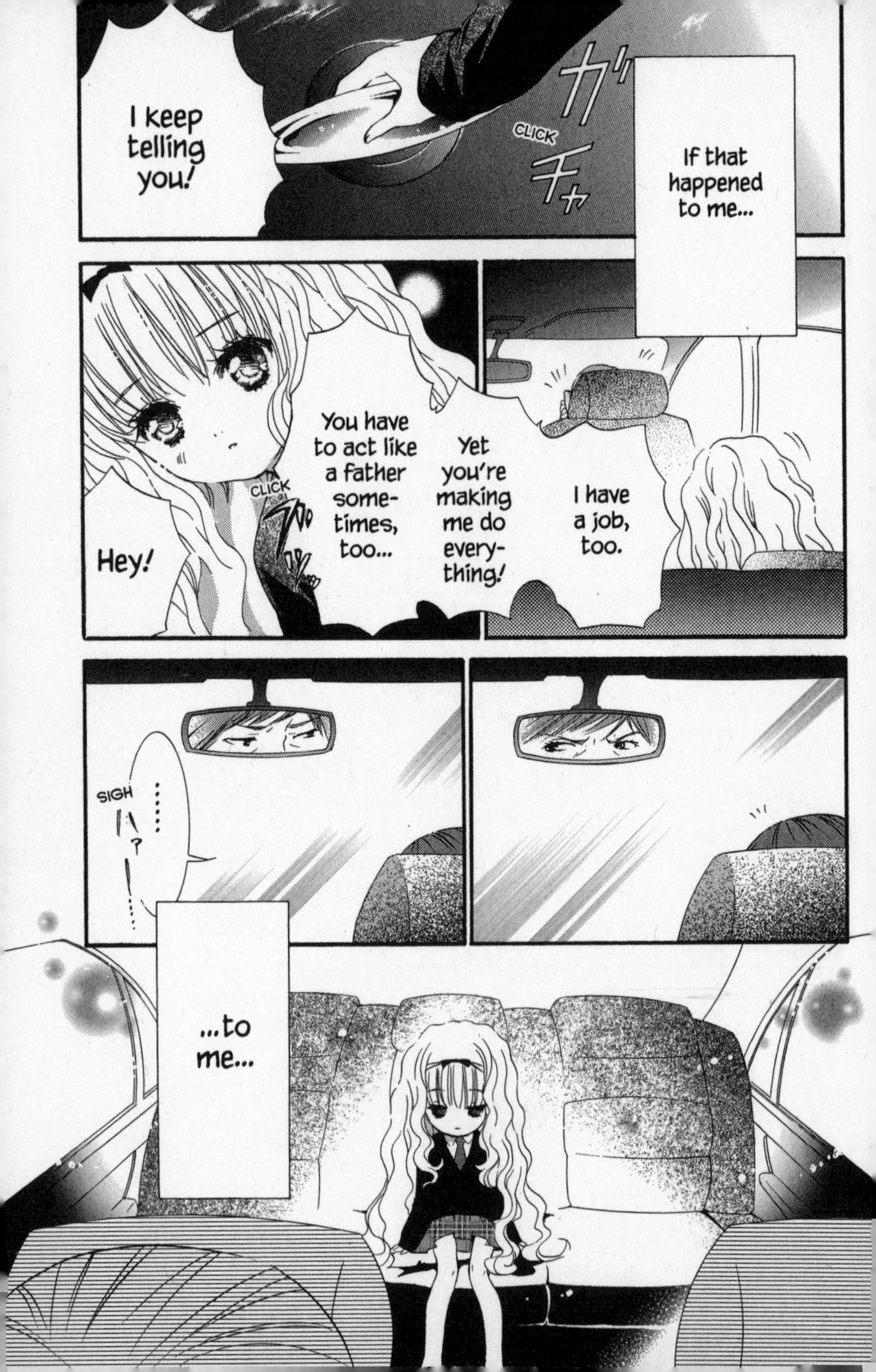

If that happened to me...
CLICK
I keep telling you!
I have a job, too.
Yet you're making me do everything!
You have to act like a father sometimes, too...
CLICK
Hey!
SIGH
......?
...to me...

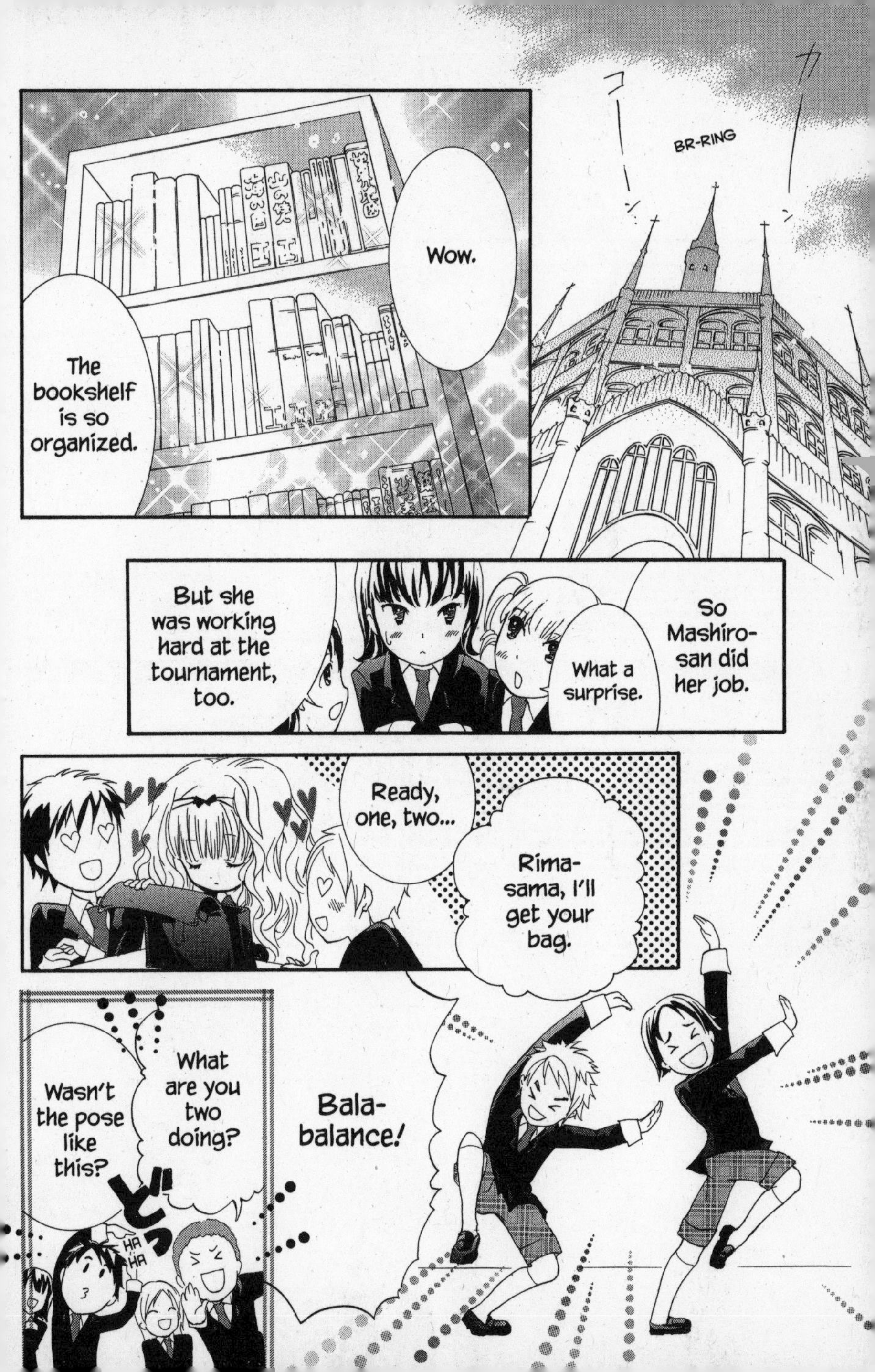
BR-RING
Wow.
The bookshelf is so organized.
So Mashiro-san did her job.
What a surprise.
But she was working hard at the tournament, too.
Ready, one, two...
Rima-sama, I'll get your bag.
Bala-balance!
What are you two doing?
Wasn't the pose like this?
HA HA

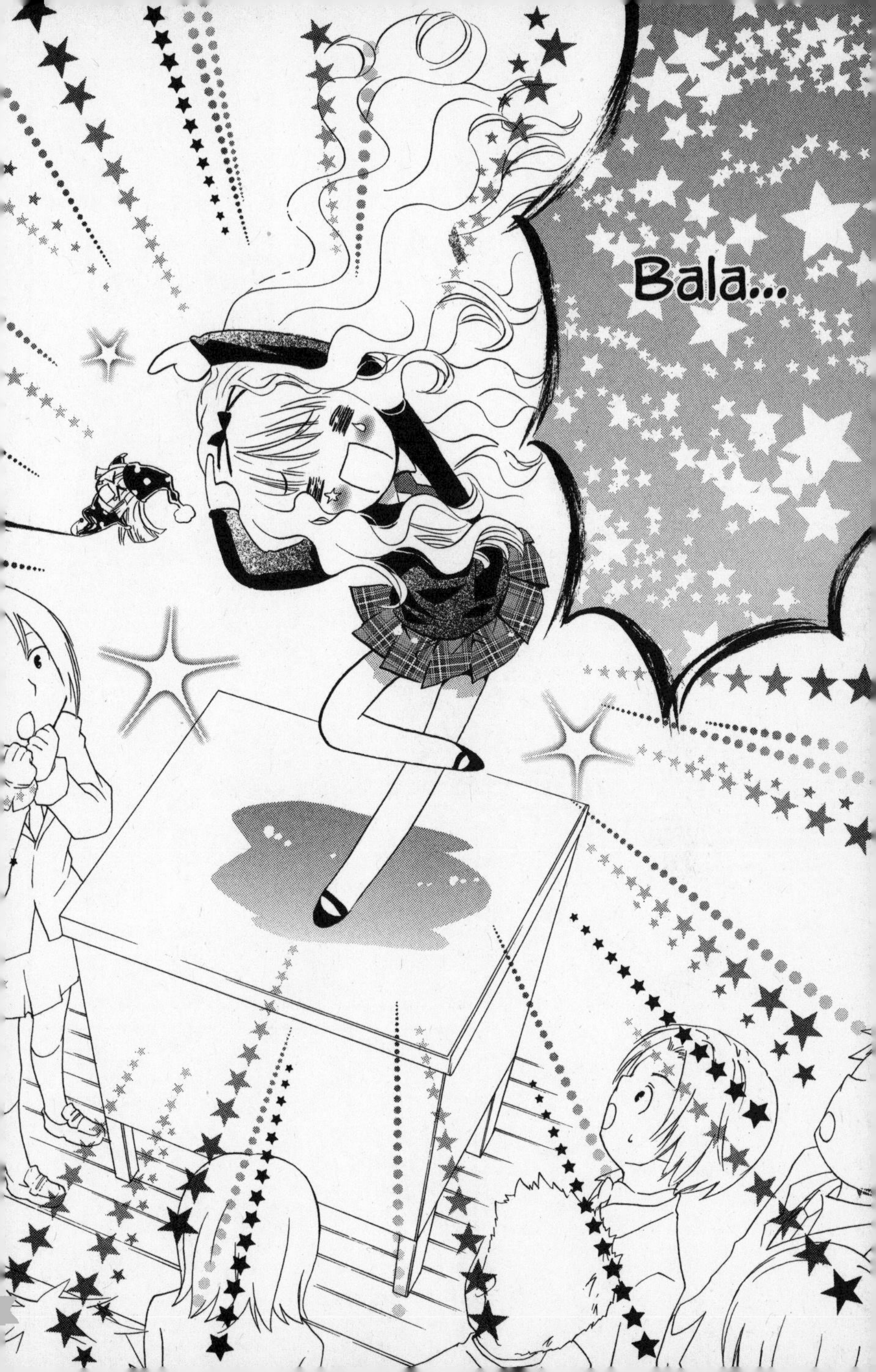
Bala...

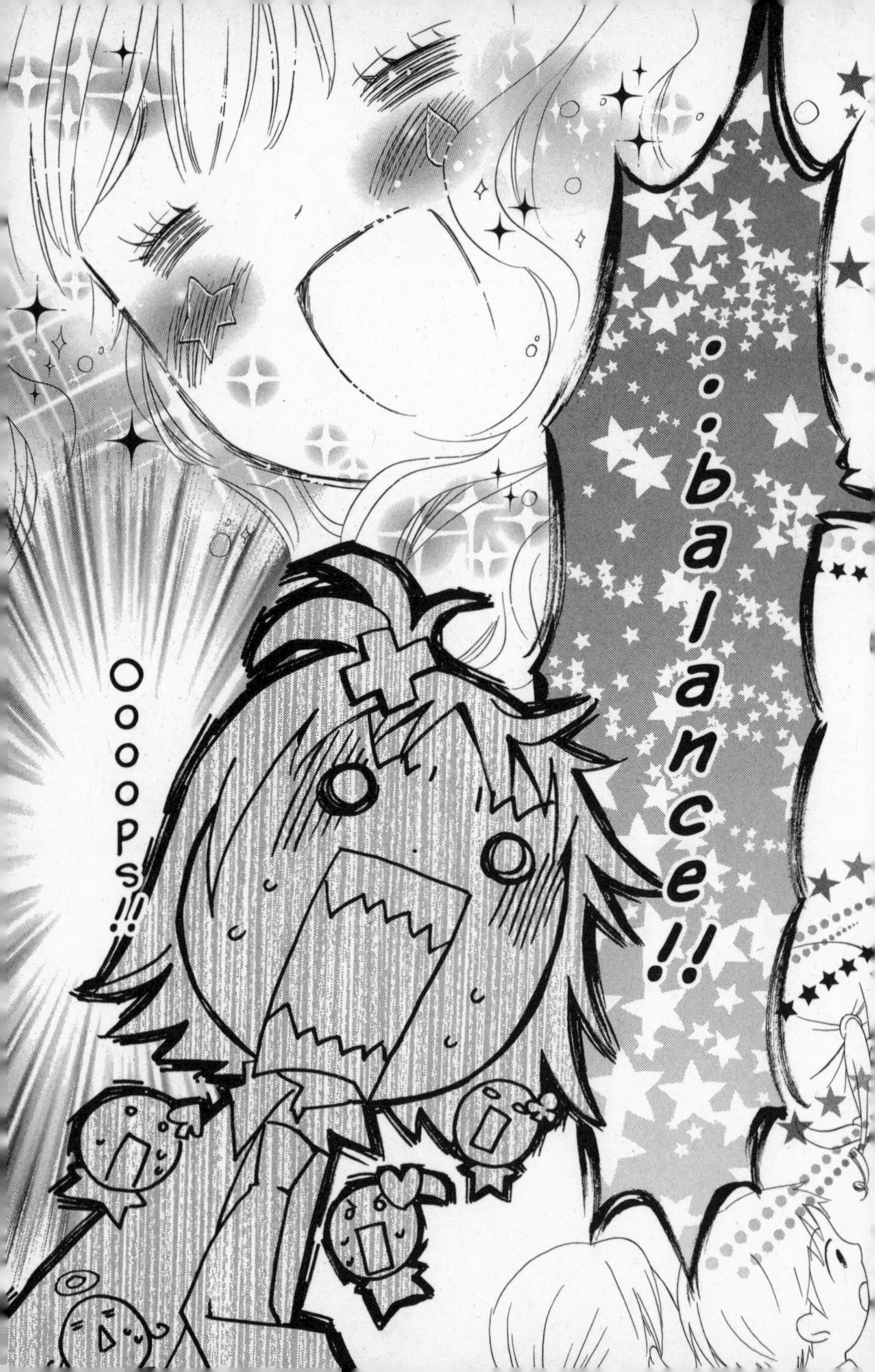
...balance!!
Oooops!!

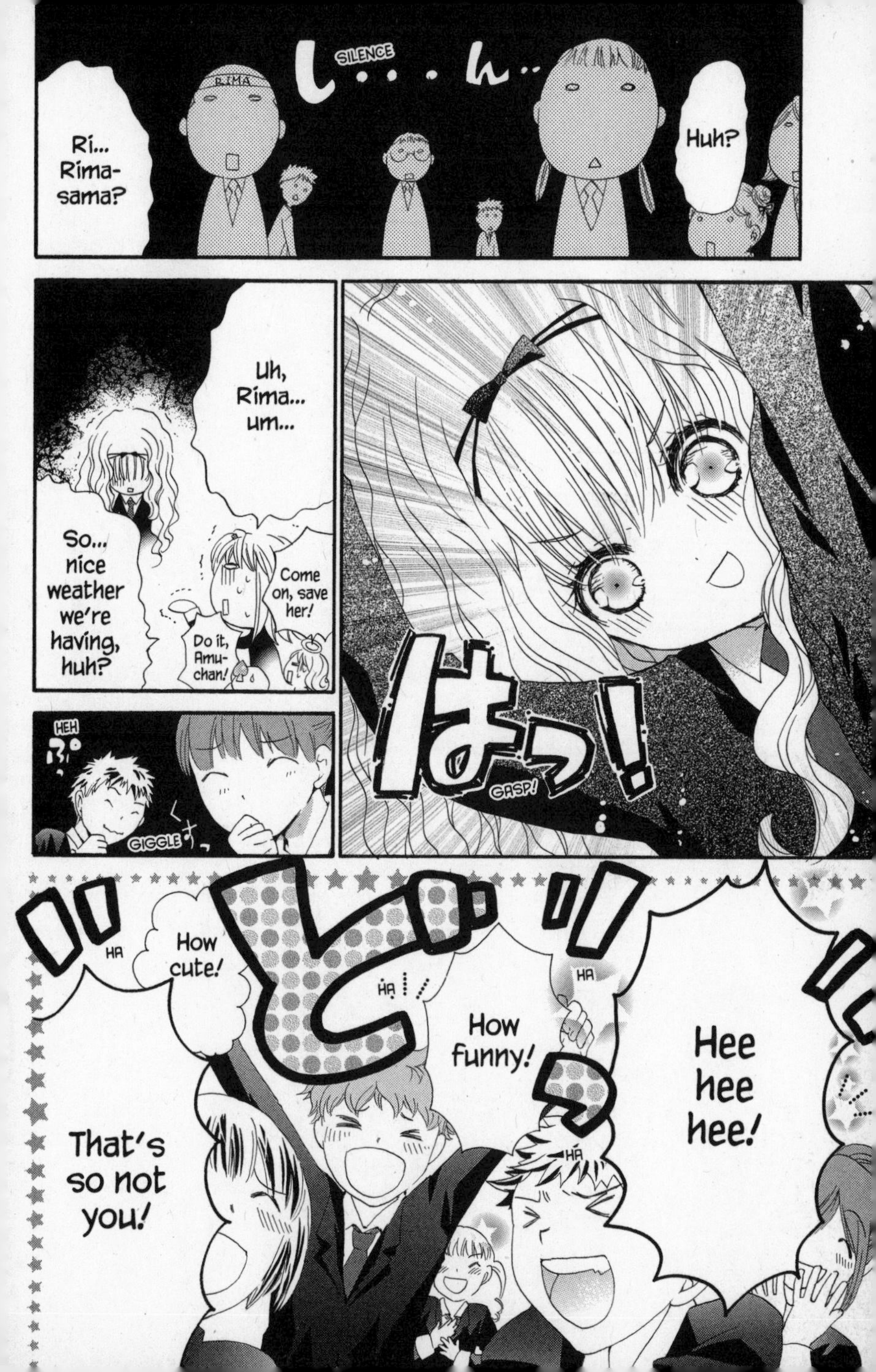
SILENCE
Huh?
Ri... Rima-sama?
GASP!
Uh, Rima... um...
So... nice weather we're having, huh?
Come on, save her!
Do it, Amu-chan!
HEH
GIGGLE
Hee hee hee!
HA
How funny!
HA
HA
How cute!
HA
That's so not you!

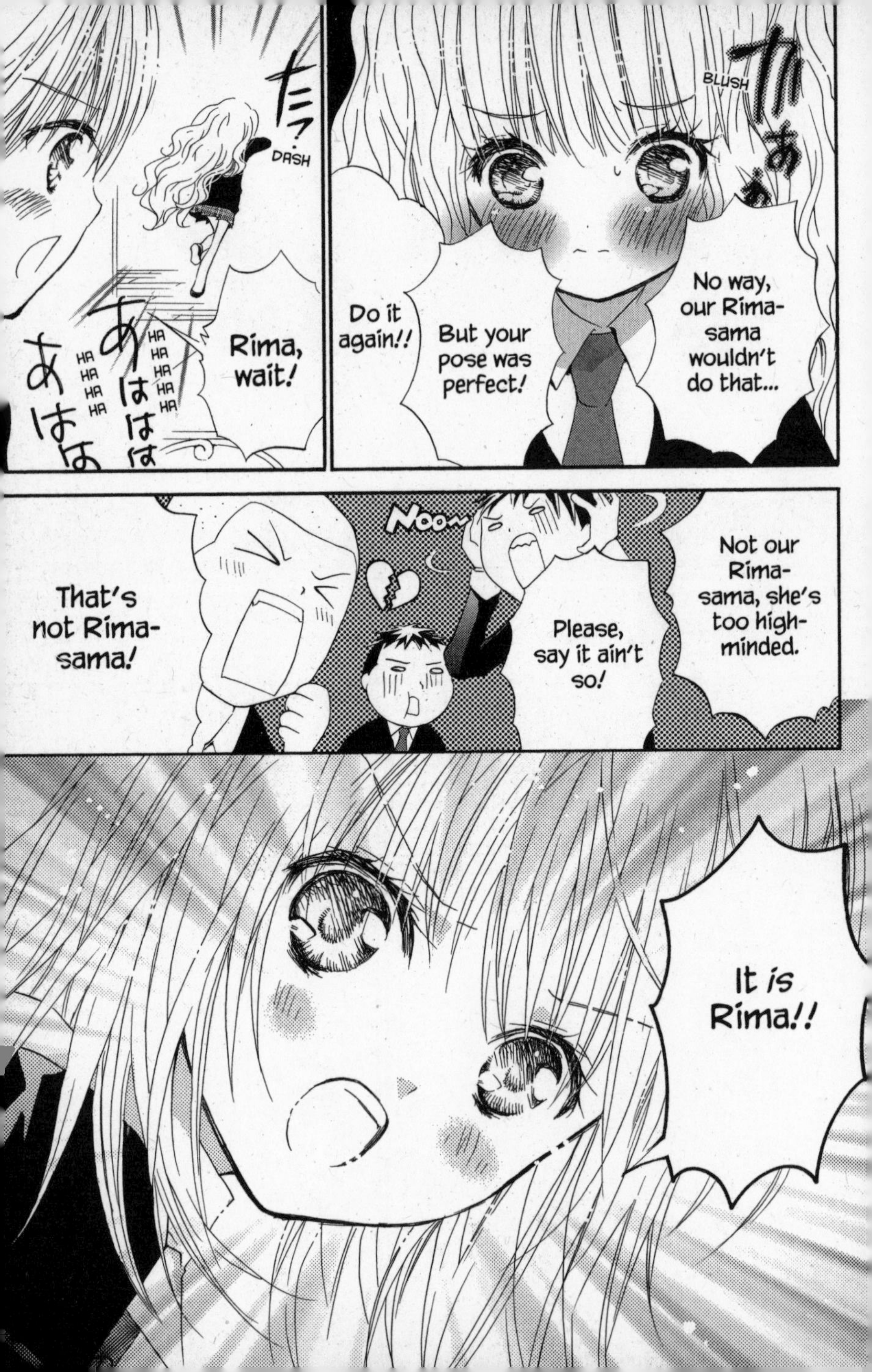
BLUSH
No way, our Rima-sama wouldn't do that...
But your pose was perfect!
Do it again!!
DASH
Rima, wait!
HA HA HA HA HA
HA HA HA HA
Not our Rima-sama, she's too high-minded.
NOO~
Please, say it ain't so!
That's not Rima-sama!
It *is* Rima!!

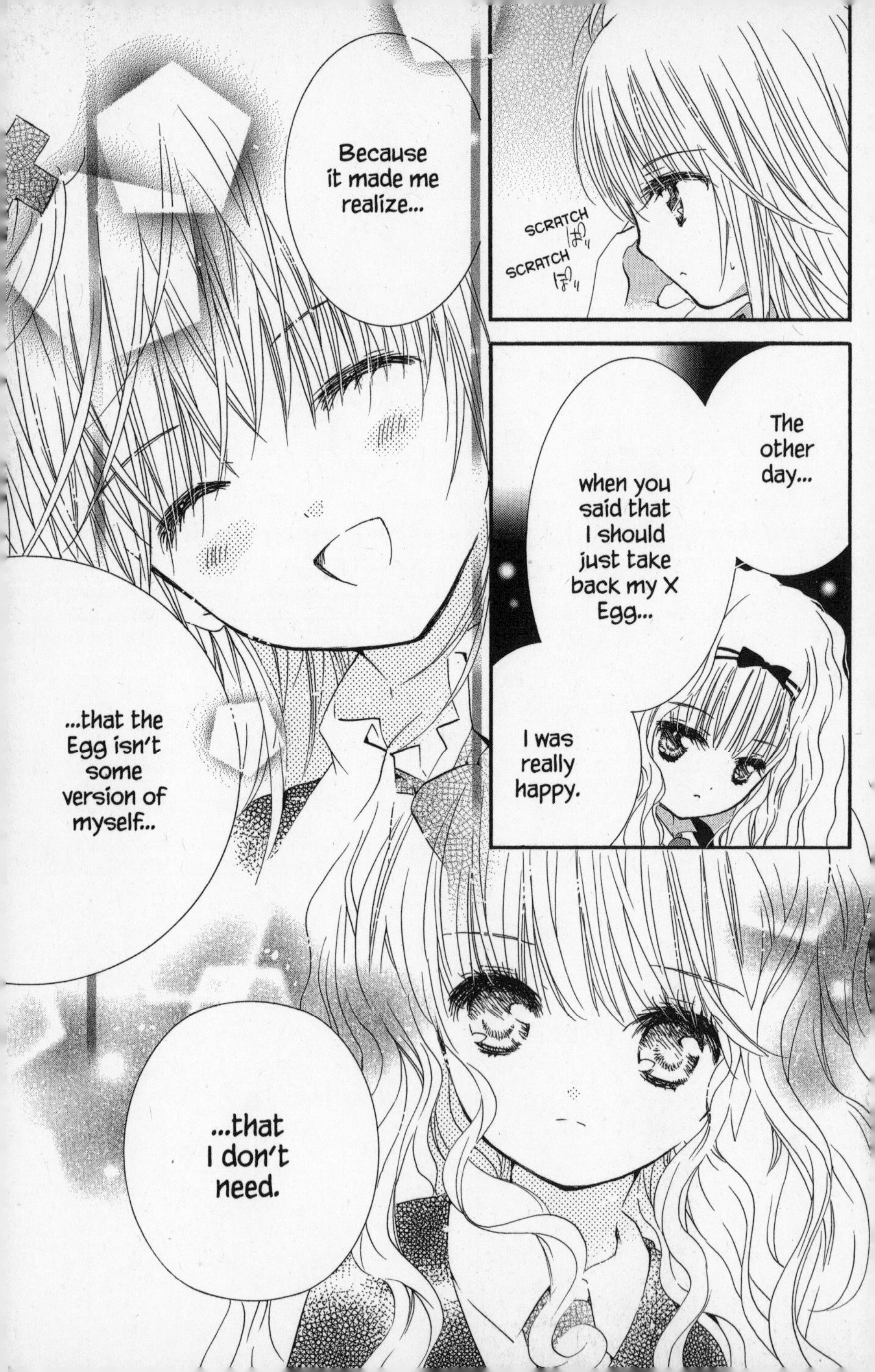
SCRATCH
SCRATCH
The other day...
when you said that I should just take back my X Egg...
I was really happy.
Because it made me realize...
...that the Egg isn't some version of myself...
...that I don't need.

This will affect the contest.

It's disappointing.

To think that underneath it all, Rima-sama is so silly.

They never stop, do they?

Ugh, those guys again...

DODGE

I'm going to announce the results.

The 2nd Cutest in our Class

1st place

Huh!?

SLIDE

First place is...

GLANCE

Hey, hide it!

CLOMP

Shoo

FLINCH

CLOMP

CL

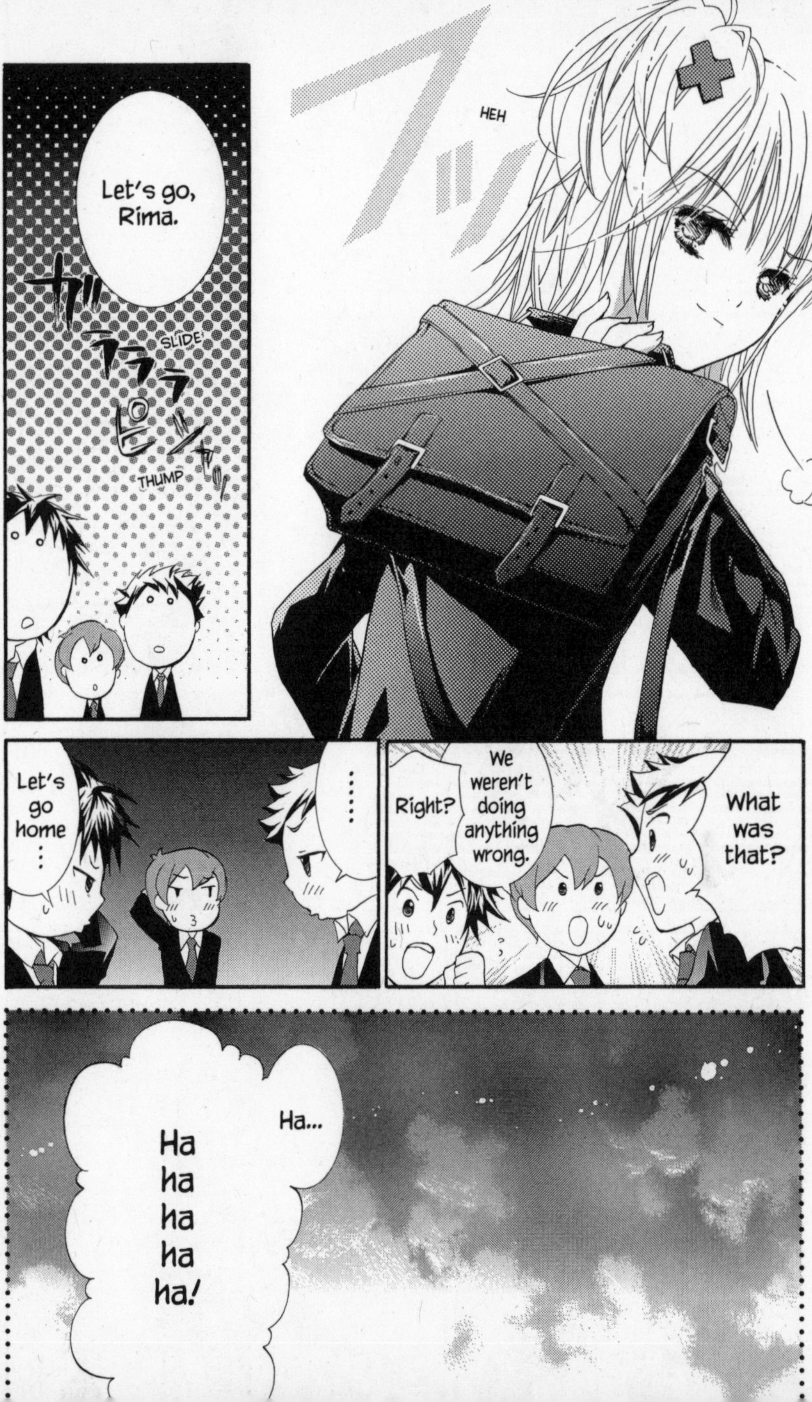
HEH
Let's go, Rima.
SLIDE
THUMP
What was that?
We weren't doing anything wrong.
Right?
......
Let's go home...
Ha...
Ha ha ha ha ha!

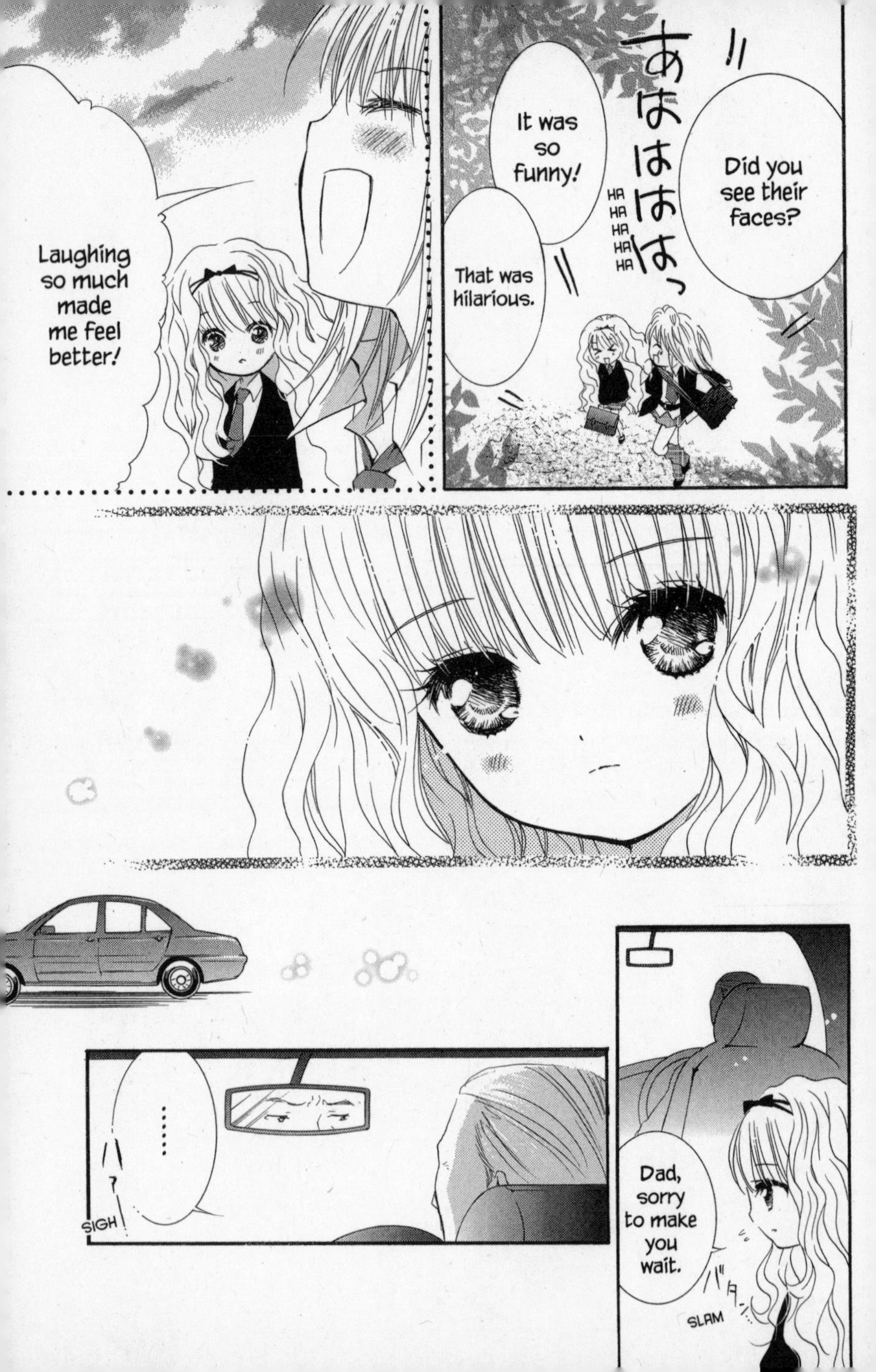
Did you see their faces?
あはははっ
HA HA HA HA HA
It was so funny!
That was hilarious.
Laughing so much made me feel better!
Dad, sorry to make you wait.
SLAM
......
SIGH

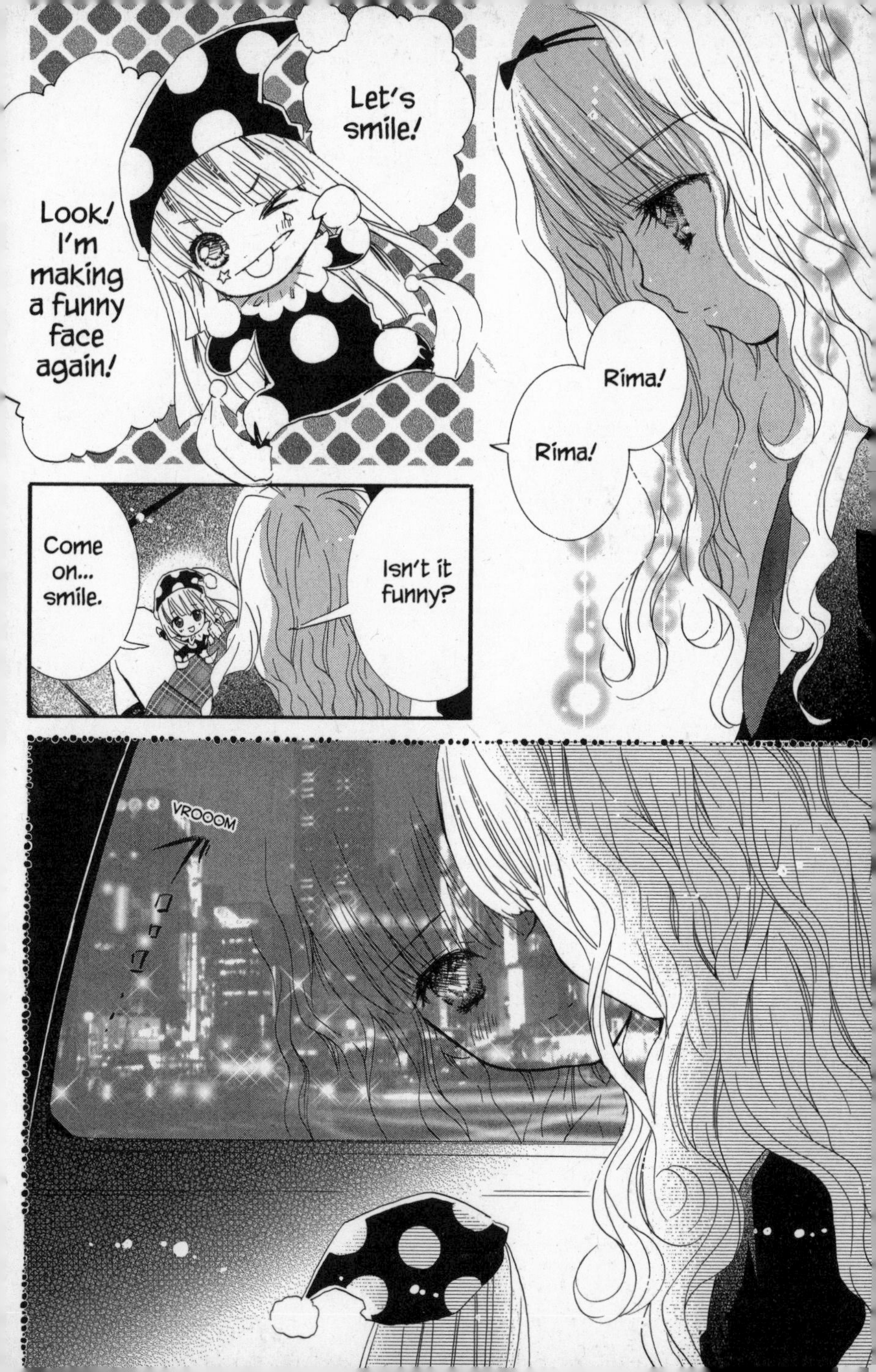
Rima!
Rima!
Let's smile!
Look! I'm making a funny face again!
Isn't it funny?
Come on... smile.
VROOOM

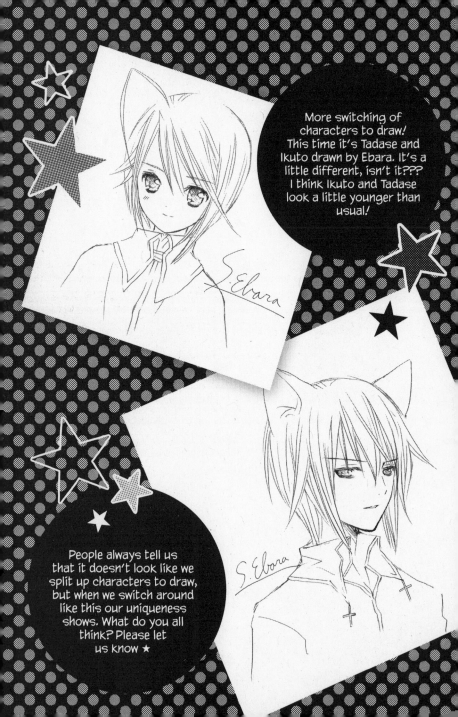

More switching of characters to draw! This time it's Tadase and Ikuto drawn by Ebara. It's a little different, isn't it??? I think Ikuto and Tadase look a little younger than usual!

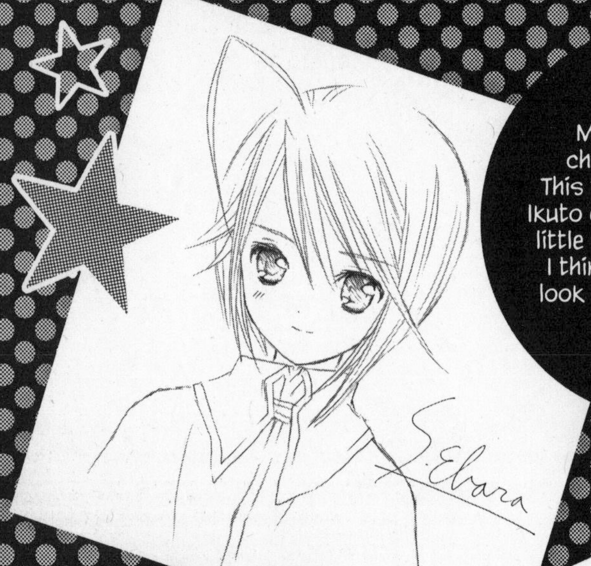
S. Ebara

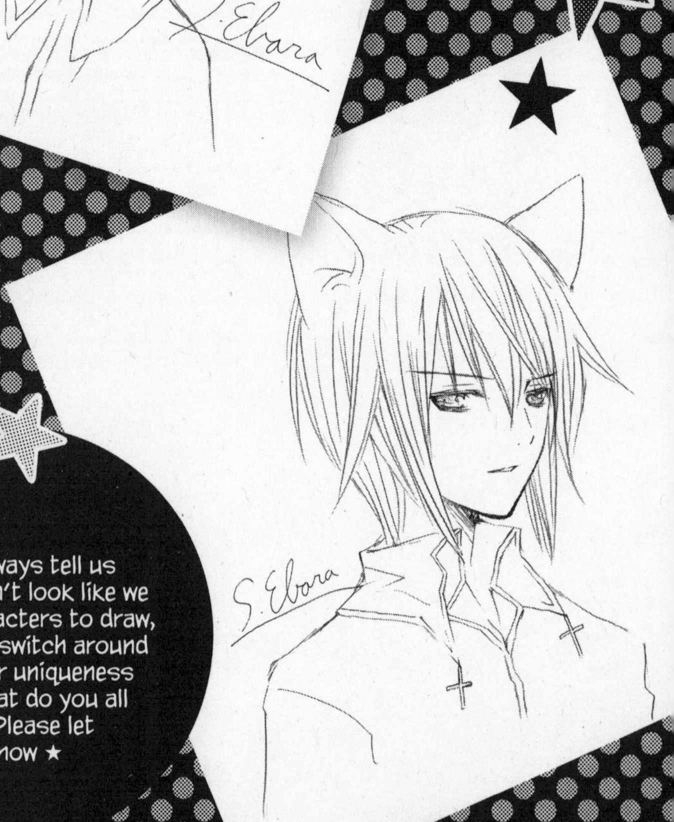
S. Ebara

People always tell us that it doesn't look like we split up characters to draw, but when we switch around like this our uniqueness shows. What do you all think? Please let us know ★

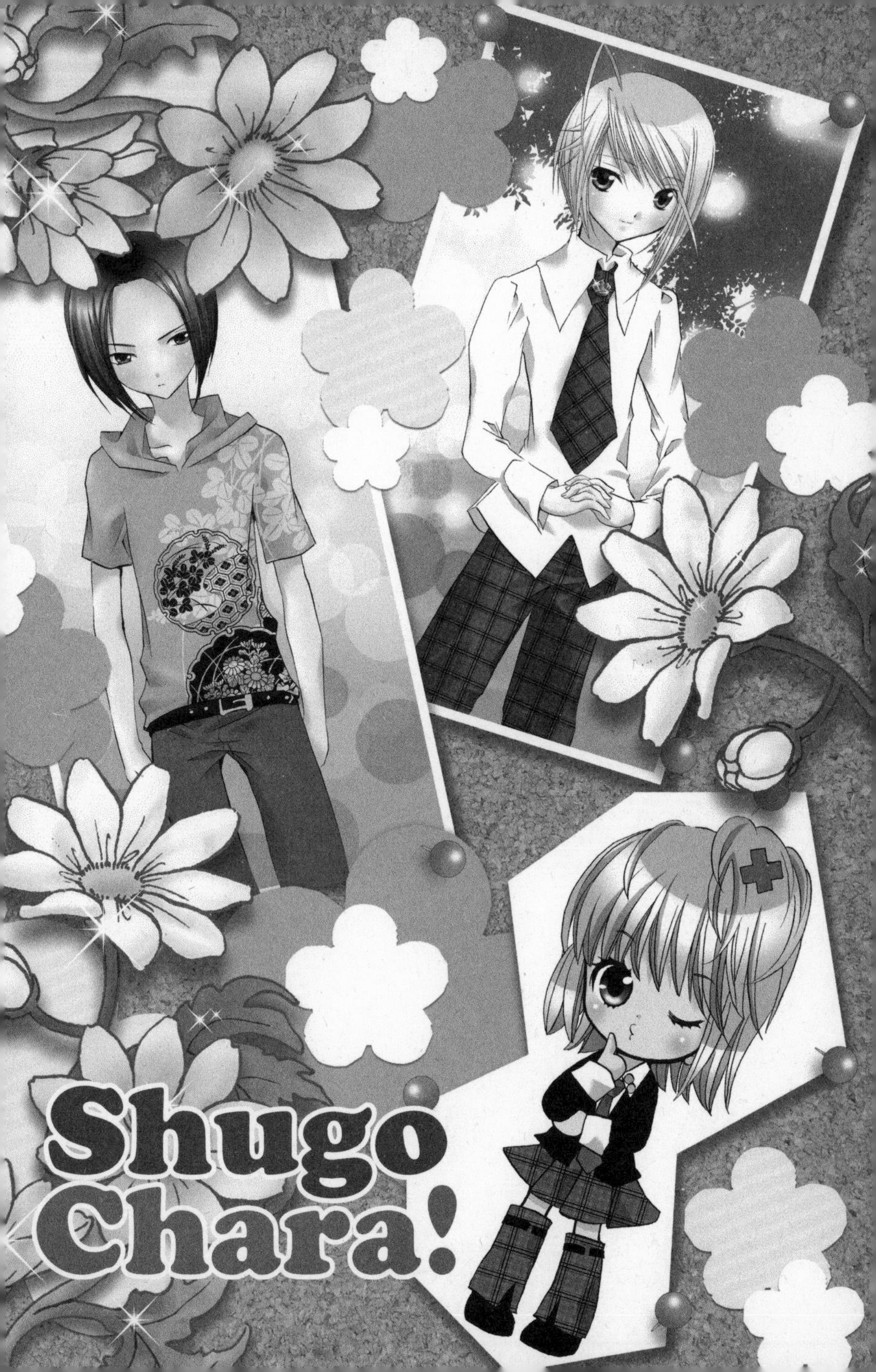
Shugo
Chara!

TH-
THUMP

TH-
THUMP

TH-
THUMP

It's a very special day today.

Hinamori-san!

Today is Sunday.

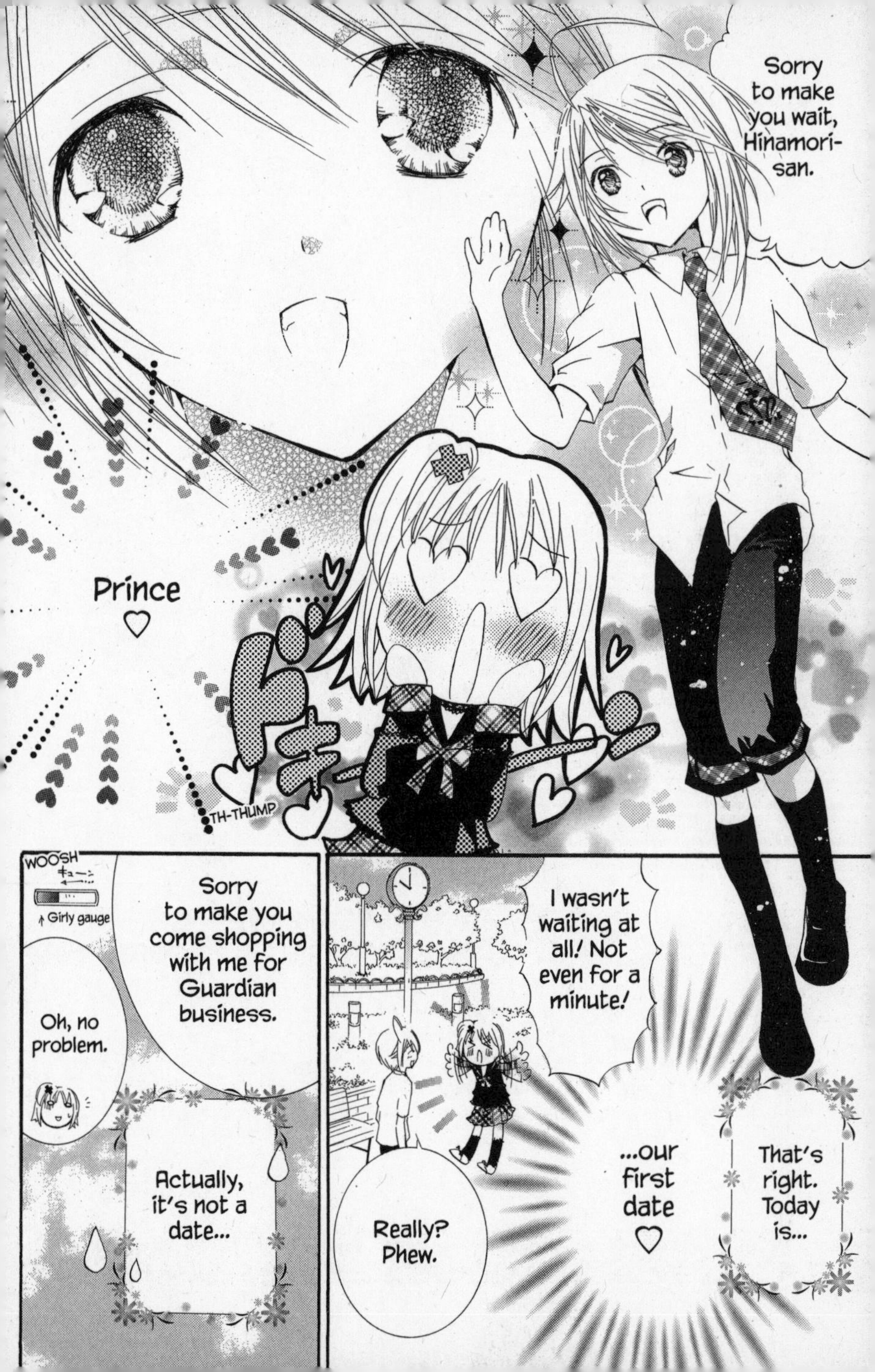
Sorry to make you wait, Hinamori-san.
Prince ♡
TH-THUMP
That's right. Today is...
...our first date ♡
I wasn't waiting at all! Not even for a minute!
Really? Phew.
Sorry to make you come shopping with me for Guardian business.
WOOSH
Girly gauge
Oh, no problem.
Actually, it's not a date...

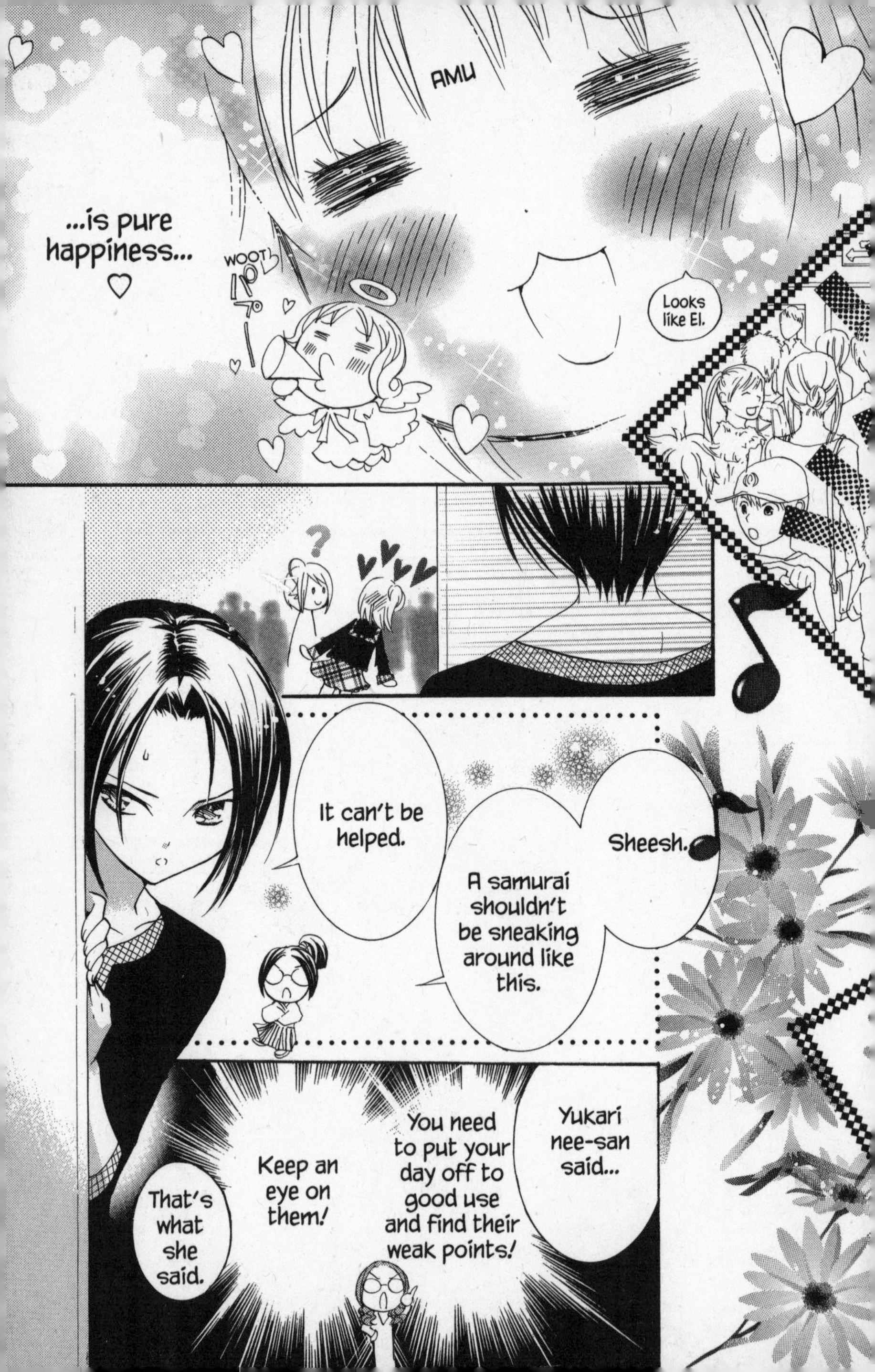
AMU
...is pure happiness...
WOOT
Looks like El.
Sheesh.
A samurai shouldn't be sneaking around like this.
It can't be helped.
Yukari nee-san said...
You need to put your day off to good use and find their weak points!
Keep an eye on them!
That's what she said.

Because I'm in disguise. Can't you tell?

By the way, how come you're not wearing glasses today?

I'm following them.

My clothes are ninja-like, too.

He's the type to dress for the occasion...

Keep an eye on her...

CHARMED

I don't think she meant it that way.

2 F
Household Goods

Oh.

What a cute store.

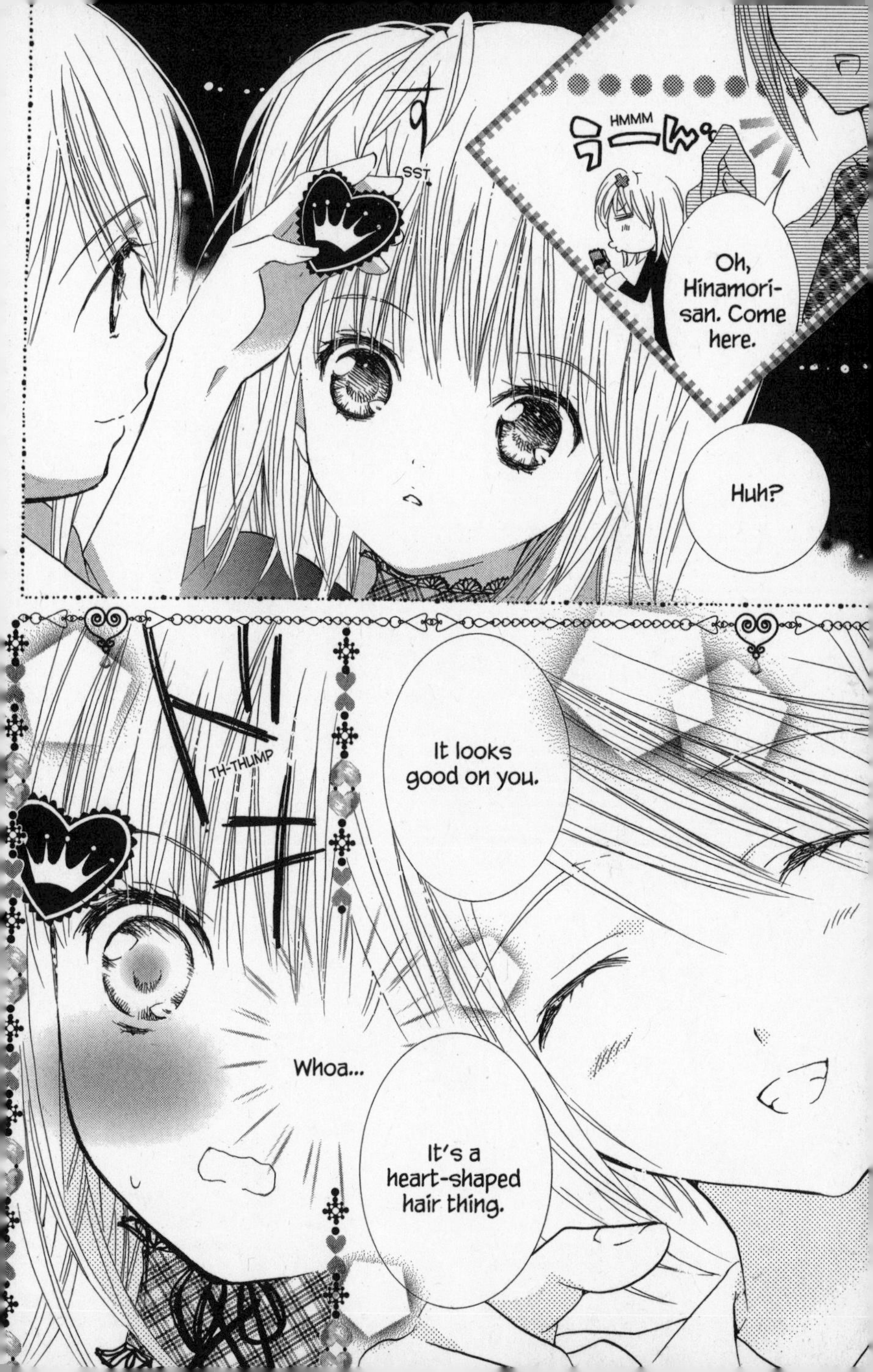
うーん。
HMMM
Oh, Hinamori-san. Come here.
Huh?
す
SST
It looks good on you.
TH-THUMP
It's a heart-shaped hair thing.
Whoa...

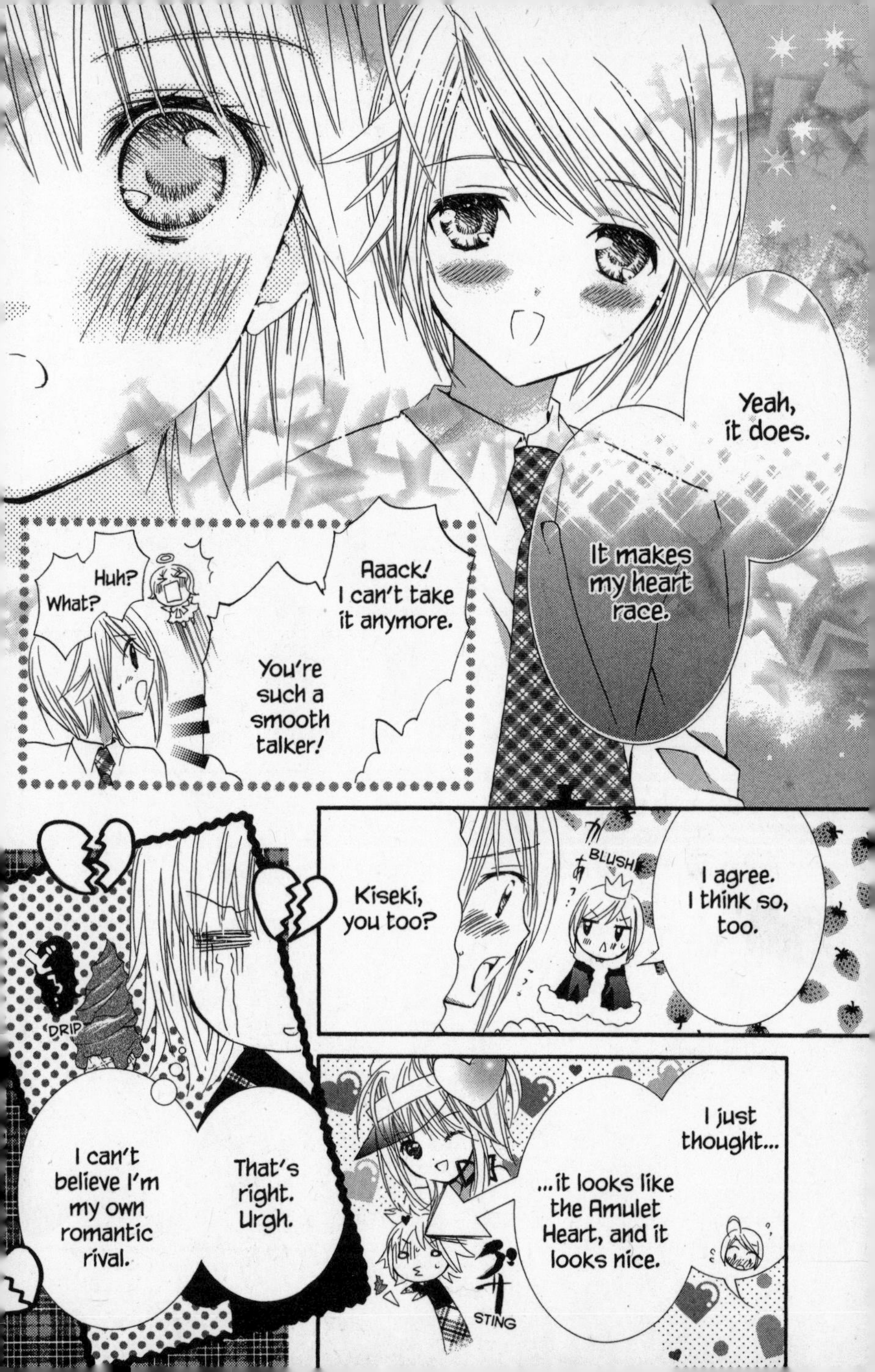
Yeah, it does.
It makes my heart race.
Aaack! I can't take it anymore.
You're such a smooth talker!
Huh?
What?
I agree. I think so, too.
BLUSH
Kiseki, you too?
I just thought...
...it looks like the Amulet Heart, and it looks nice.
STING
DRIP
That's right. Urgh.
I can't believe I'm my own romantic rival.

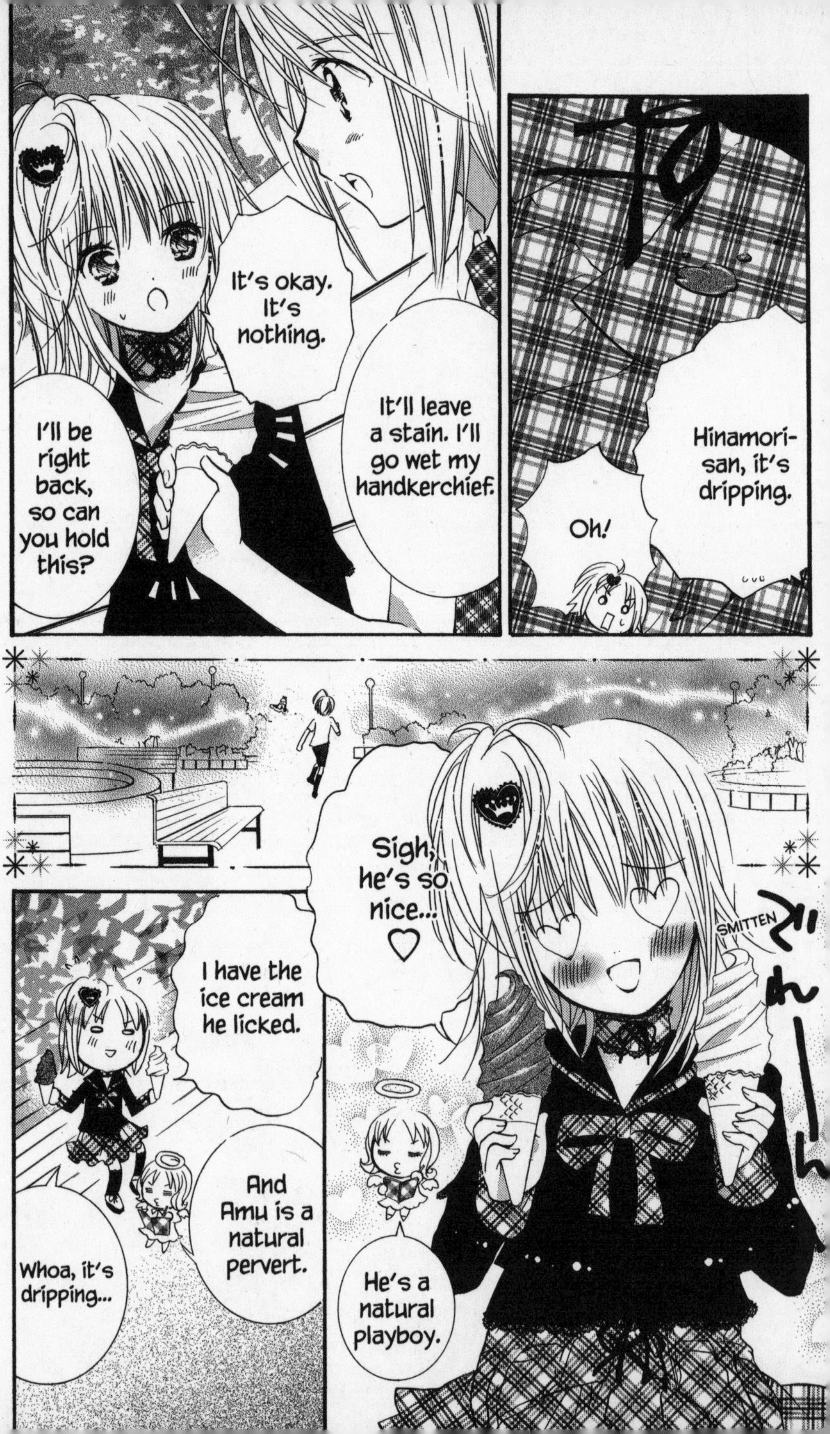

Hinamori-san, it's dripping.
Oh!
It'll leave a stain. I'll go wet my handkerchief.
It's okay. It's nothing.
I'll be right back, so can you hold this?
Sigh, he's so nice... ♡
SMITTEN
I have the ice cream he licked.
He's a natural playboy.
And Amu is a natural pervert.
Whoa, it's dripping...

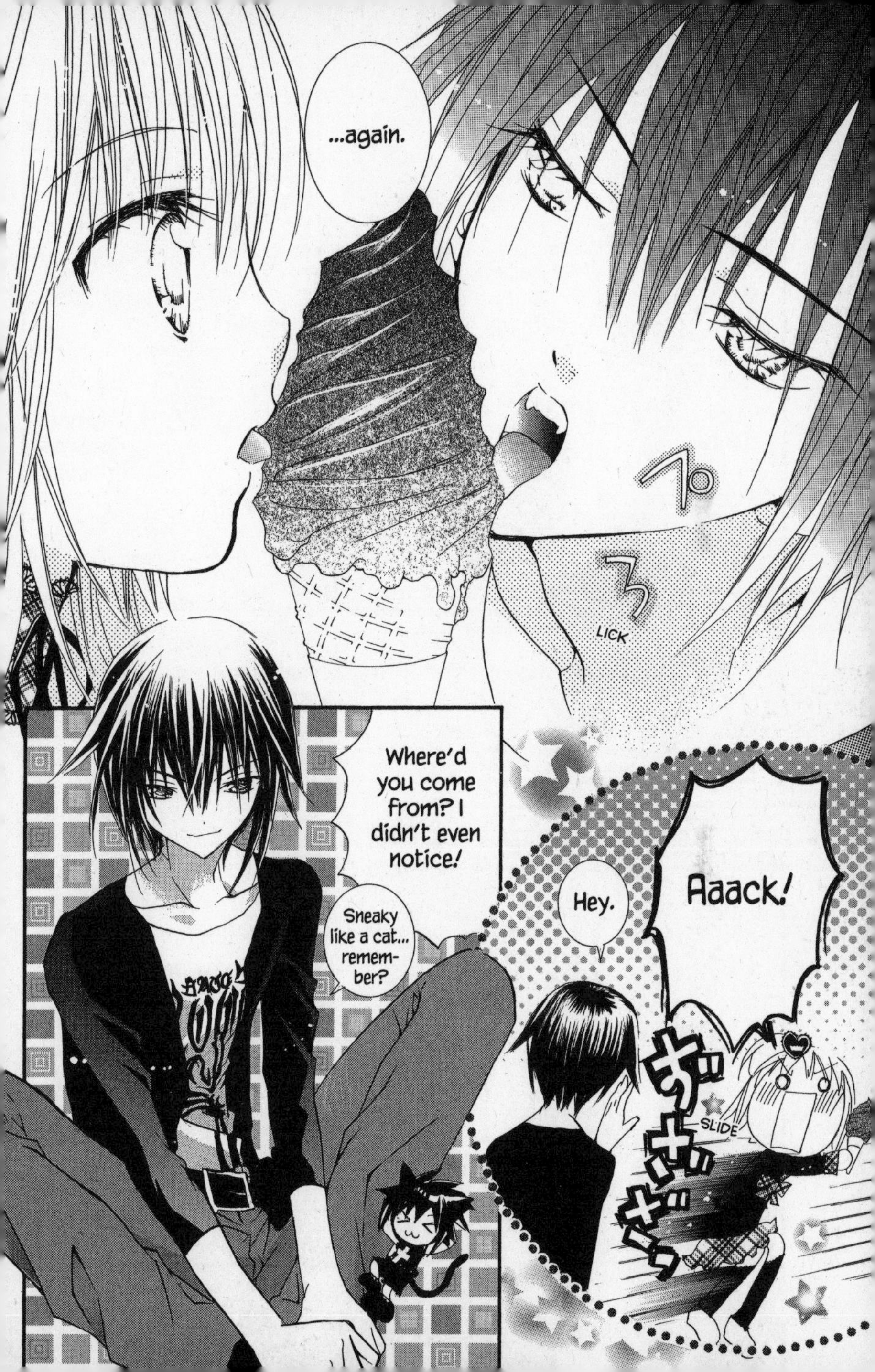
...again.
LICK
Aaack!
Hey.
SLIDE
Where'd you come from? I didn't even notice!
Sneaky like a cat... remember?

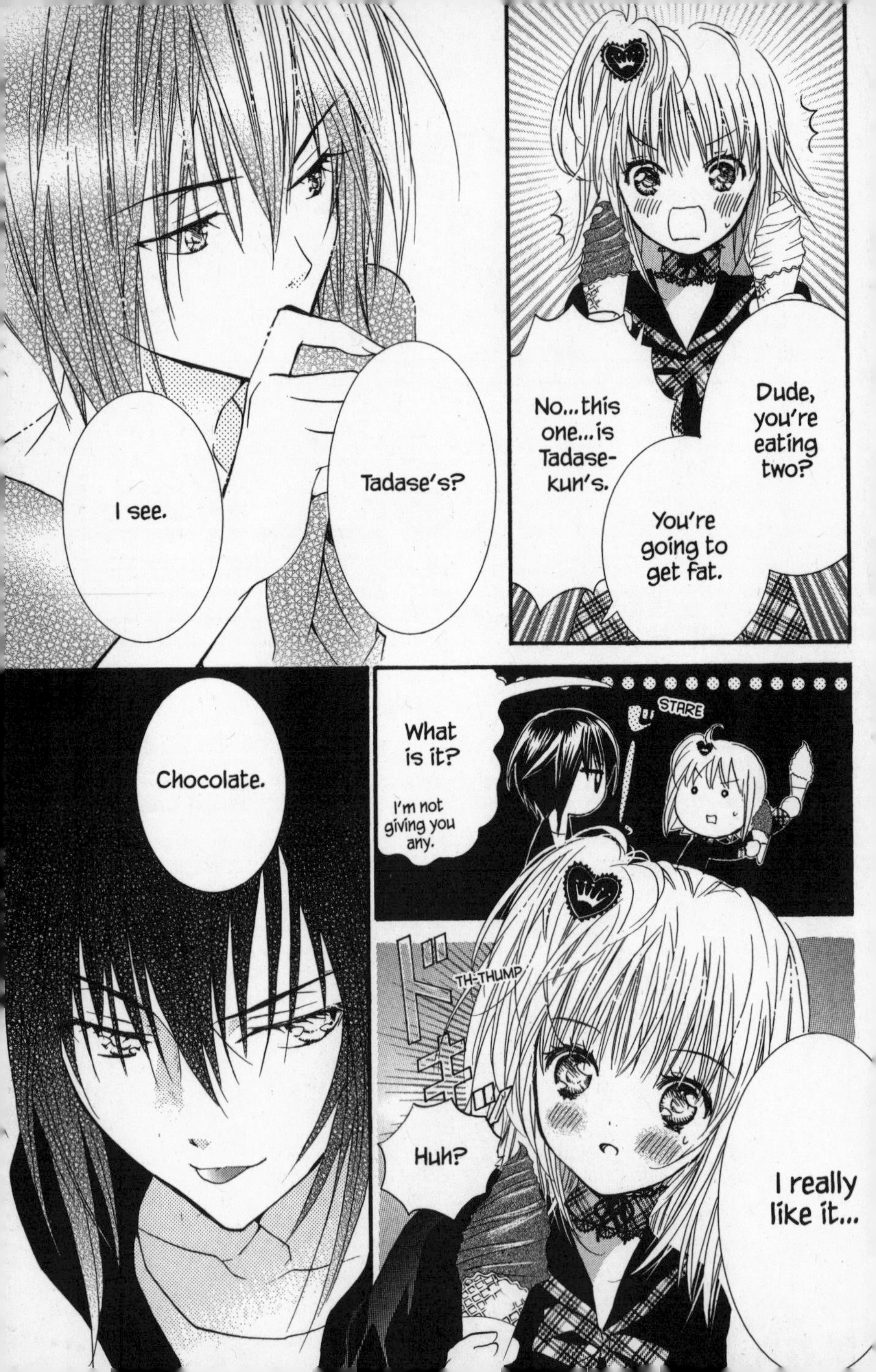

Dude, you're eating two?
You're going to get fat.
No...this one...is Tadase-kun's.
Tadase's?
I see.
STARE
What is it?
I'm not giving you any.
TH-THUMP
I really like it...
Huh?
Chocolate.

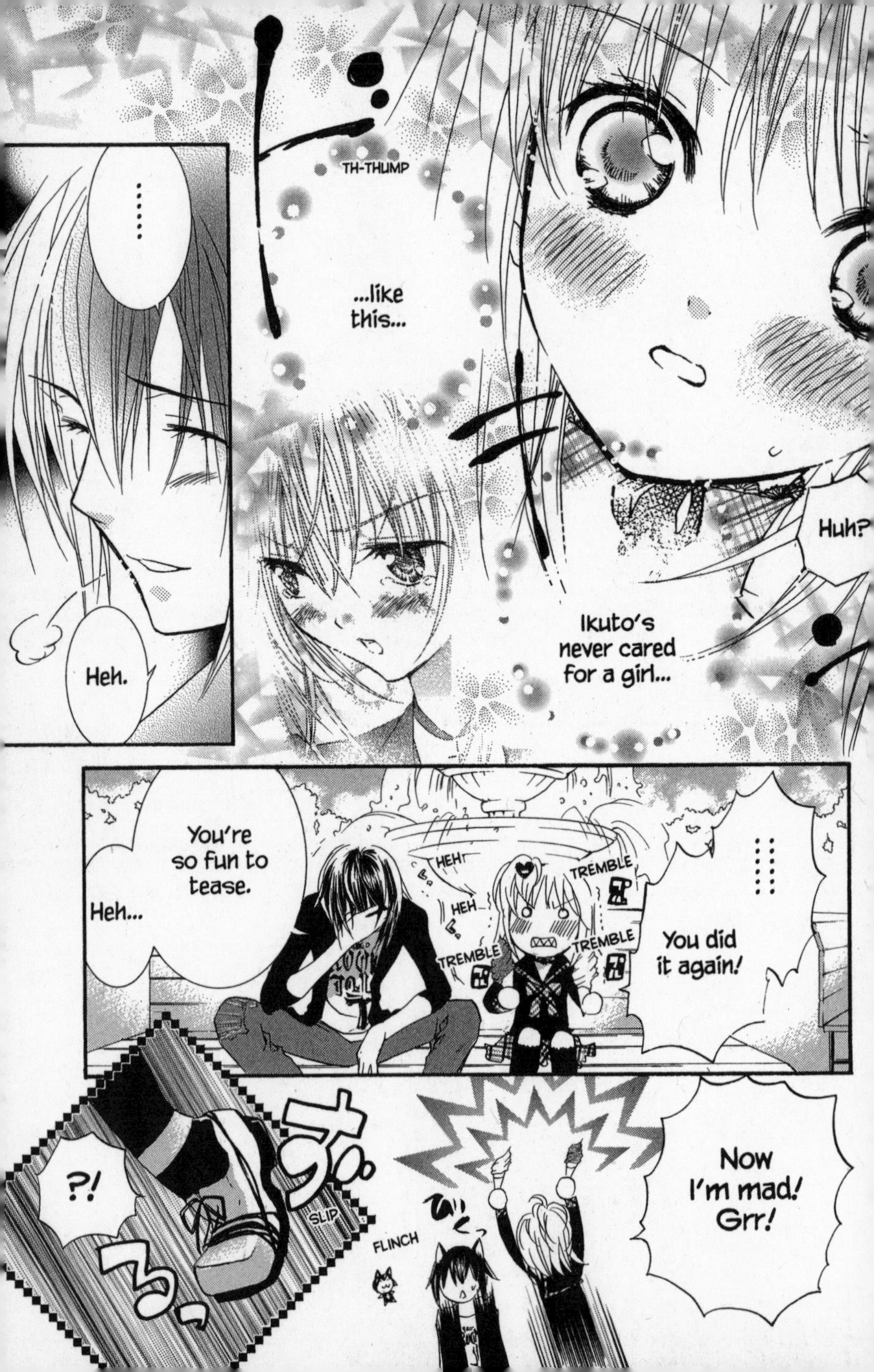
TH-THUMP
Huh?
...like this...
Ikuto's never cared for a girl...
......
Heh.
......
You did it again!
TREMBLE
TREMBLE
TREMBLE
HEH
HEH
You're so fun to tease.
Heh...
Now I'm mad! Grr!
FLINCH
SLIP
?!

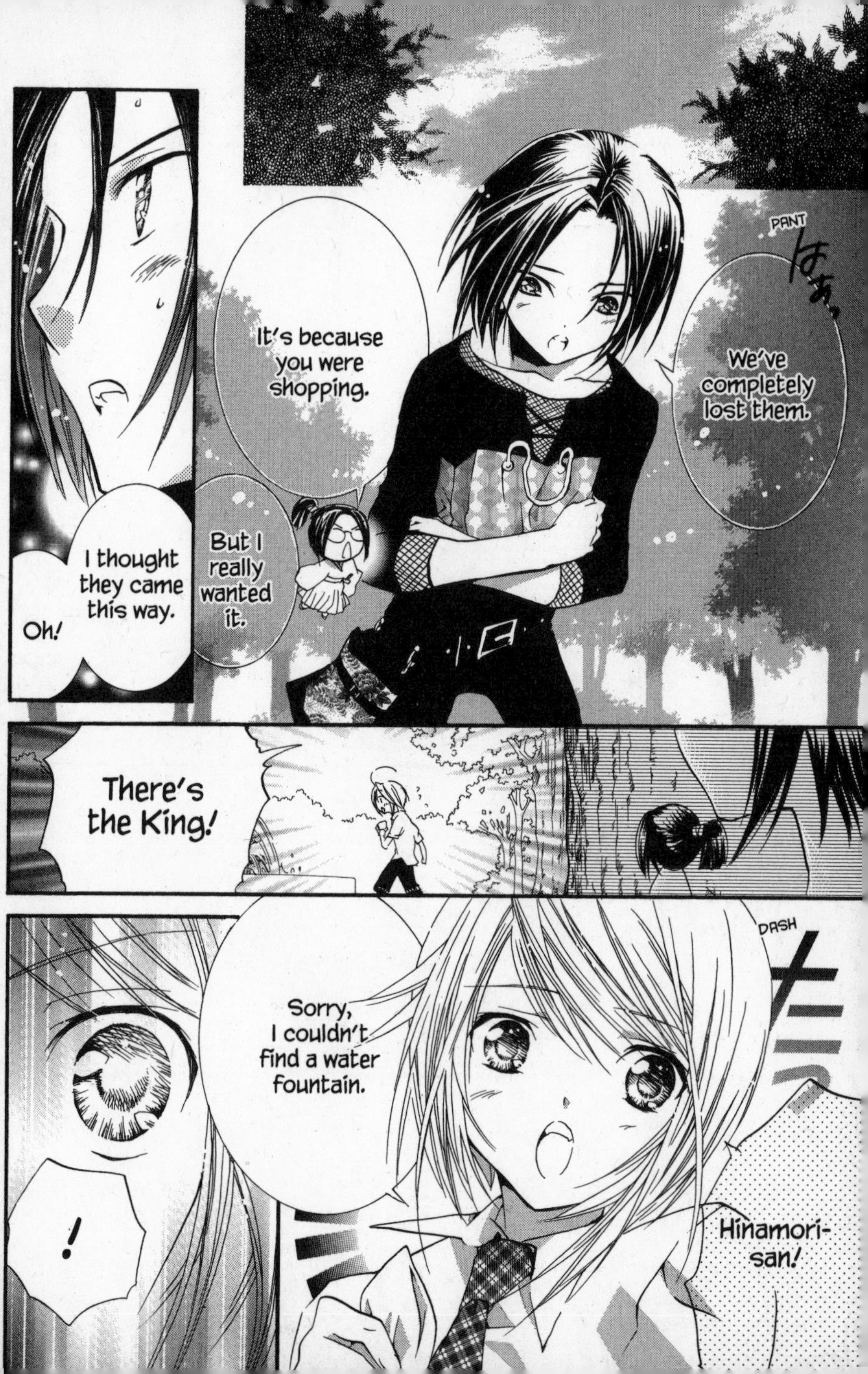
PANT
We've completely lost them.
It's because you were shopping.
But I really wanted it.
I thought they came this way.
Oh!
There's the King!
DASH
Hinamori-san!
Sorry, I couldn't find a water fountain.
!

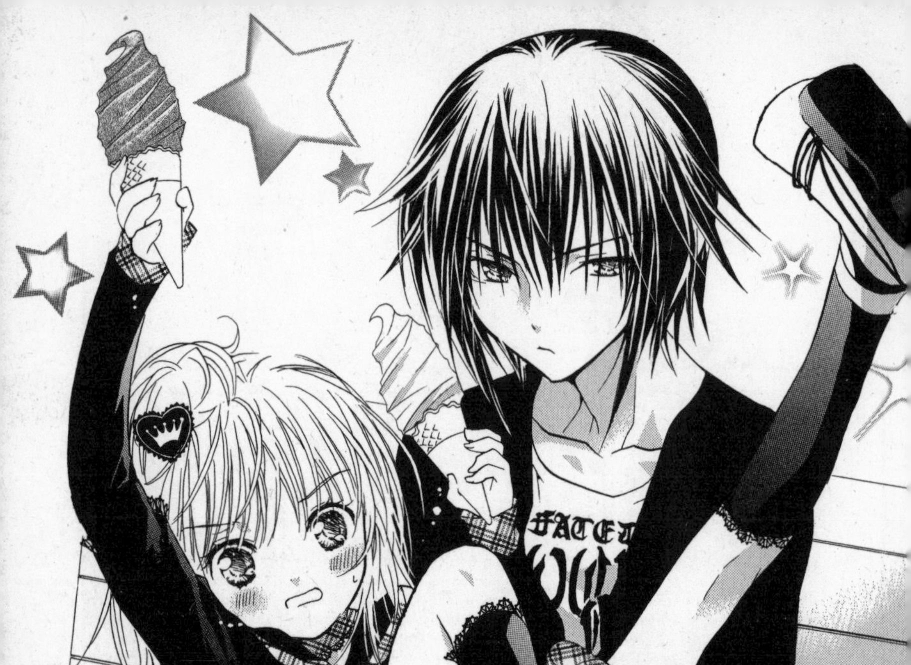
Ta..dase-
kun...

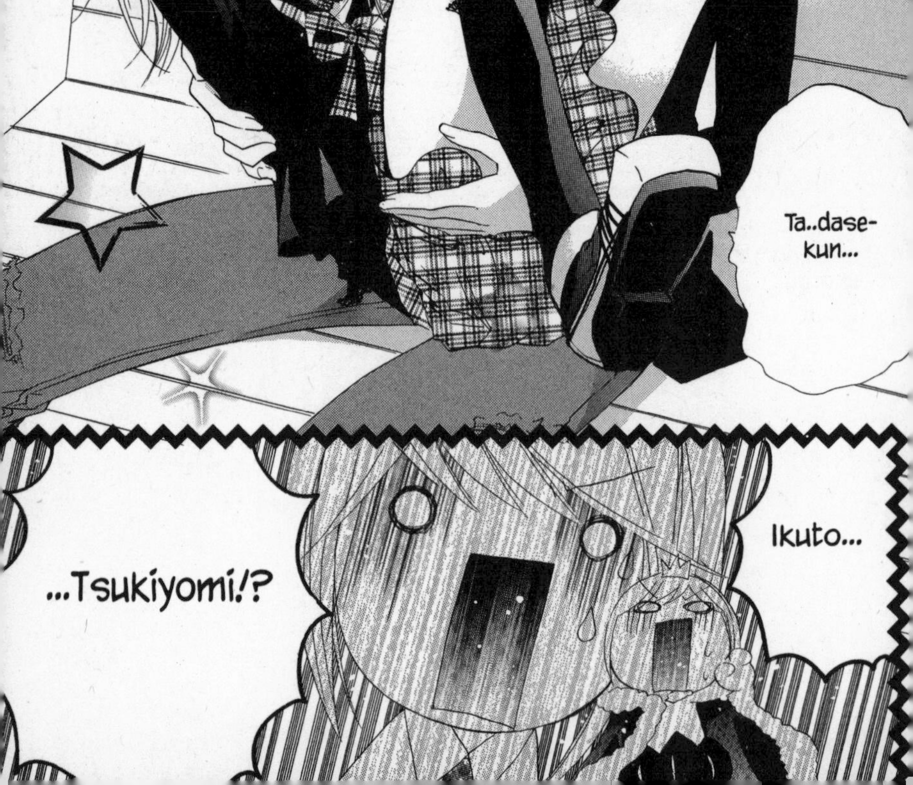
Ikuto...
...Tsukiyomi!?

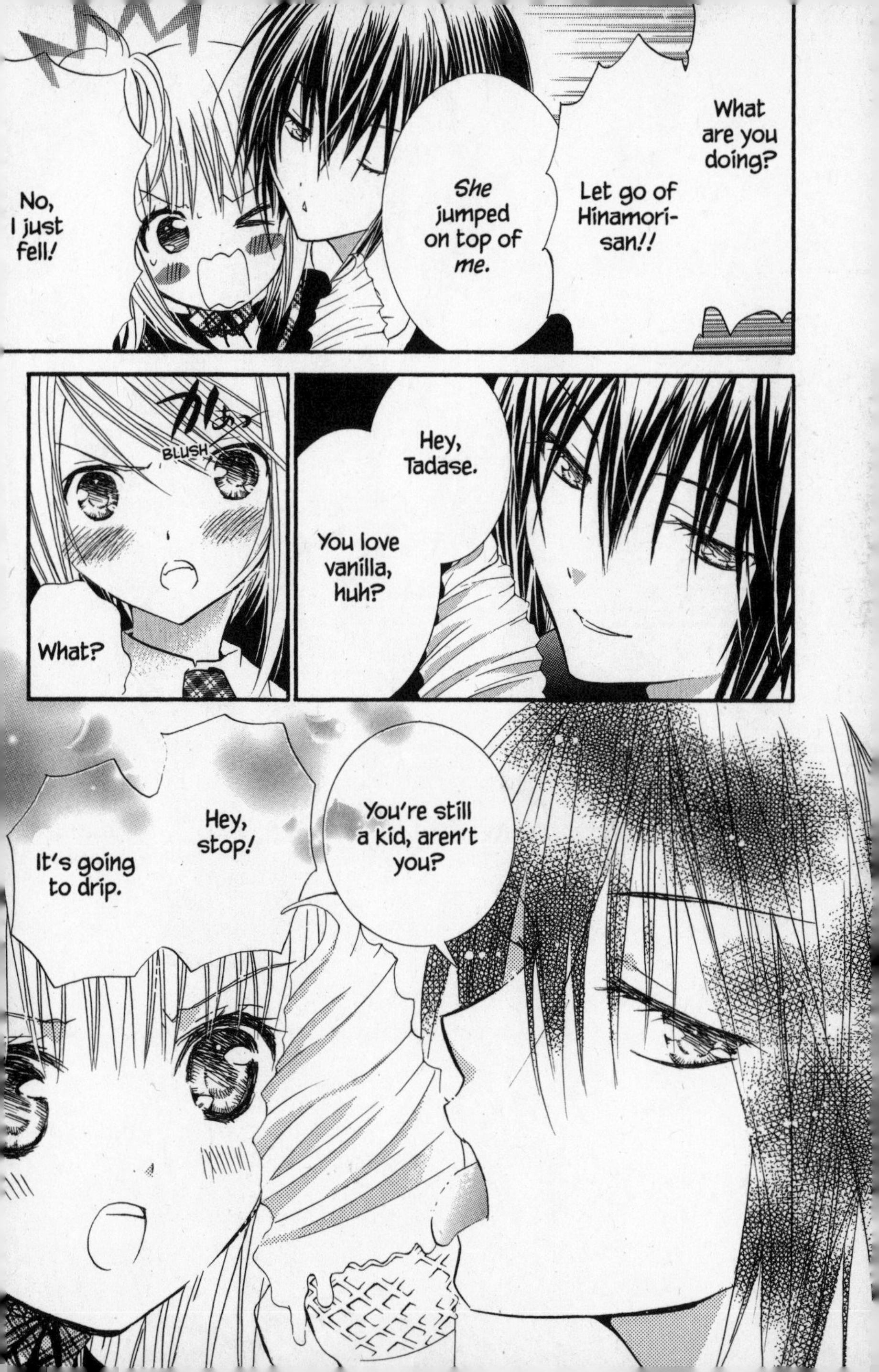
What are you doing?
Let go of Hinamori-san!!
She jumped on top of me.
No, I just fell!
Hey, Tadase.
You love vanilla, huh?
BLUSH
What?
You're still a kid, aren't you?
Hey, stop!
It's going to drip.

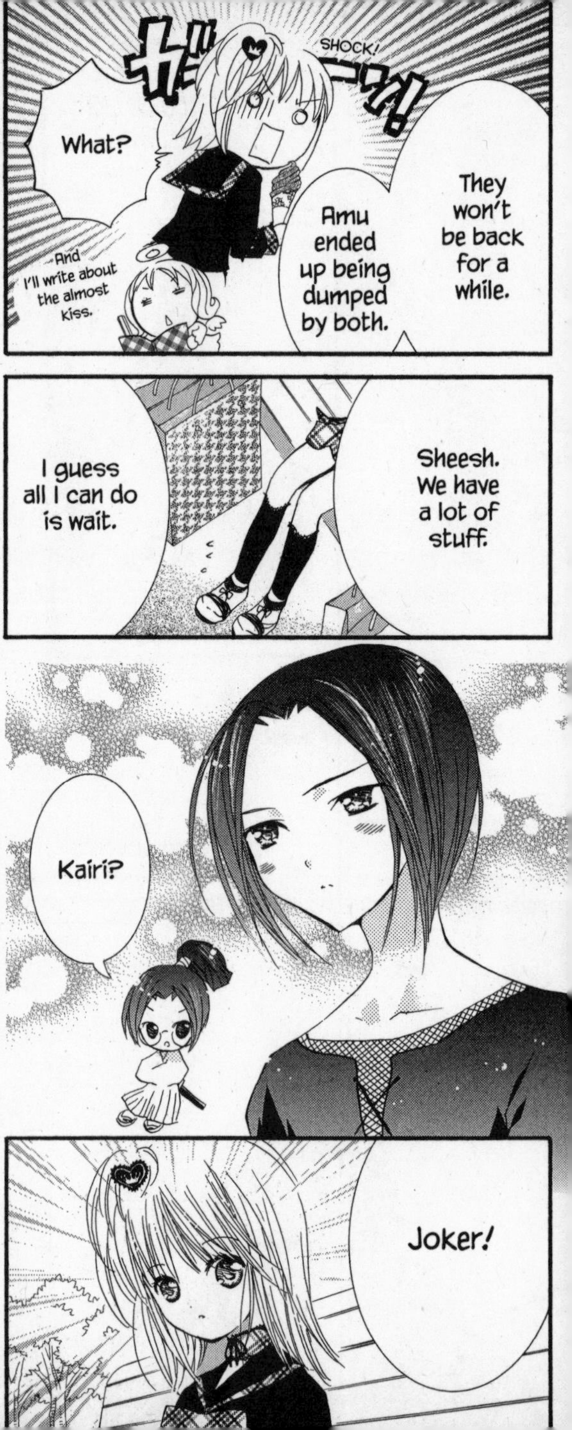
They won't be back for a while.
Amu ended up being dumped by both.
SHOCK!
What?
And I'll write about the almost kiss.
Sheesh. We have a lot of stuff.
I guess all I can do is wait.
Kairi?
Joker!

character profile

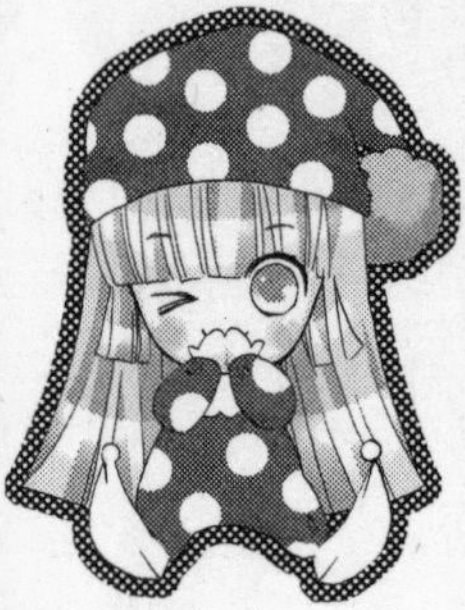

KUSUKUSU

Guardian Character of: Rima
Special Skill: Comedy
Hates: Staring

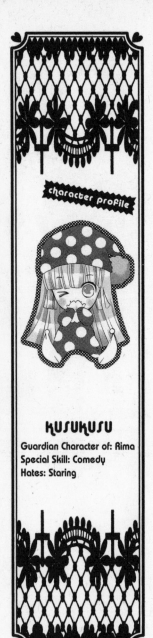

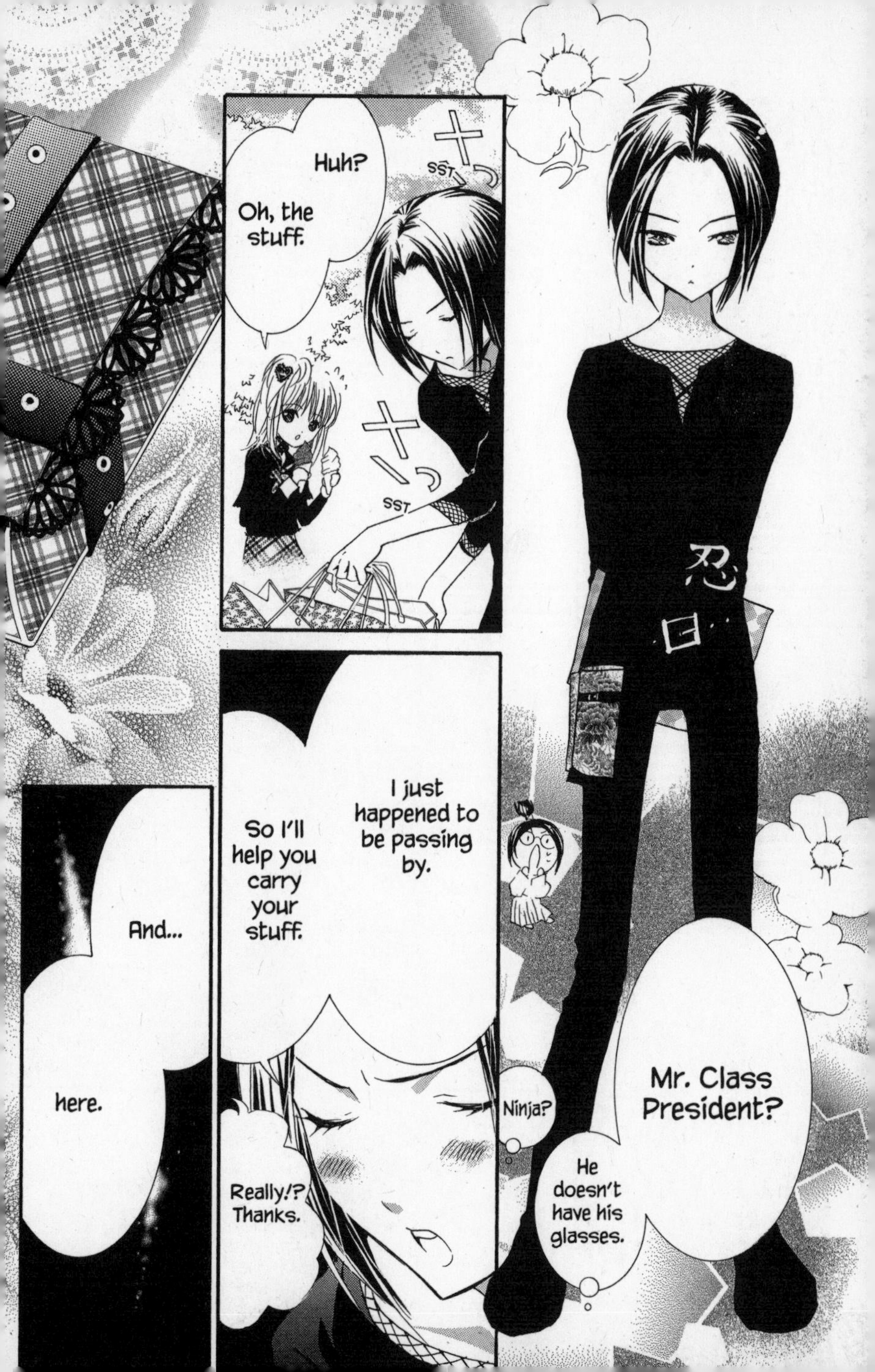
Mr. Class President?
Ninja?
He doesn't have his glasses.
Huh?
SST
Oh, the stuff.
SST
I just happened to be passing by.
So I'll help you carry your stuff.
Really!? Thanks.
And...
here.

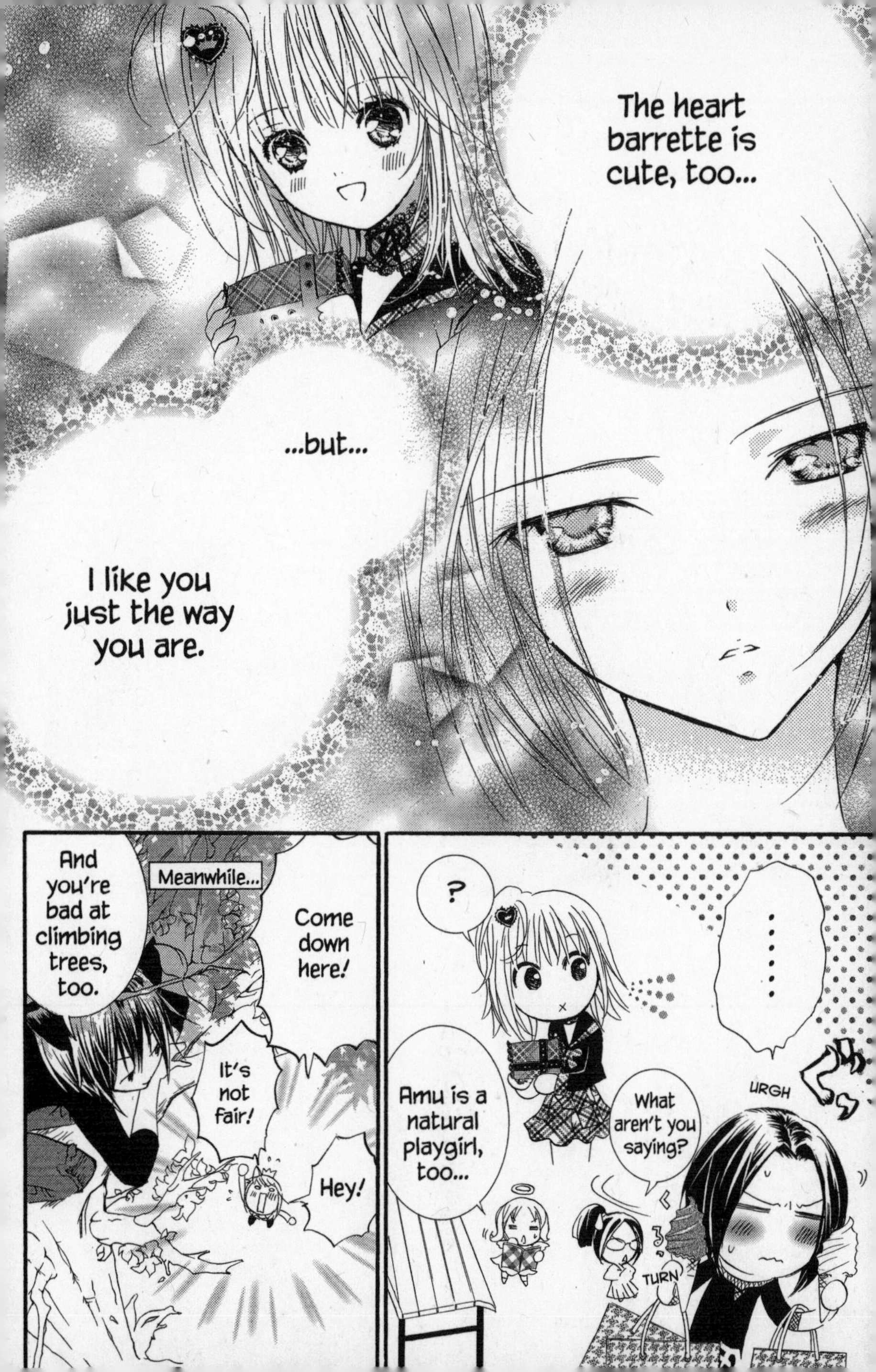
The heart barrette is cute, too...
...but...
I like you just the way you are.
......
?
URGH
What aren't you saying?
Amu is a natural playgirl, too...
TURN
Meanwhile...
Come down here!
And you're bad at climbing trees, too.
It's not fair!
Hey!

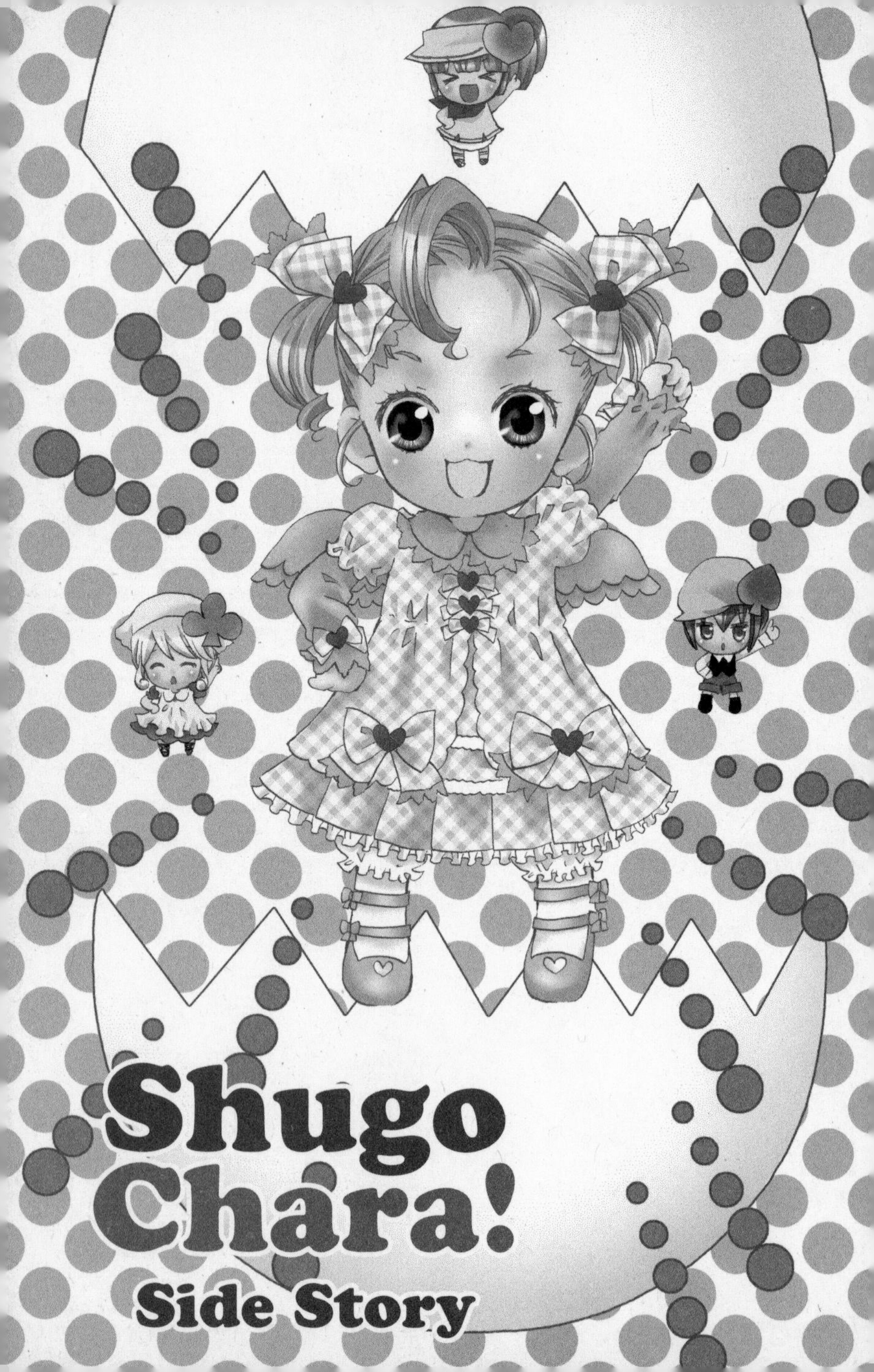
Shugo Chara!
Side Story

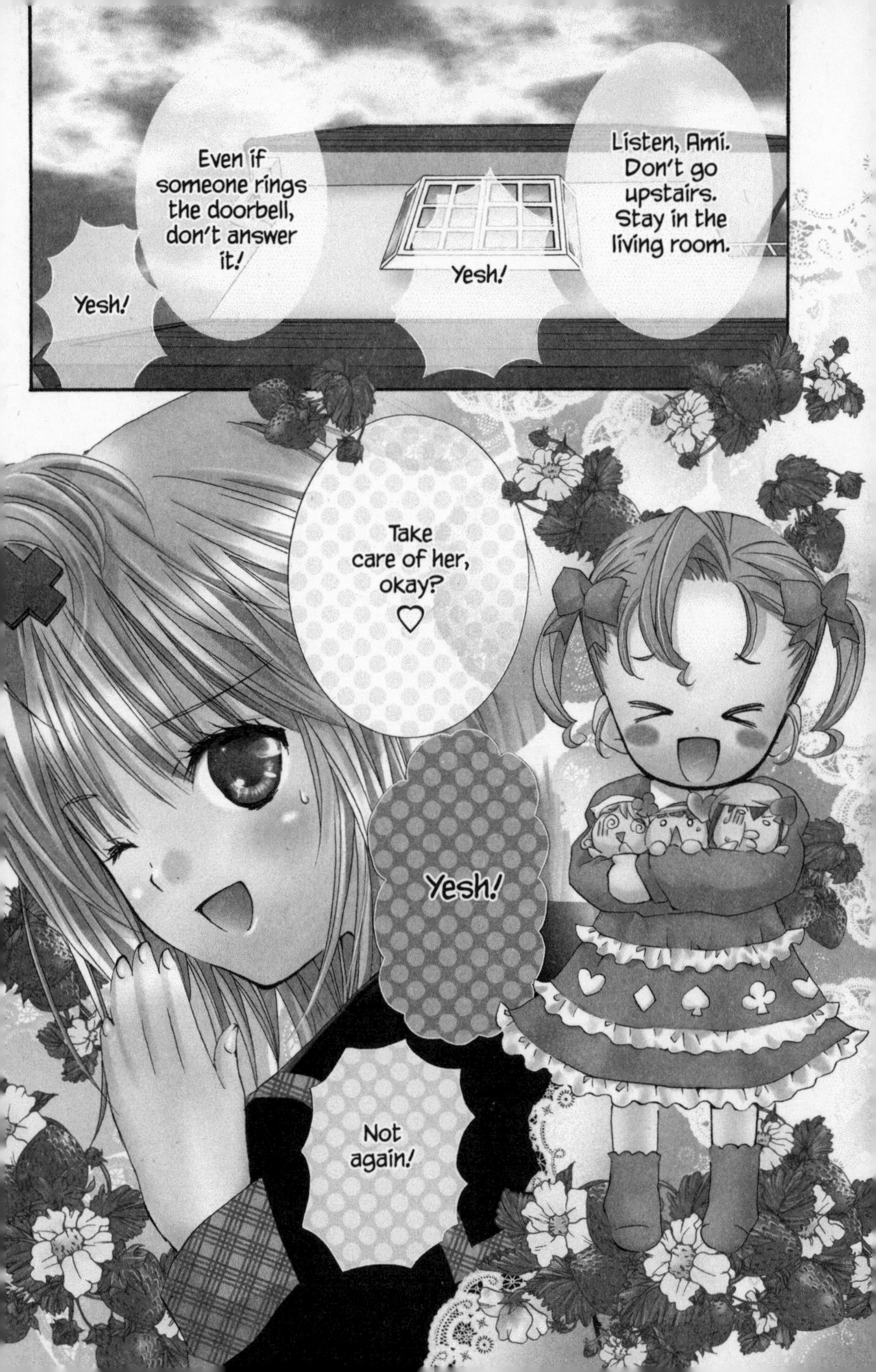
Listen, Ami. Don't go upstairs. Stay in the living room.
Yesh!
Even if someone rings the doorbell, don't answer it!
Yesh!
Take care of her, okay? ♡
Yesh!
Not again!

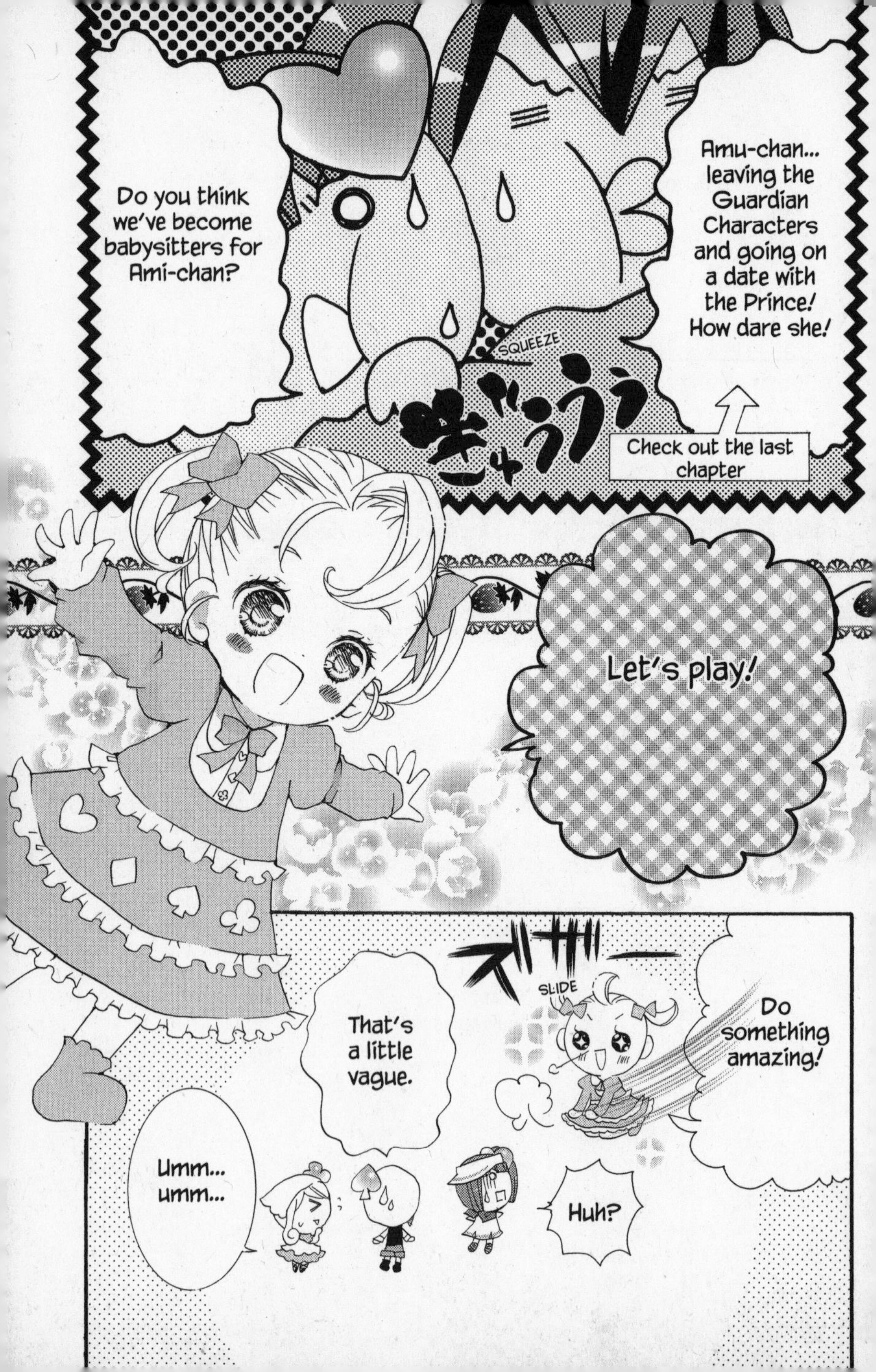
Amu-chan... leaving the Guardian Characters and going on a date with the Prince! How dare she!
Do you think we've become babysitters for Ami-chan?
SQUEEZE
Check out the last chapter
Let's play!
SLIDE
Do something amazing!
That's a little vague.
Huh?
Umm... umm...

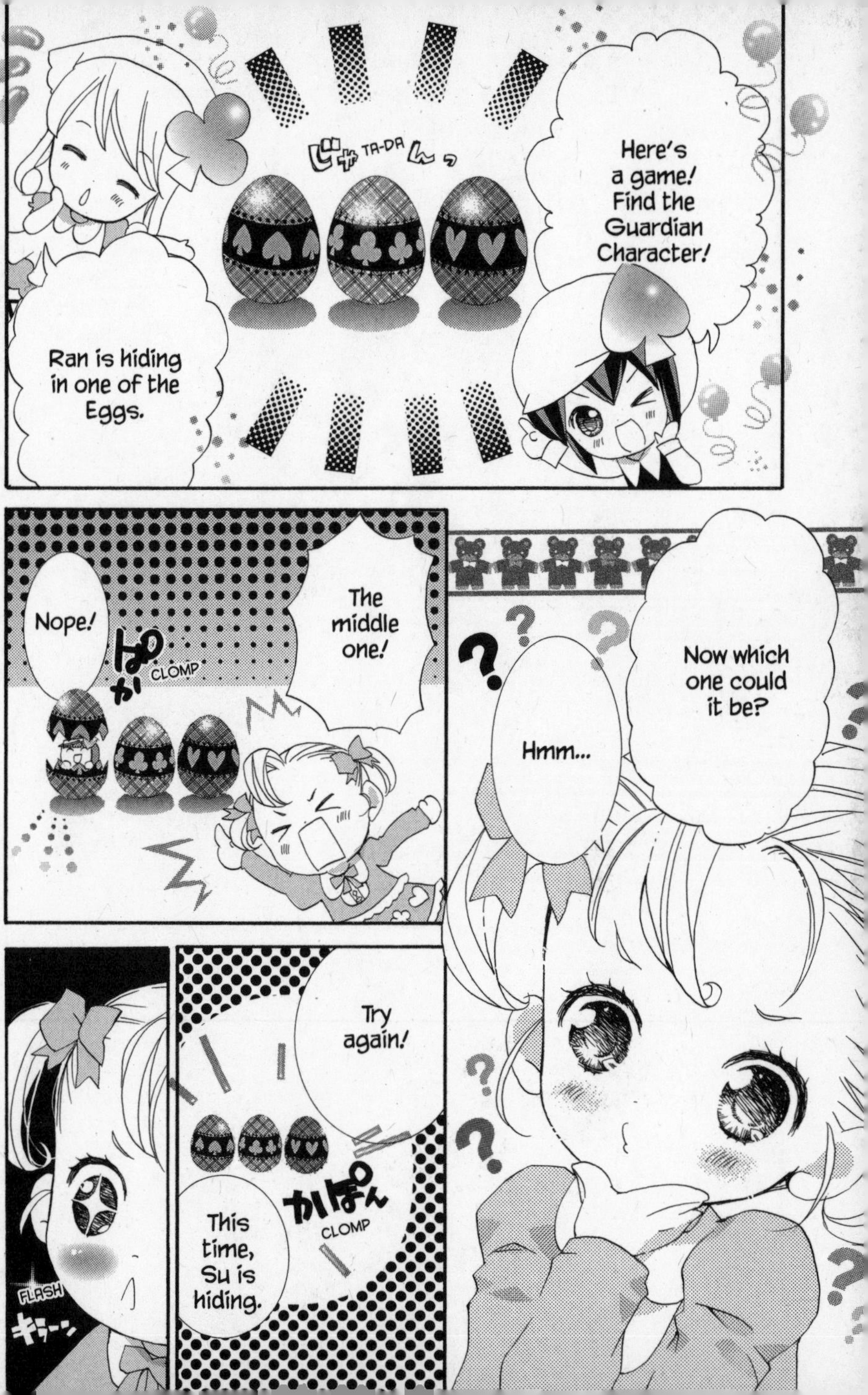
Here's a game! Find the Guardian Character!
じゃ TA-DA ん
Ran is hiding in one of the Eggs.
Now which one could it be?
Hmm...
The middle one!
Nope!
ぱか CLOMP
Try again!
かぱん CLOMP
This time, Su is hiding.
キラーン FLASH

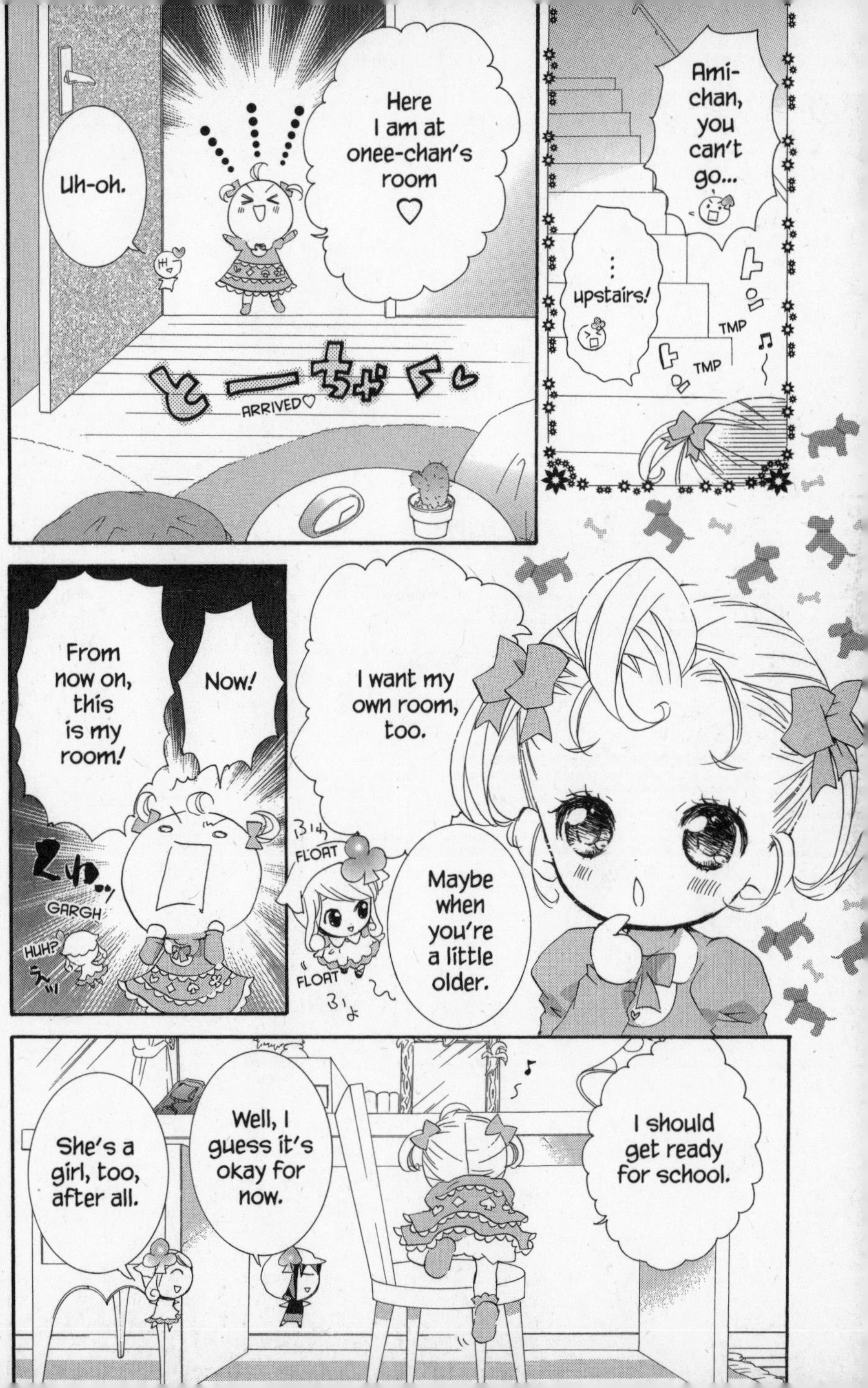
Ami-chan, you can't go...
...upstairs!
TMP
TMP
Here I am at onee-chan's room ♡
ARRIVED♡
Uh-oh.
I want my own room, too.
FLOAT
FLOAT
Maybe when you're a little older.
Now!
From now on, this is my room!
GARGH
HUH?
I should get ready for school.
Well, I guess it's okay for now.
She's a girl, too, after all.

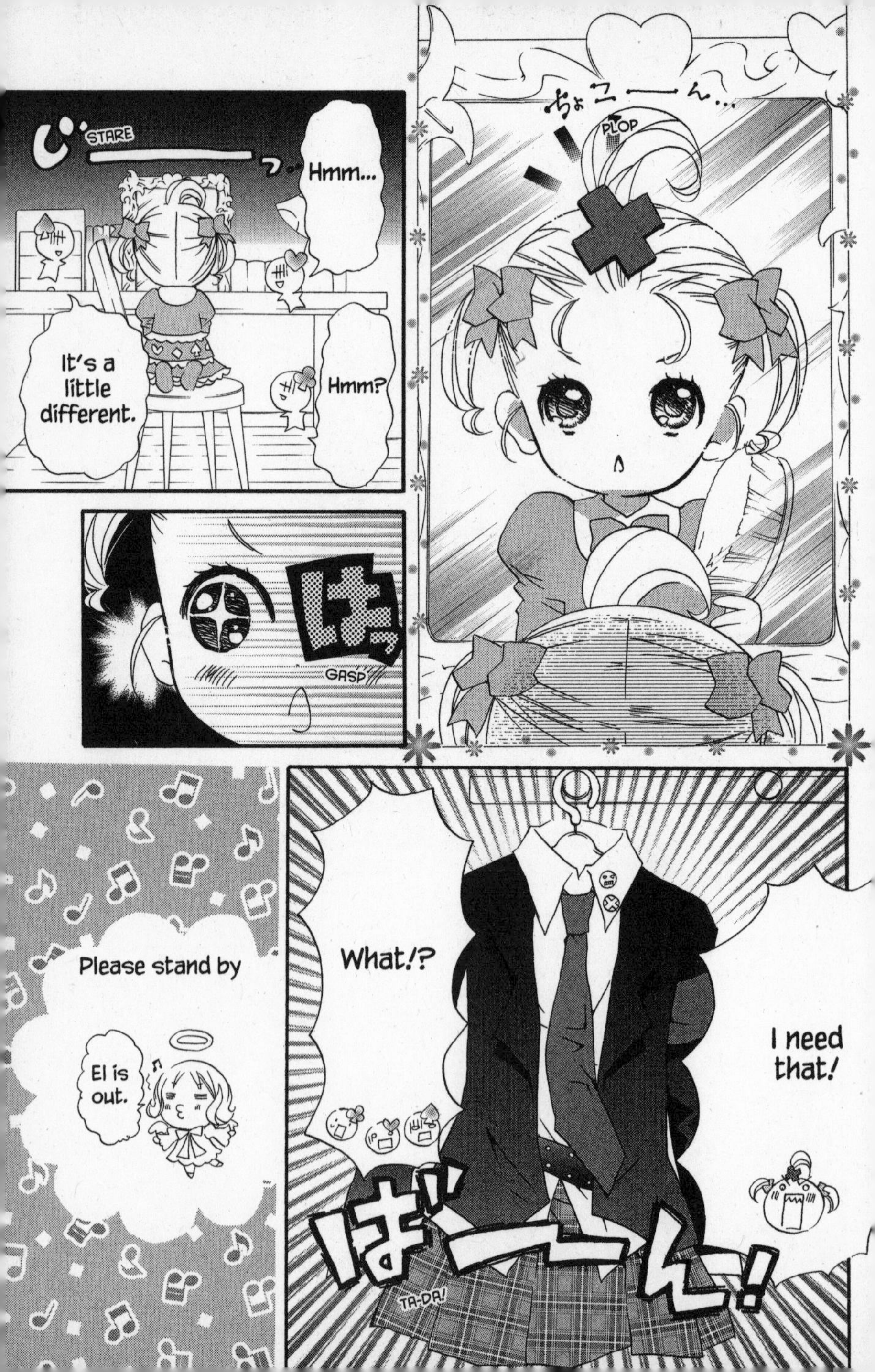
ちょこーん…
PLOP
じー
STARE
Hmm...
Hmm?
It's a little different.
は
GASP
I need that!
What!?
ばーん!
TA-DA!
Please stand by
El is out.

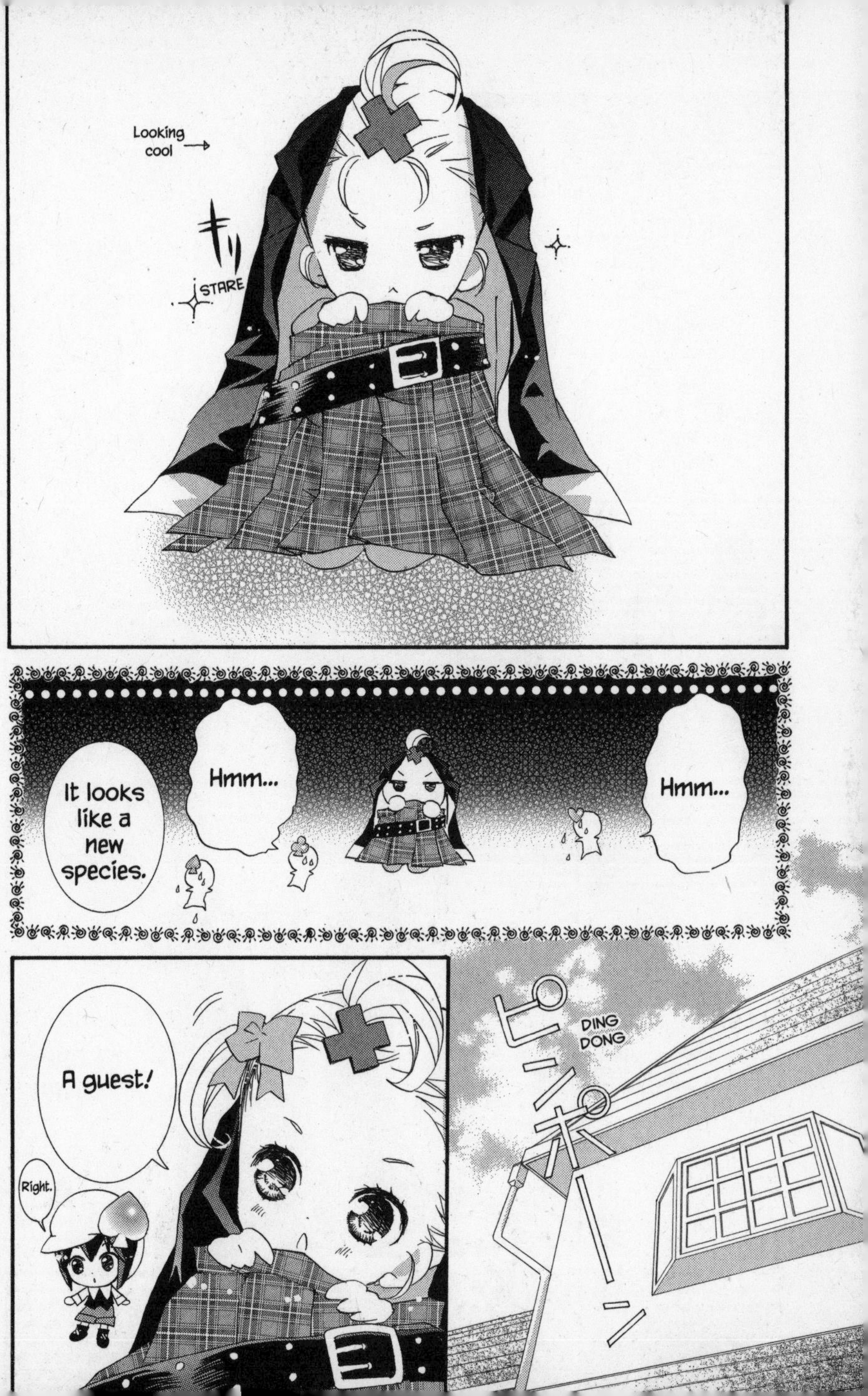
Looking cool
STARE
Hmm...
Hmm...
It looks like a new species.
DING DONG
A guest!
Right.

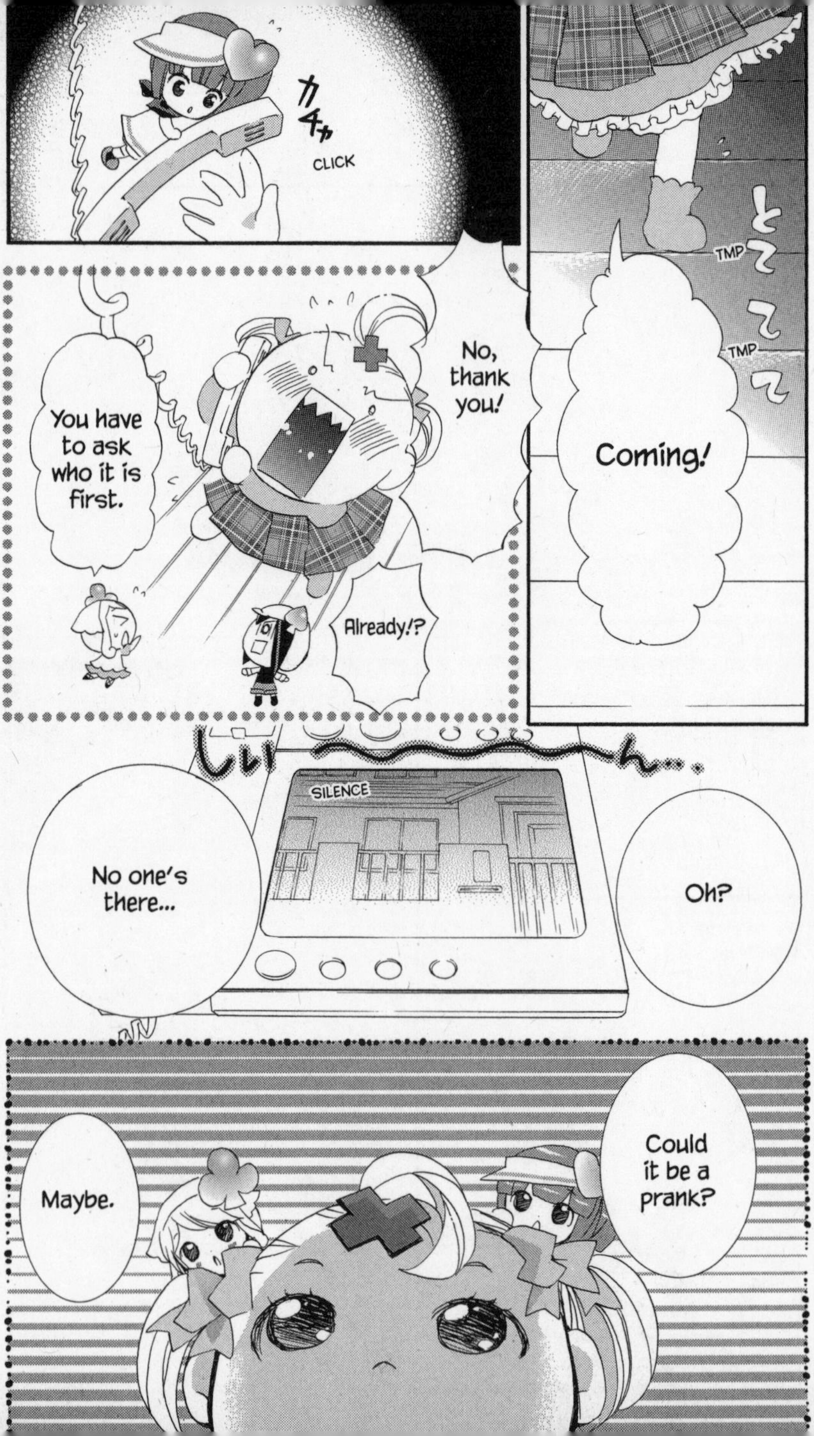

とてとて
TMP
TMP
Coming!
カチャ
CLICK
No, thank you!
You have to ask who it is first.
Already!?
しぃ〜ん…
SILENCE
Oh?
No one's there...
Could it be a prank?
Maybe.

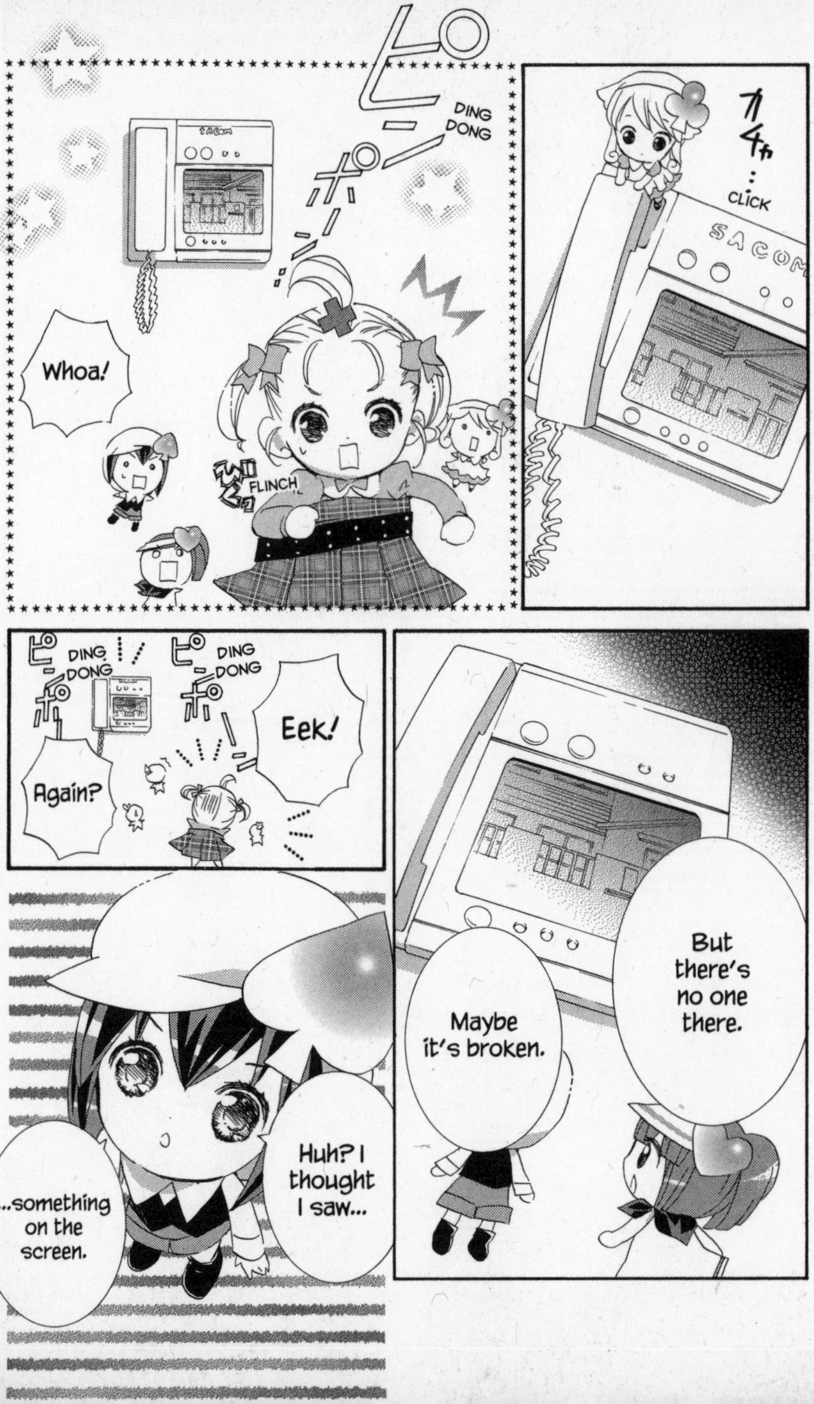
CLICK
DING DONG
FLINCH
Whoa!
But there's no one there.
Maybe it's broken.
DING DONG
DING DONG
Eek!
Again?
Huh? I thought I saw...
...something on the screen.

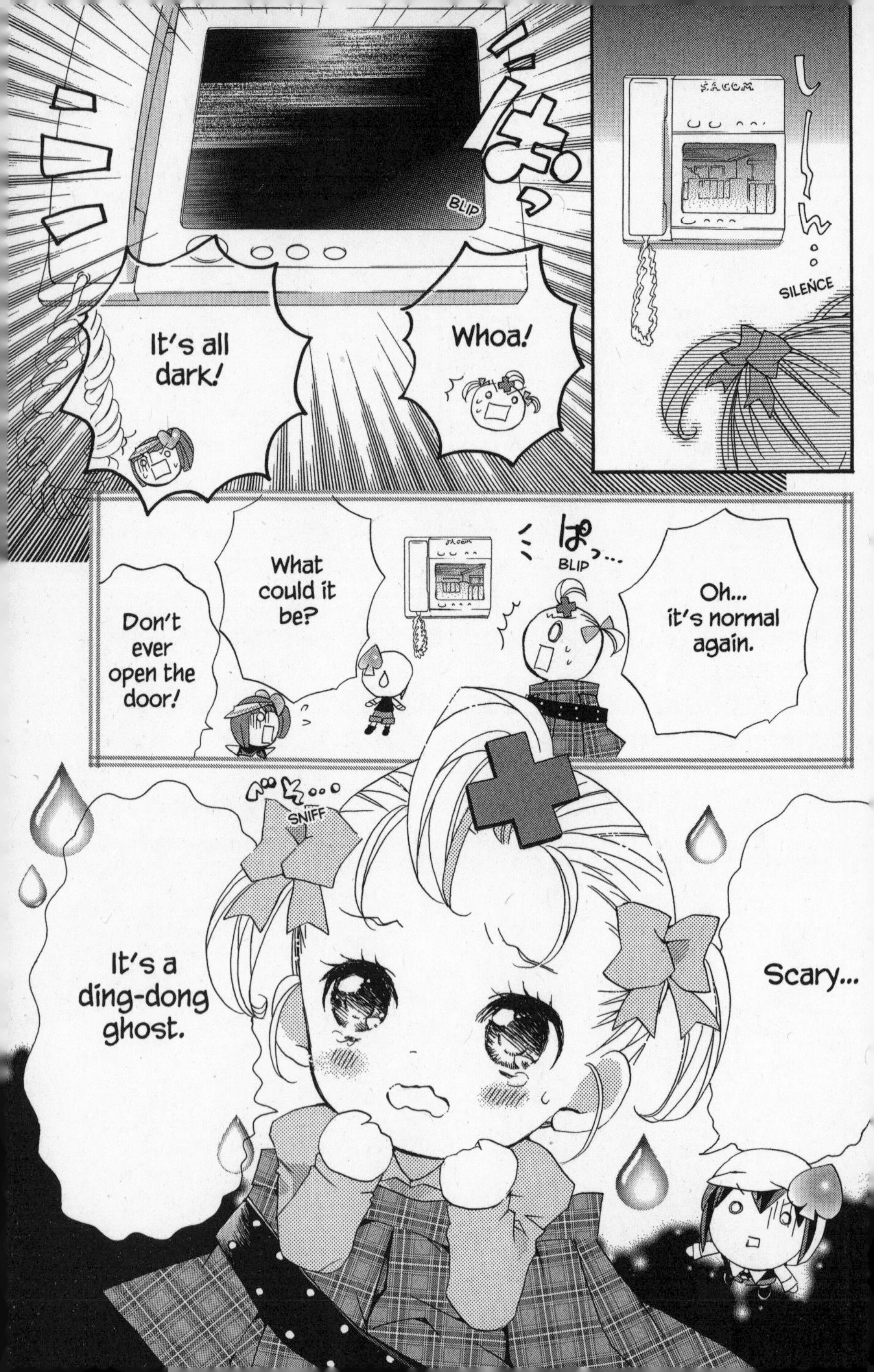

SACOM
しーん。
SILENCE
ぱっ
BLIP
Whoa!
It's all dark!
Oh... it's normal again.
ぱっ...
BLIP
What could it be?
Don't ever open the door!
SNIFF
Scary...
It's a ding-dong ghost.

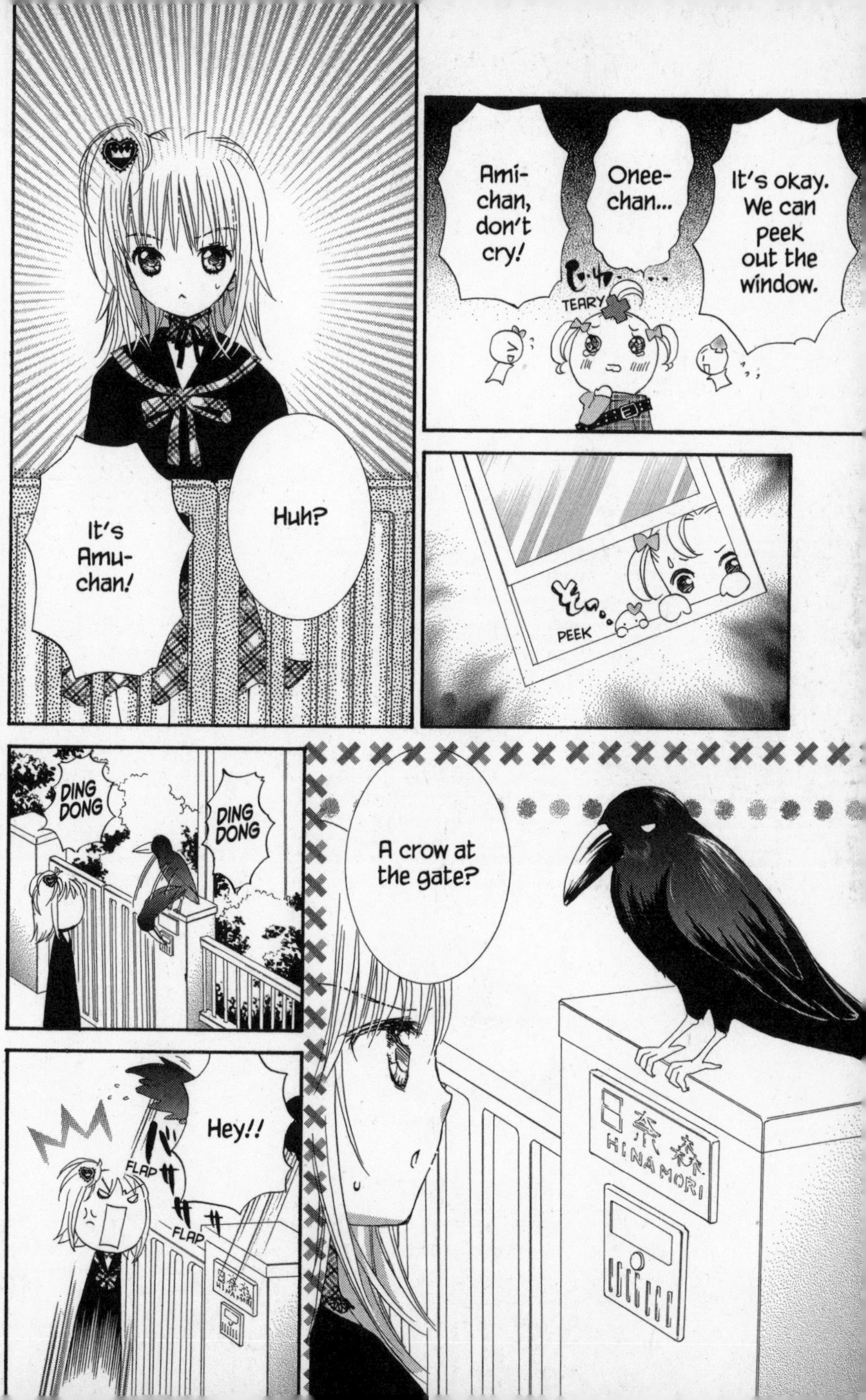
It's okay. We can peek out the window.
Onee-chan...
Ami-chan, don't cry!
TEARY
PEEK
Huh?
It's Amu-chan!
A crow at the gate?
HINAMORI
DING DONG
DING DONG
Hey!!
FLAP
FLAP

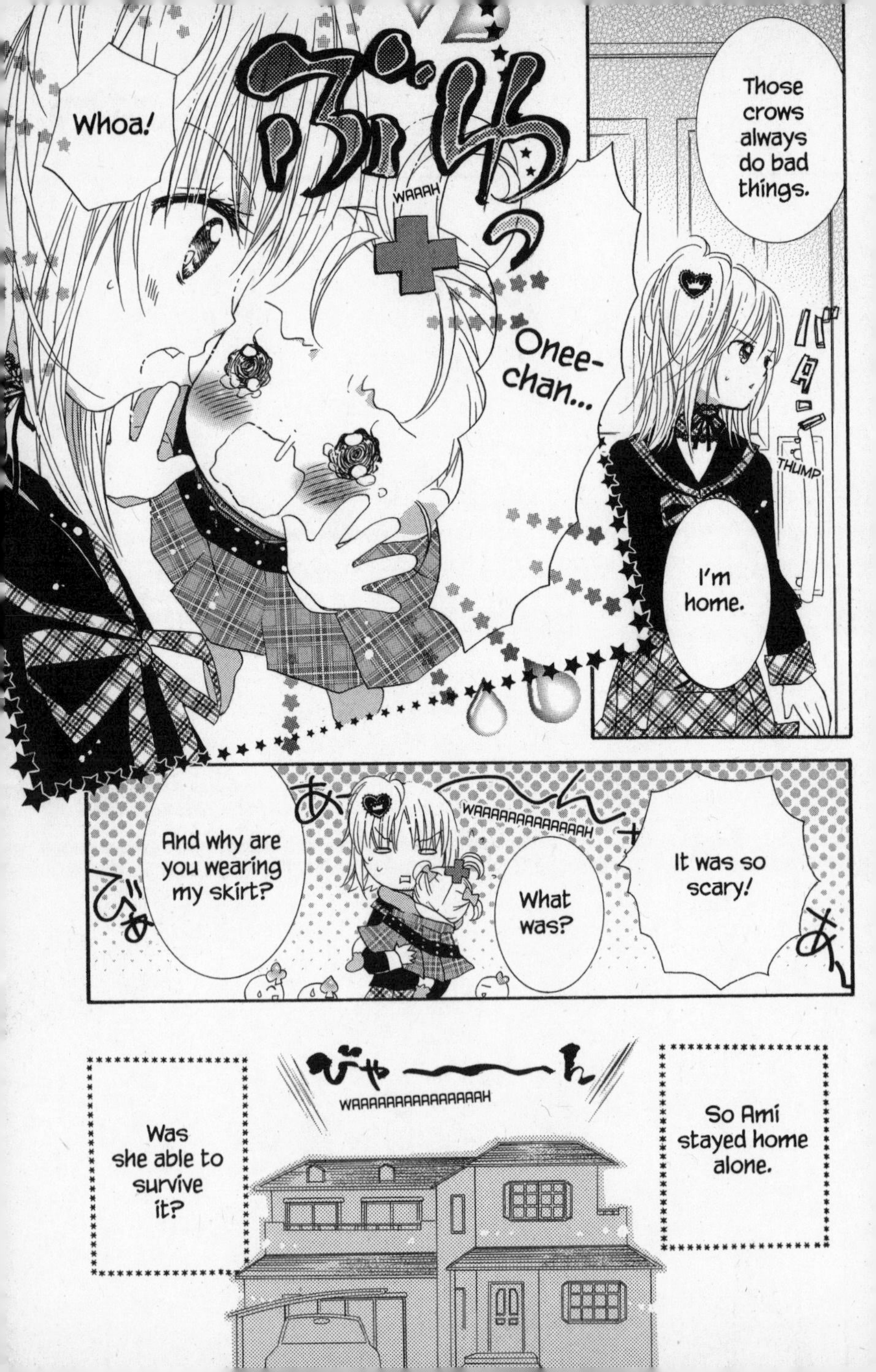
Those crows always do bad things.
THUMP
I'm home.
WAAAH
Onee-chan...
Whoa!
It was so scary!
WAAAAAAAAAAAAAAH
What was?
And why are you wearing my skirt?
So Ami stayed home alone.
WAAAAAAAAAAAAAAAAH
Was she able to survive it?

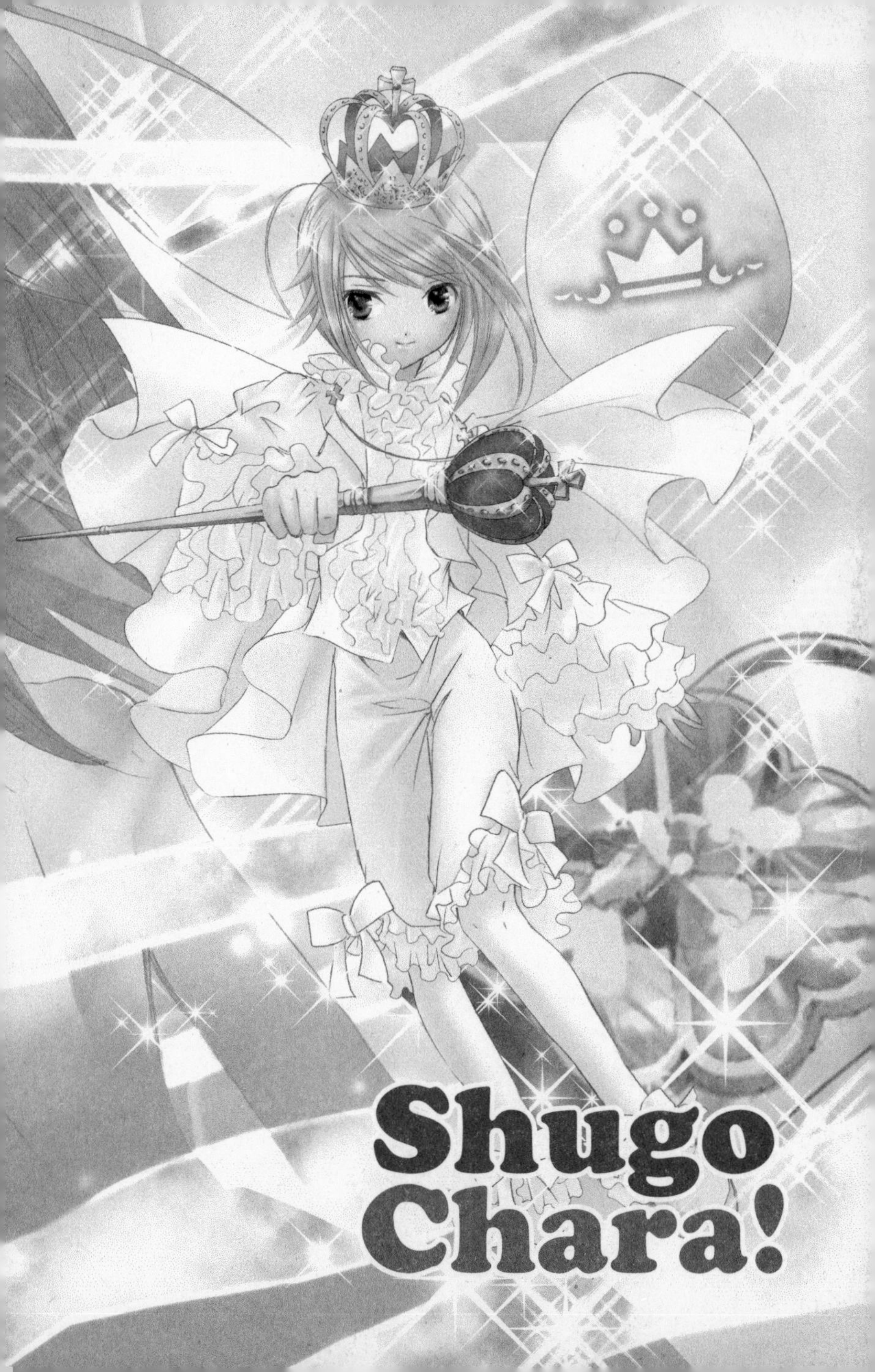
Shugo
Chara!

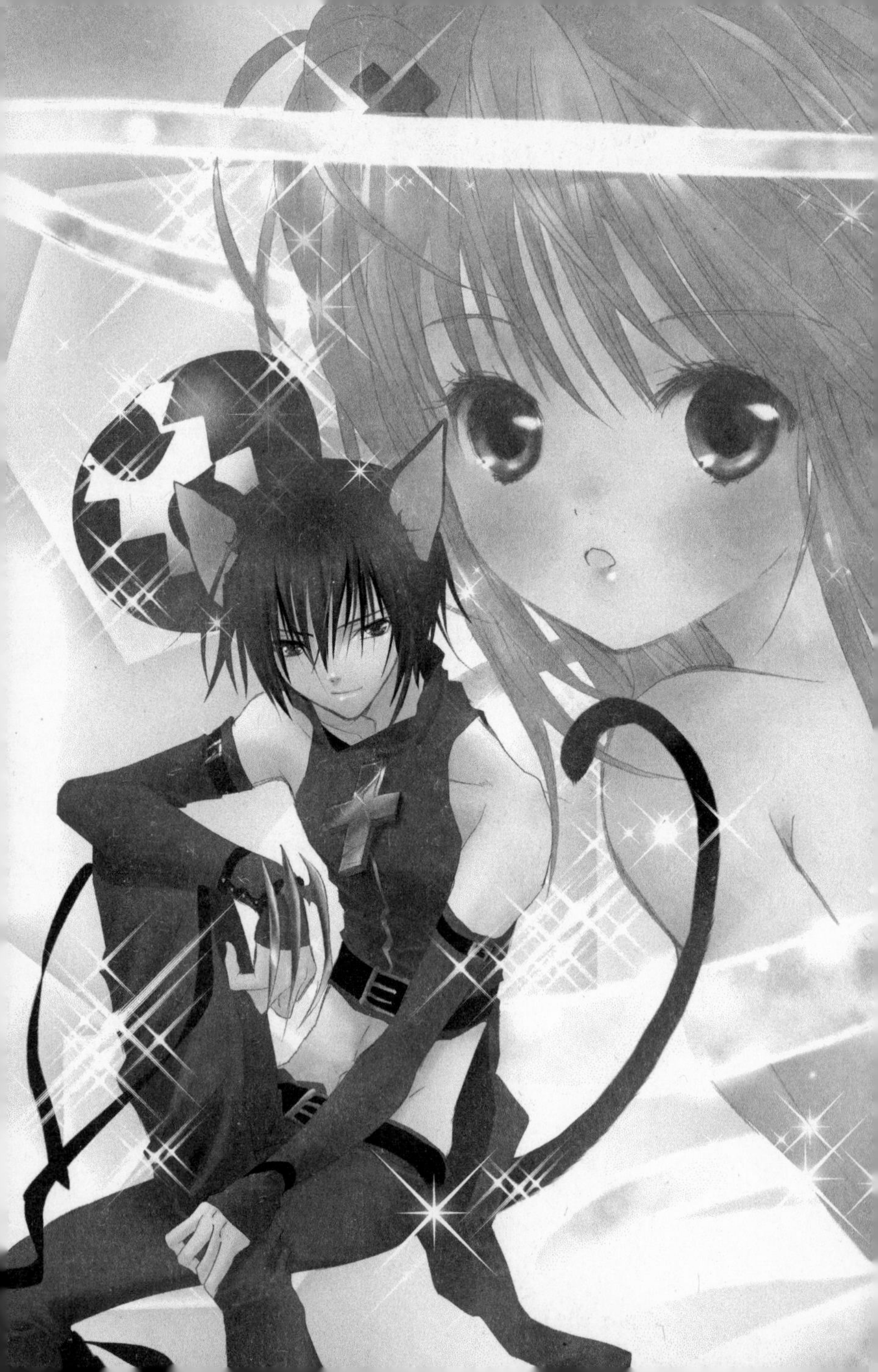

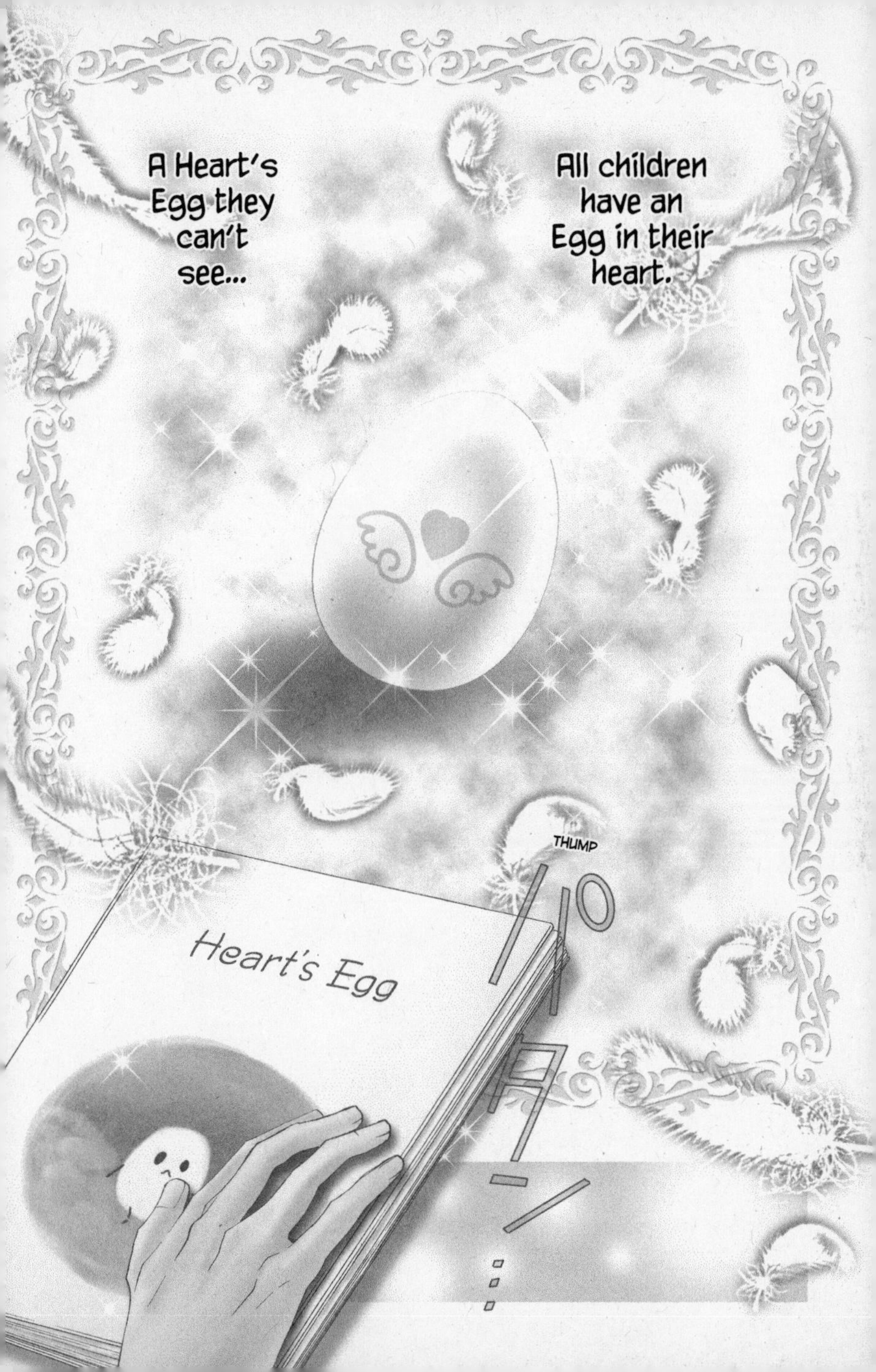
All children have an Egg in their heart.
A Heart's Egg they can't see...
THUMP
Heart's Egg

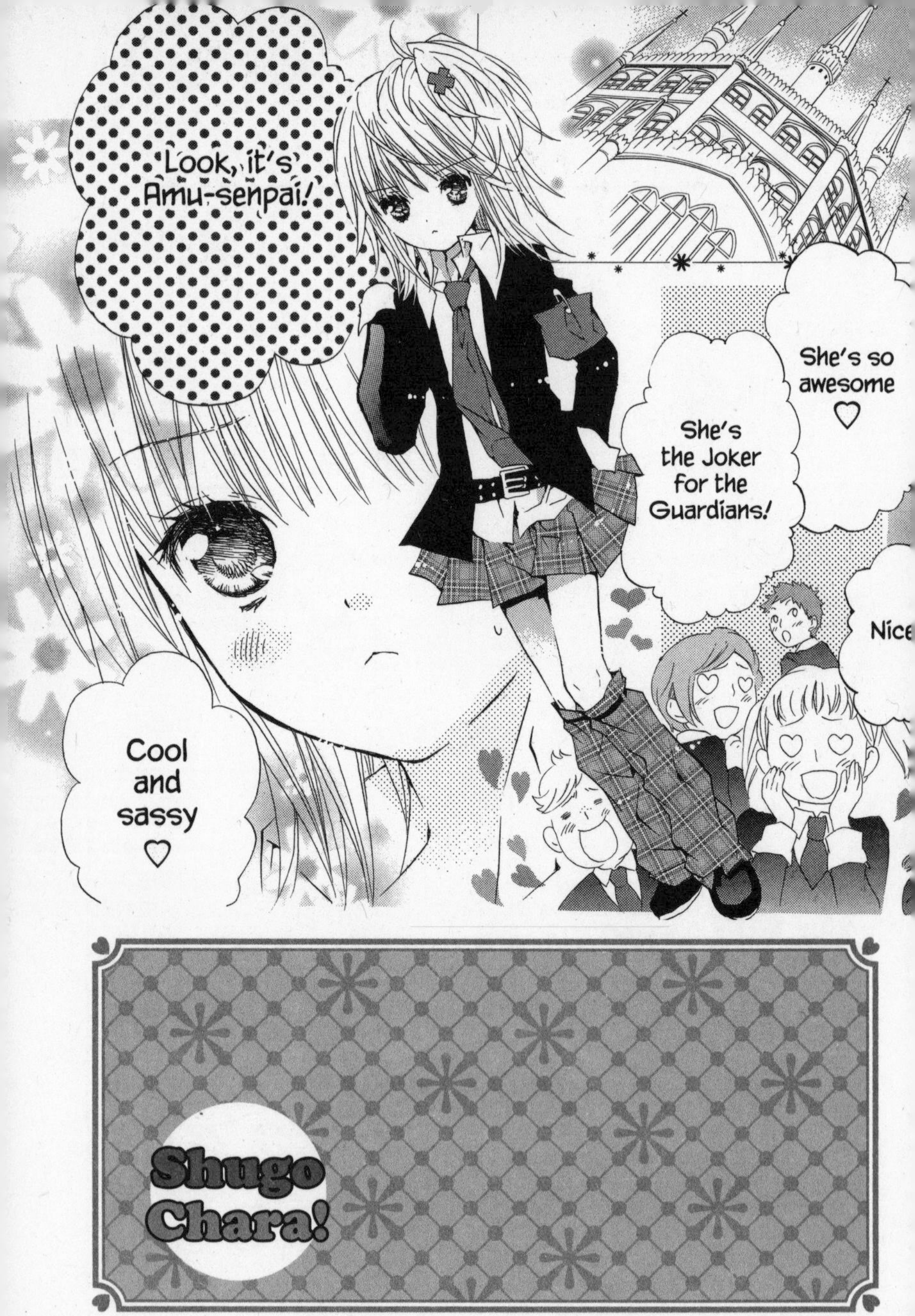
Look, it's Amu-senpai!
She's so awesome ♡
She's the Joker for the Guardians!
Nice
Cool and sassy ♡

Shugo Chara!

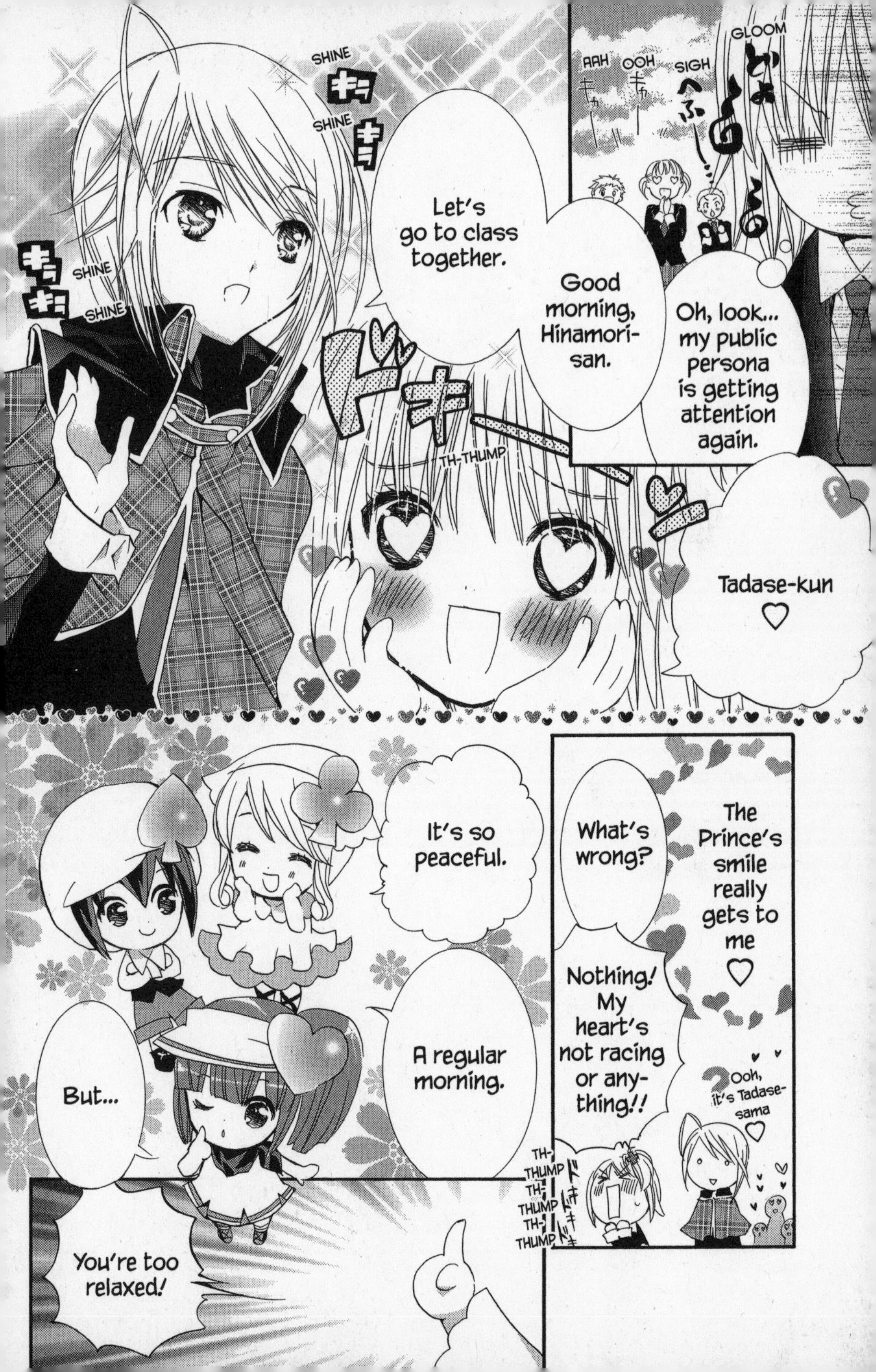
GLOOM
SIGH
OOH
AAH
Oh, look... my public persona is getting attention again.
SHINE
SHINE
SHINE
SHINE
Good morning, Hinamori-san.
Let's go to class together.
TH-THUMP
Tadase-kun ♡
The Prince's smile really gets to me ♡
What's wrong?
Nothing! My heart's not racing or anything!!
Ooh, it's Tadase-sama ♡
TH-THUMP TH-THUMP TH-THUMP
It's so peaceful.
A regular morning.
But...
You're too relaxed!

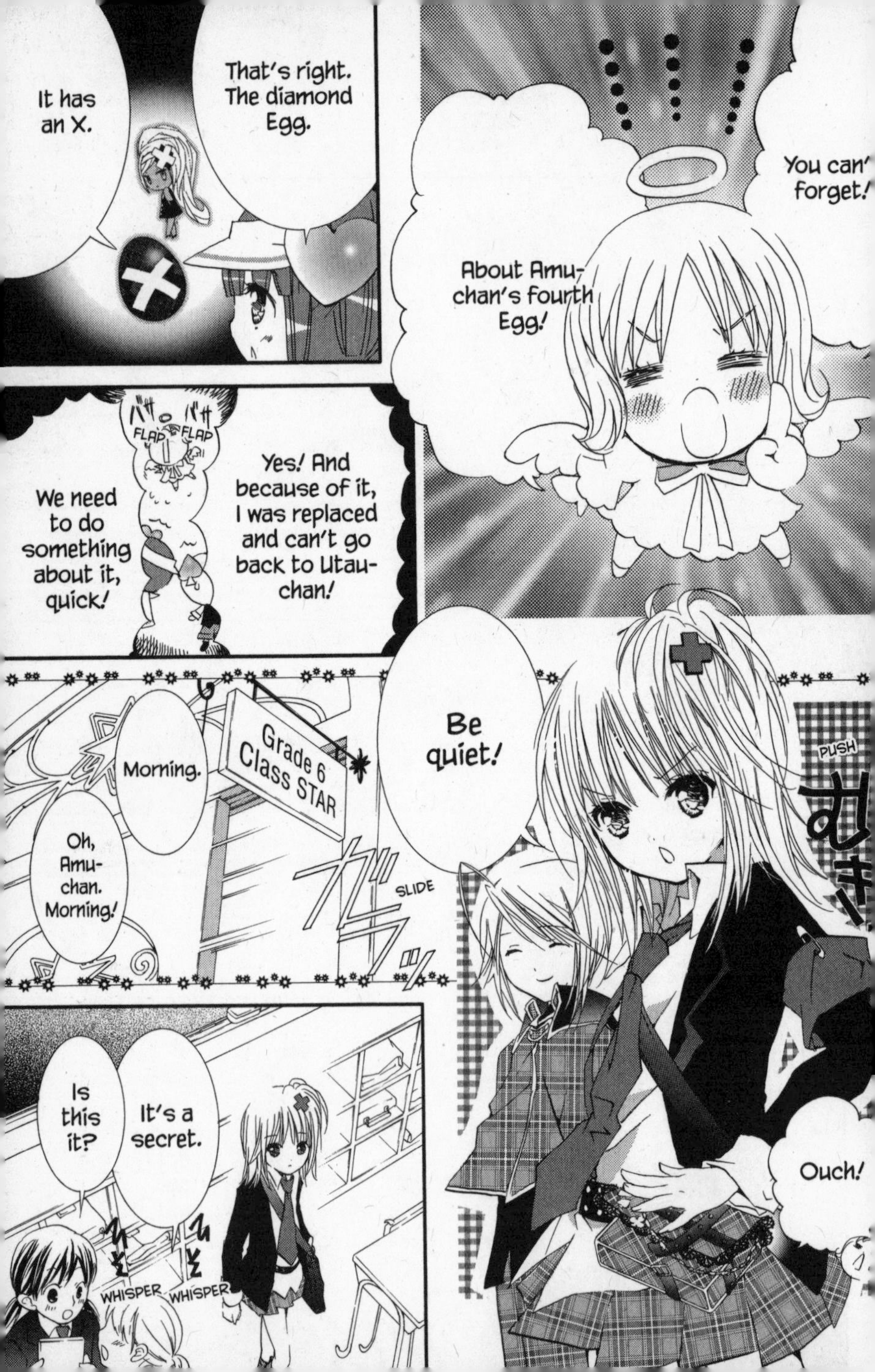

You can'
forget!
About Amu-chan's fourth Egg!
That's right. The diamond Egg.
It has an X.
FLAP FLAP
Yes! And because of it, I was replaced and can't go back to Utau-chan!
We need to do something about it, quick!
Be quiet!
PUSH
Ouch!
Grade 6 Class STAR
SLIDE
Morning.
Oh, Amu-chan. Morning!
It's a secret.
Is this it?
WHISPER WHISPER

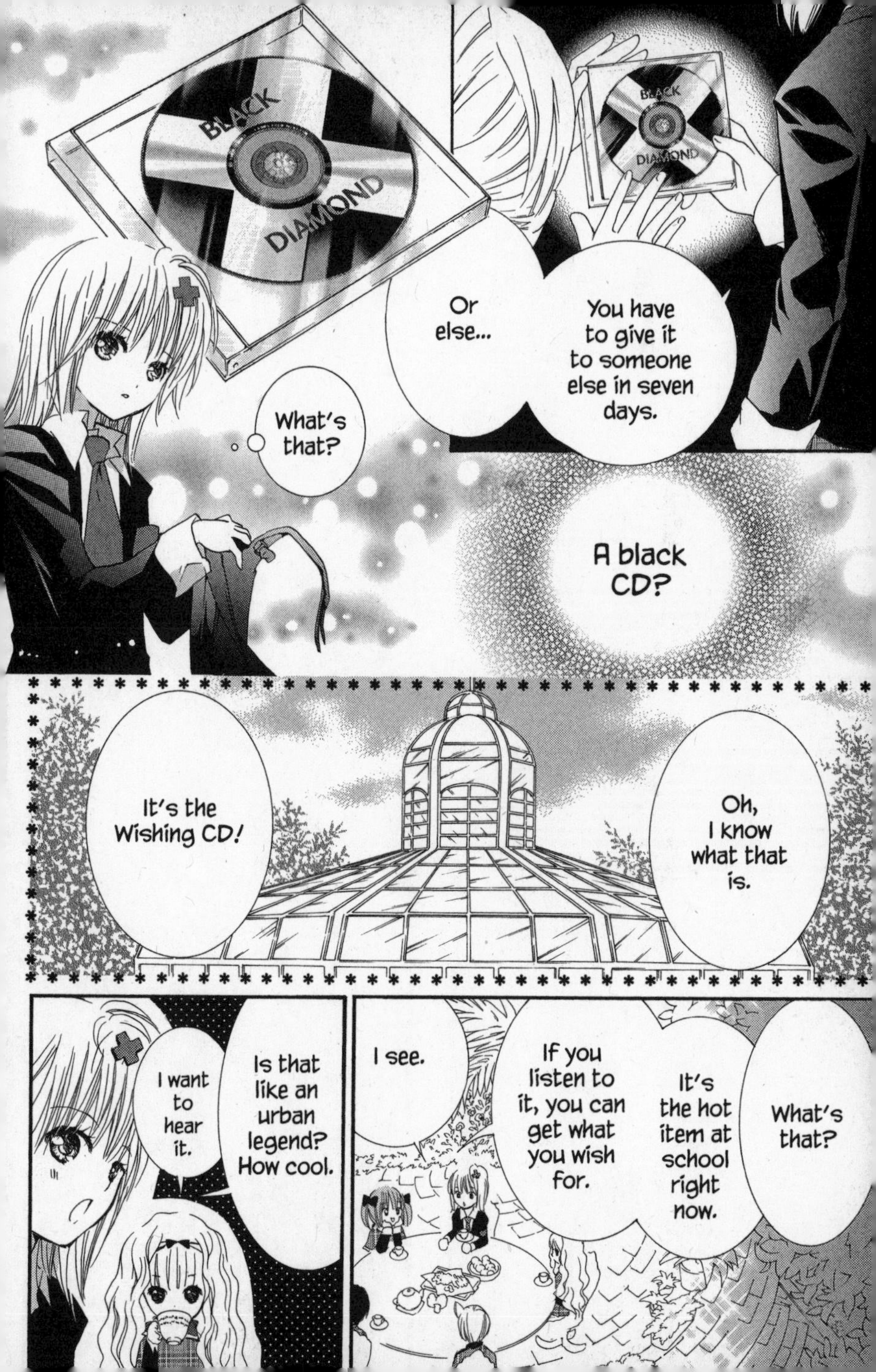
BLACK DIAMOND
You have to give it to someone else in seven days.
Or else...
BLACK DIAMOND
What's that?
A black CD?
Oh, I know what that is.
It's the Wishing CD!
What's that?
It's the hot item at school right now.
If you listen to it, you can get what you wish for.
I see.
Is that like an urban legend? How cool.
I want to hear it.

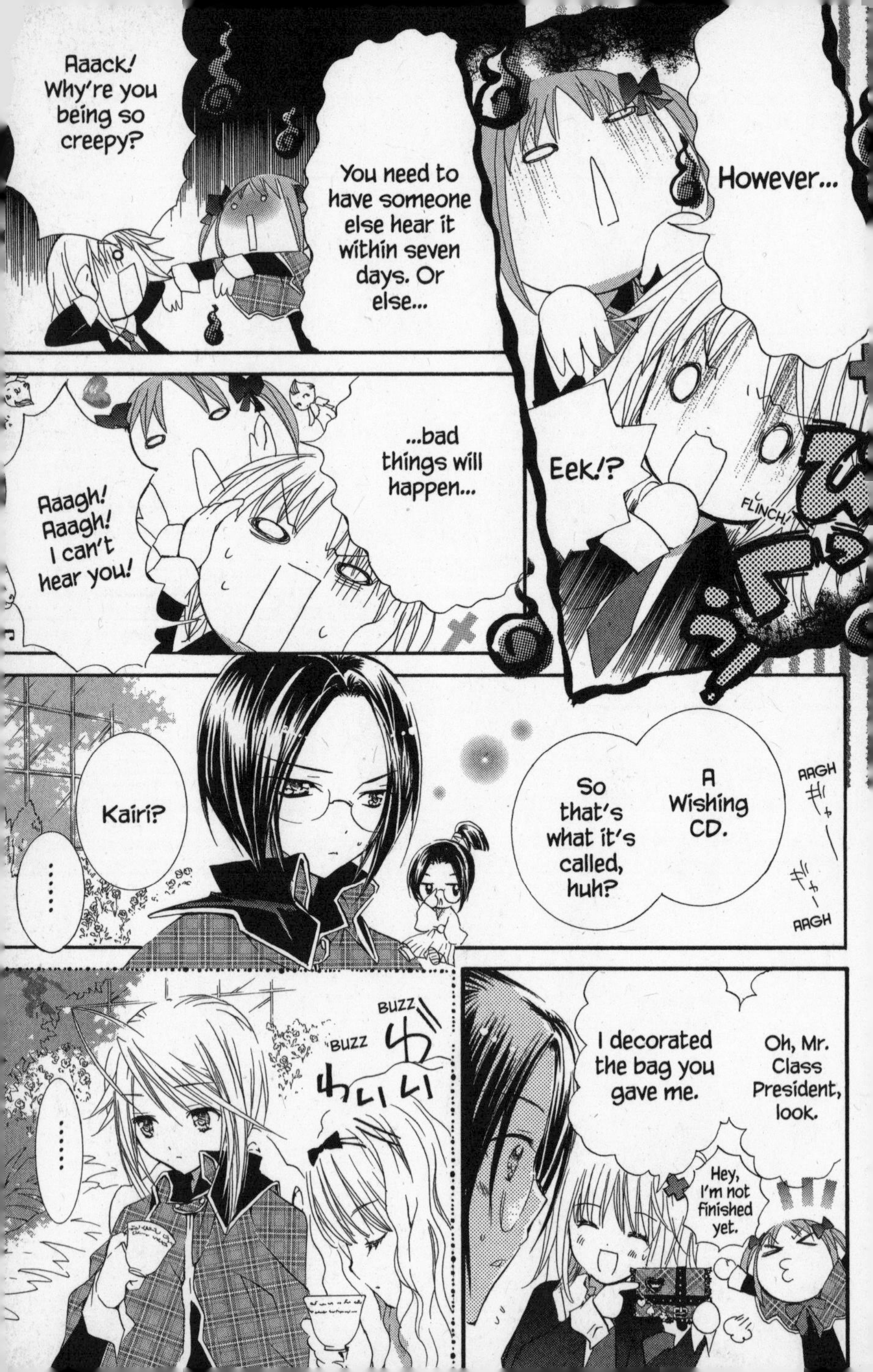
However...
Eek!?
FLINCH!
You need to have someone else hear it within seven days. Or else...
Aaack! Why're you being so creepy?
...bad things will happen...
Aaagh! Aaagh! I can't hear you!
A Wishing CD.
So that's what it's called, huh?
AAGH
AAGH
Kairi?
......
Oh, Mr. Class President, look.
I decorated the bag you gave me.
Hey, I'm not finished yet.
BUZZ
BUZZ
......

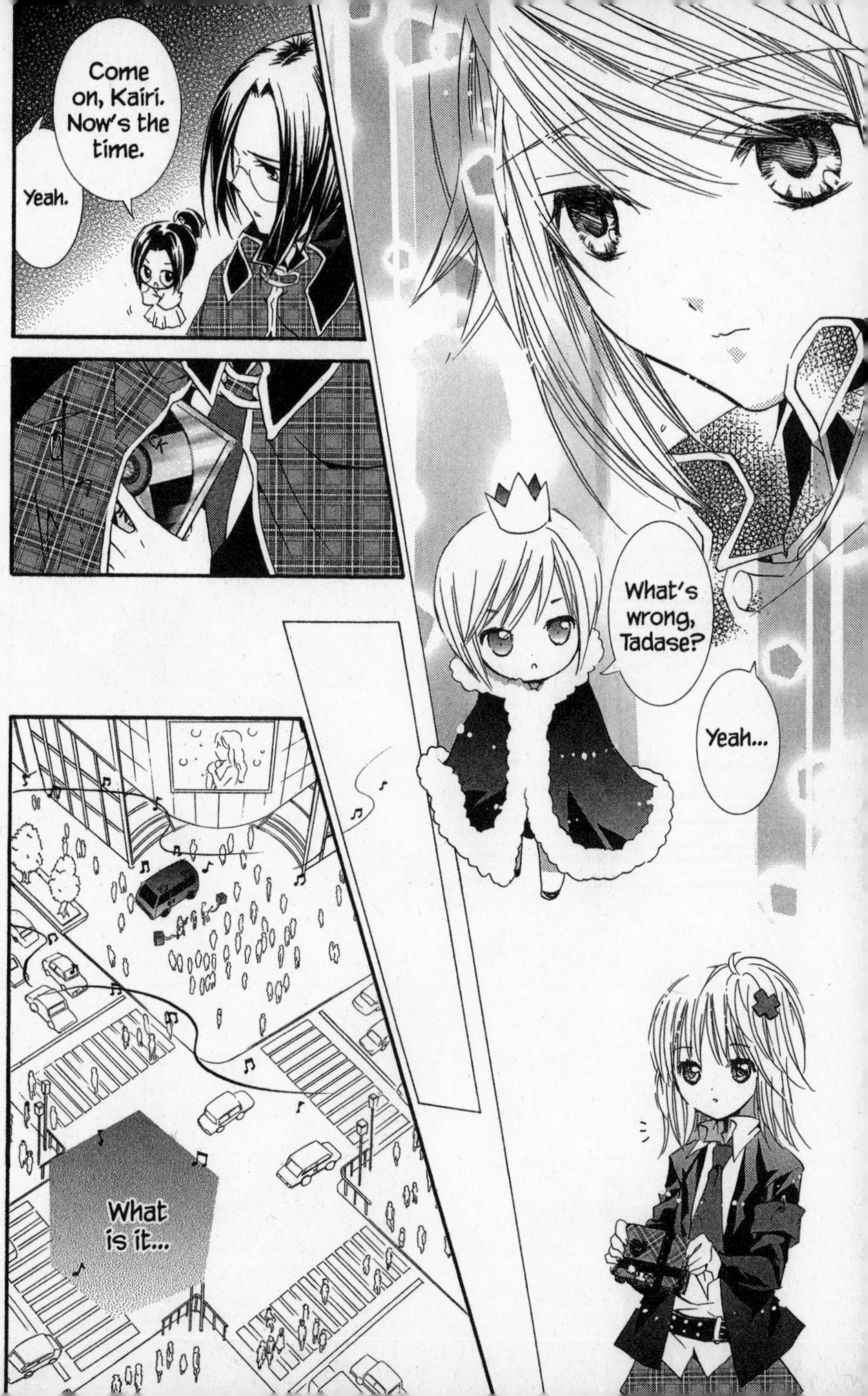
What's wrong, Tadase?
Yeah...
Come on, Kairi. Now's the time.
Yeah.
What is it...

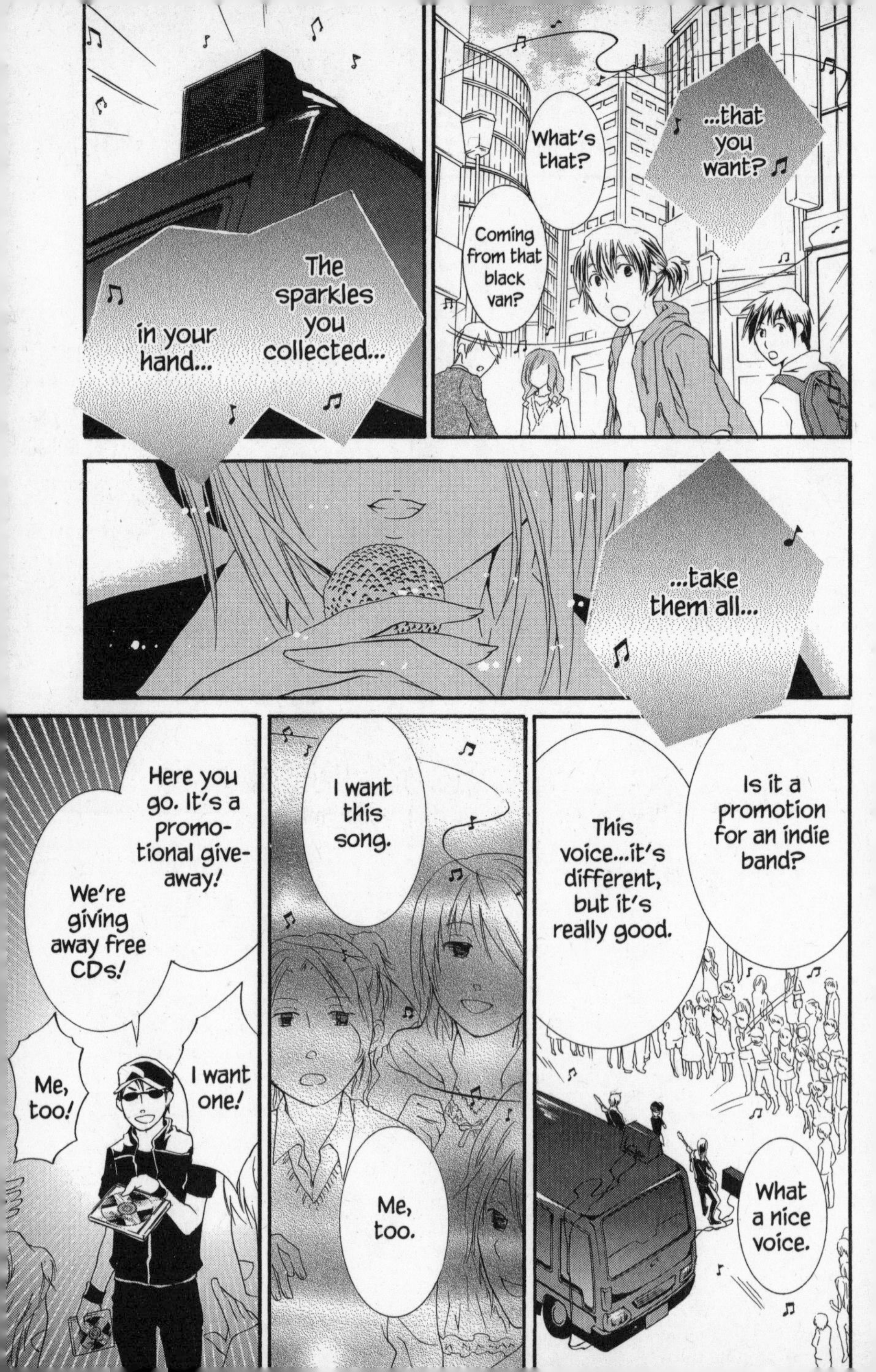
...that you want?
What's that?
Coming from that black van?
The sparkles you collected...
in your hand...
...take them all...
Is it a promotion for an indie band?
This voice...it's different, but it's really good.
What a nice voice.
I want this song.
Me, too.
Here you go. It's a promotional give-away!
We're giving away free CDs!
I want one!
Me, too!

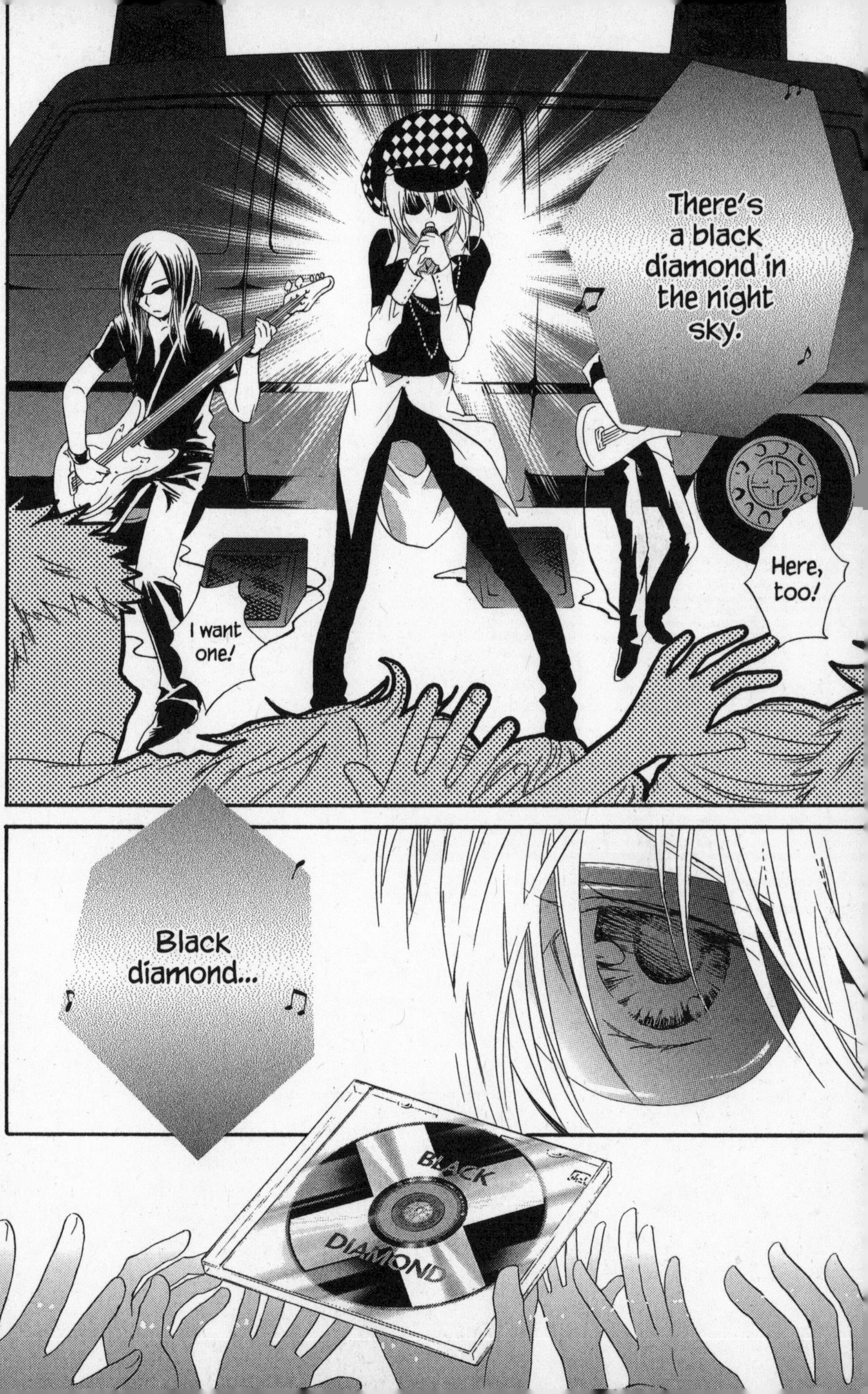
There's a black diamond in the night sky.
Here, too!
I want one!
Black diamond...
BLACK DIAMOND

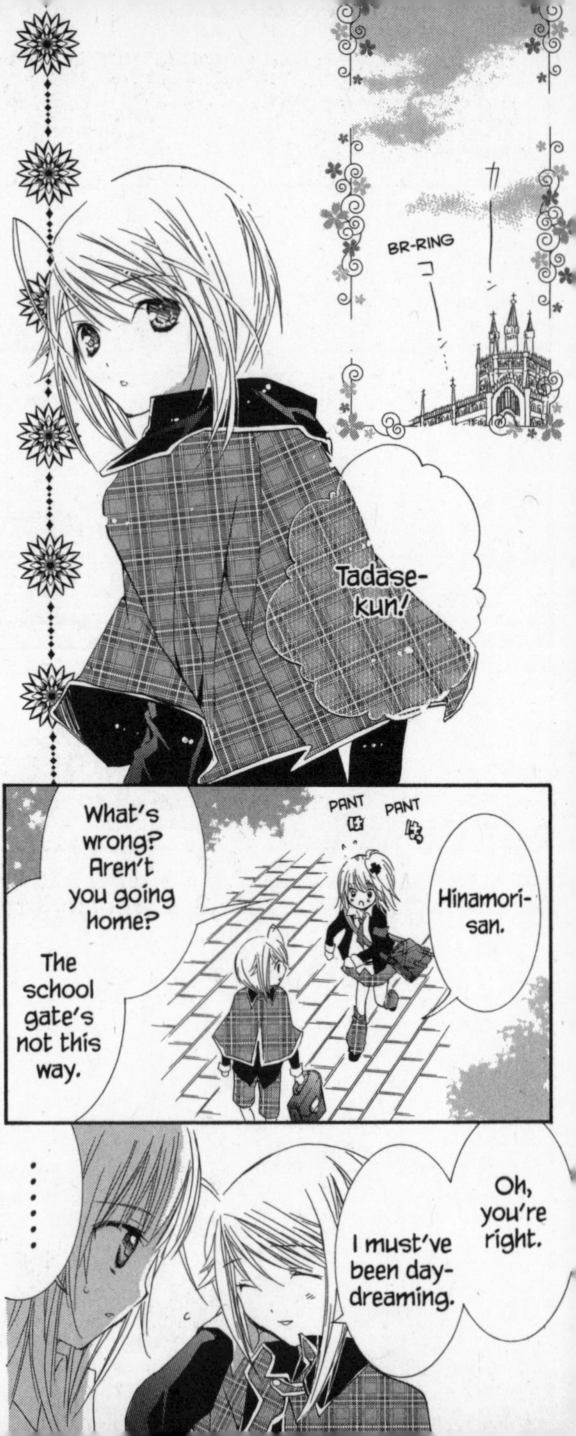
BR-RING
Tadase-kun!
Hinamori-san.
PANT PANT
What's wrong? Aren't you going home?
The school gate's not this way.
Oh, you're right.
I must've been day-dreaming.
......

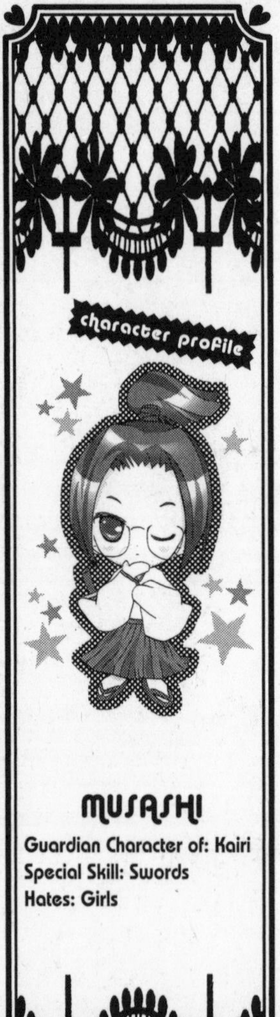
character profile
MUSASHI
Guardian Character of: Kairi
Special Skill: Swords
Hates: Girls

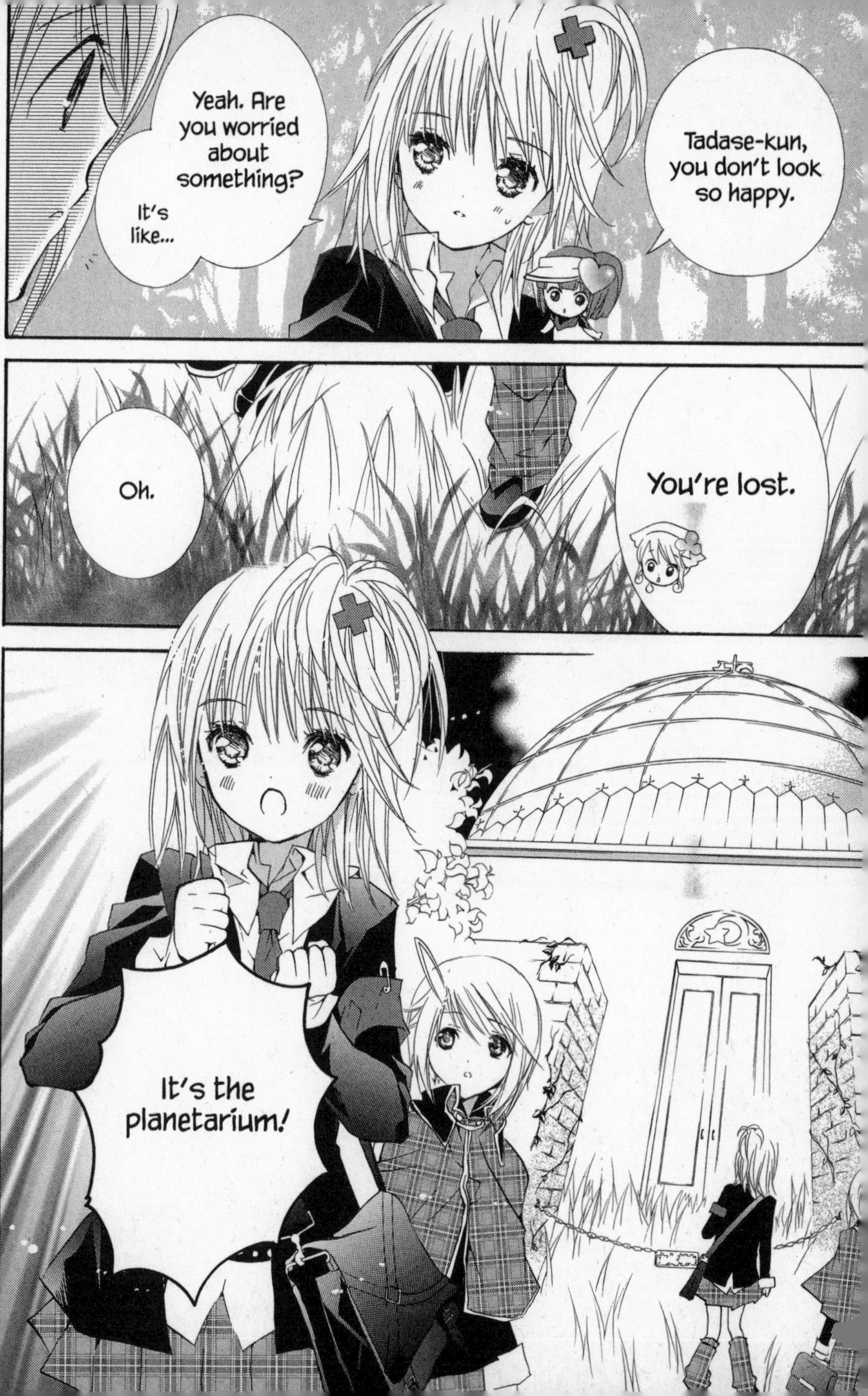
Tadase-kun, you don't look so happy.
Yeah. Are you worried about something?
It's like...
You're lost.
Oh.
It's the planetarium!

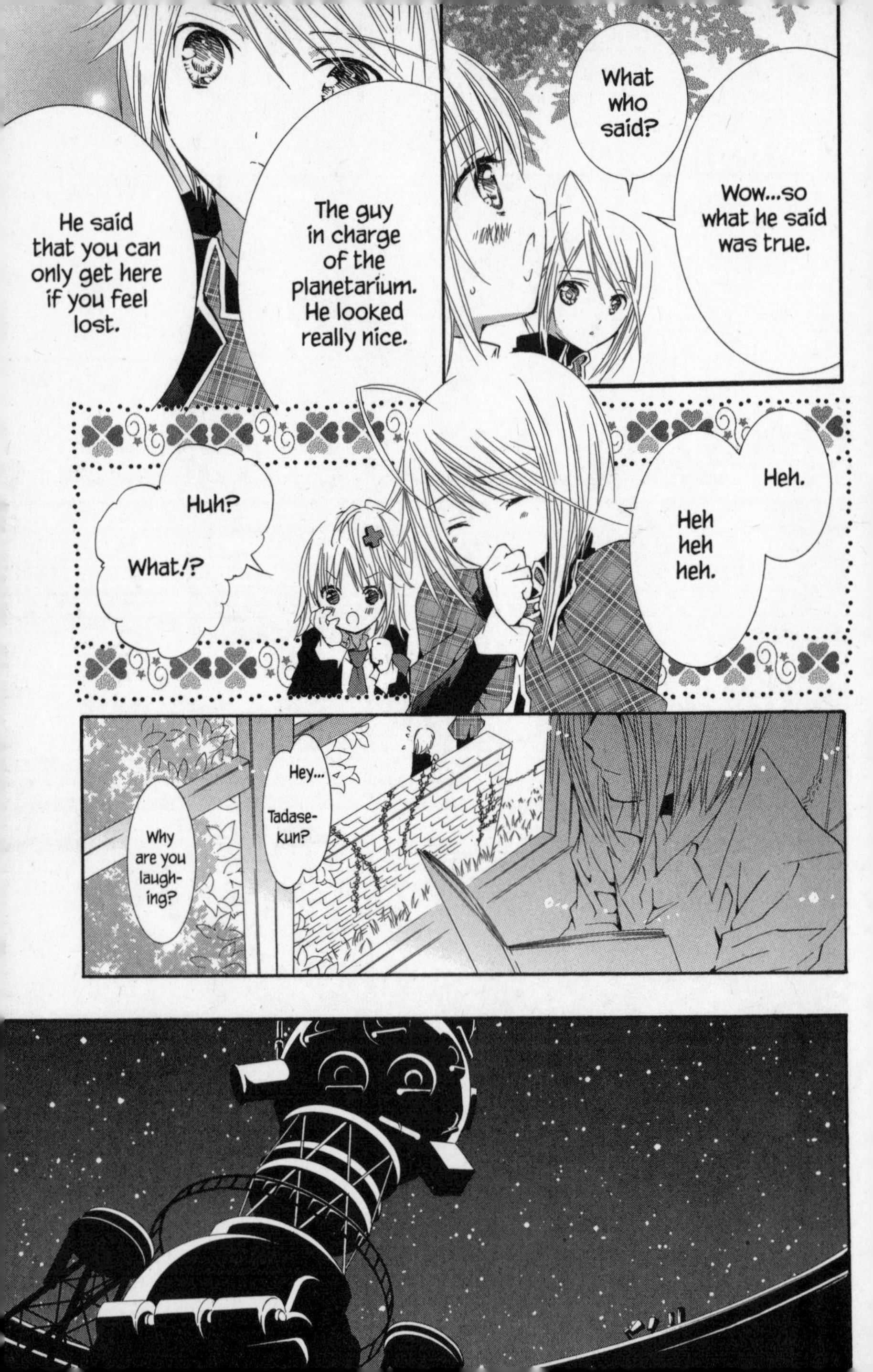
Wow...so what he said was true.
What who said?
The guy in charge of the planetarium. He looked really nice.
He said that you can only get here if you feel lost.
Heh. Heh heh heh.
Huh? What!?
Hey... Tadase-kun?
Why are you laughing?

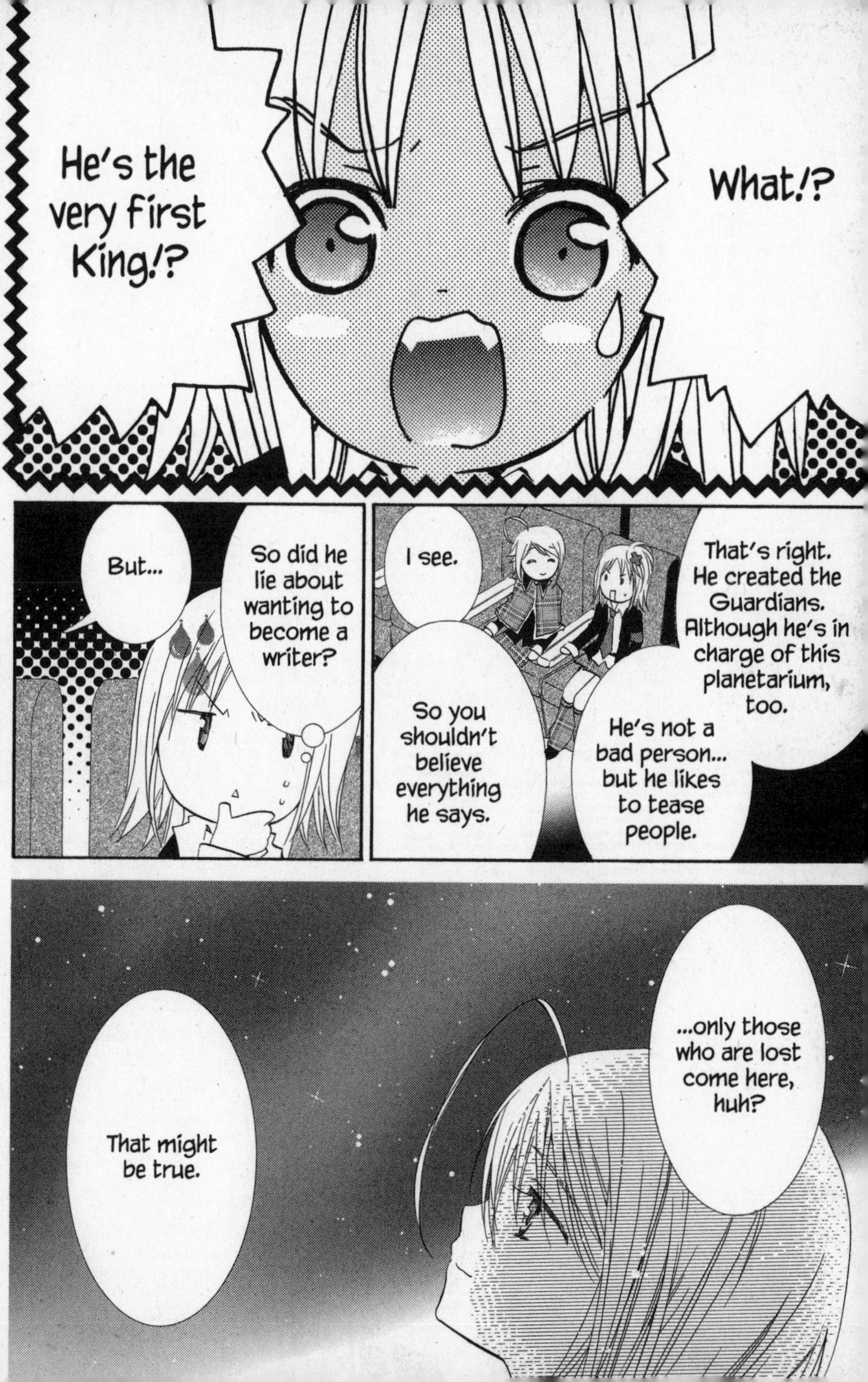
What!?
He's the very first King!?
That's right. He created the Guardians. Although he's in charge of this planetarium, too.
He's not a bad person... but he likes to tease people.
So you shouldn't believe everything he says.
I see.
So did he lie about wanting to become a writer?
But...
...only those who are lost come here, huh?
That might be true.

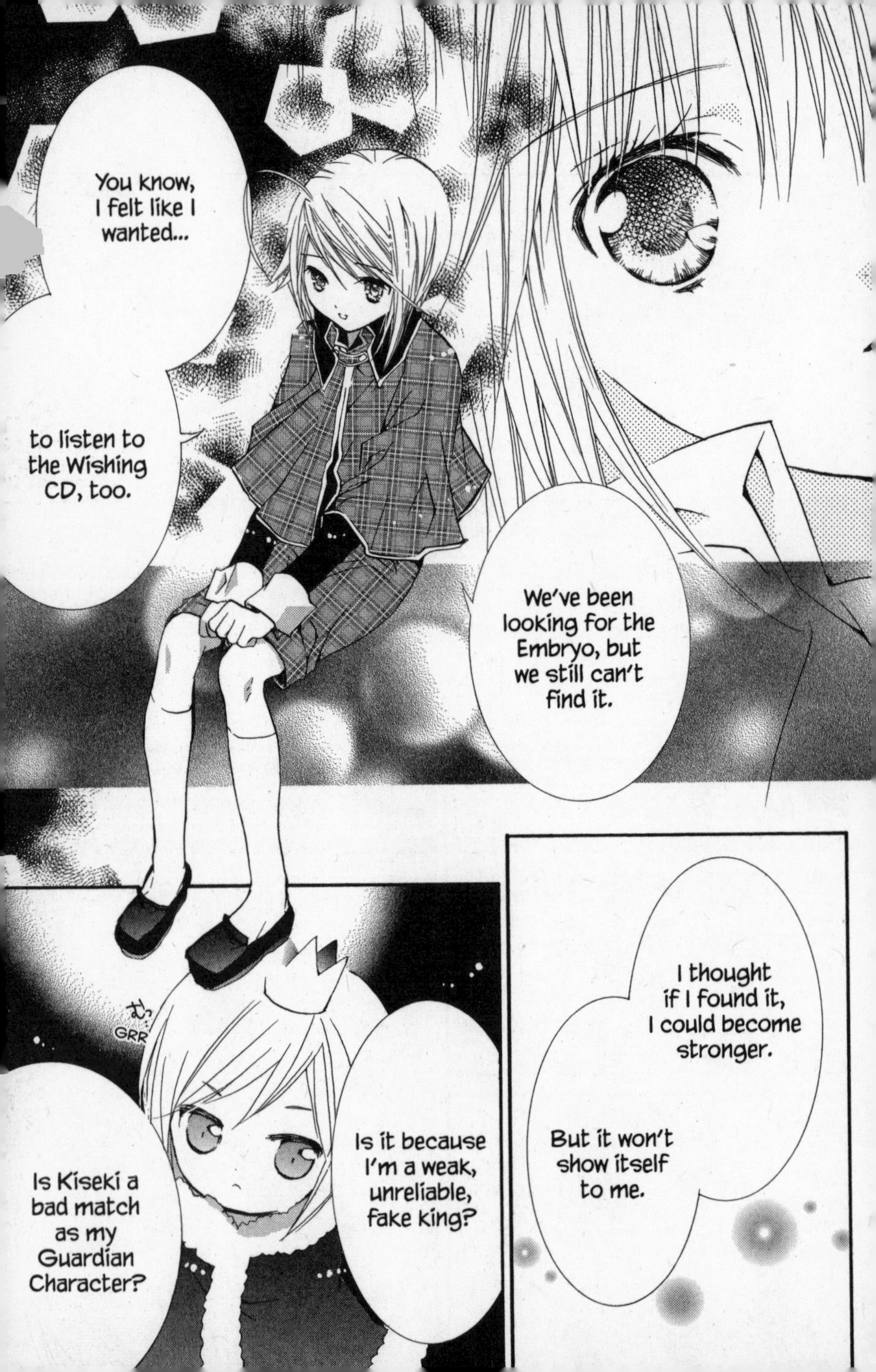
You know, I felt like I wanted...
to listen to the Wishing CD, too.
We've been looking for the Embryo, but we still can't find it.
I thought if I found it, I could become stronger.
But it won't show itself to me.
GRR
Is it because I'm a weak, unreliable, fake king?
Is Kiseki a bad match as my Guardian Character?

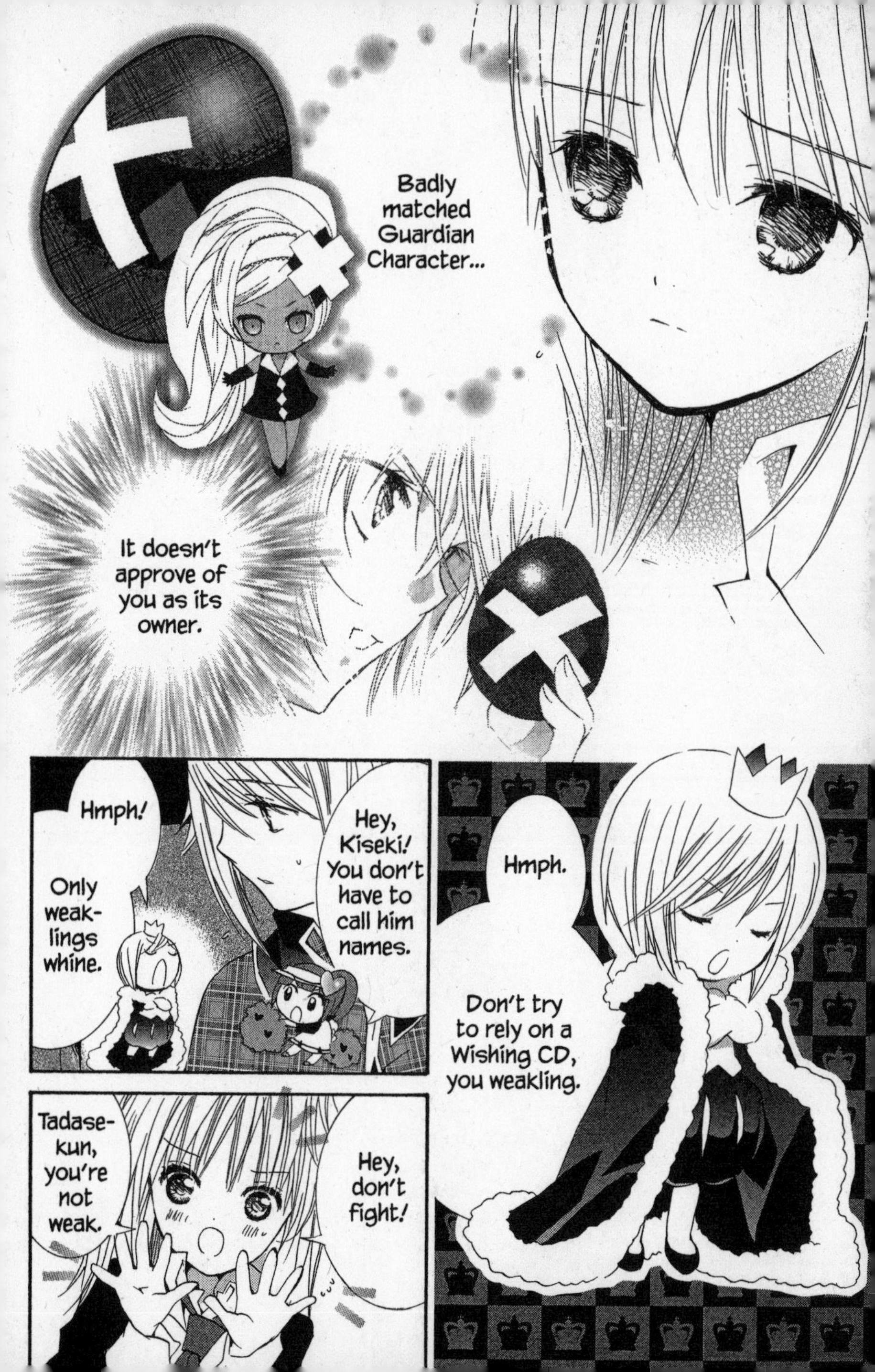
Badly matched Guardian Character...
It doesn't approve of you as its owner.
Hmph.
Don't try to rely on a Wishing CD, you weakling.
Hey, Kiseki! You don't have to call him names.
Hmph!
Only weak-lings whine.
Hey, don't fight!
Tadase-kun, you're not weak.

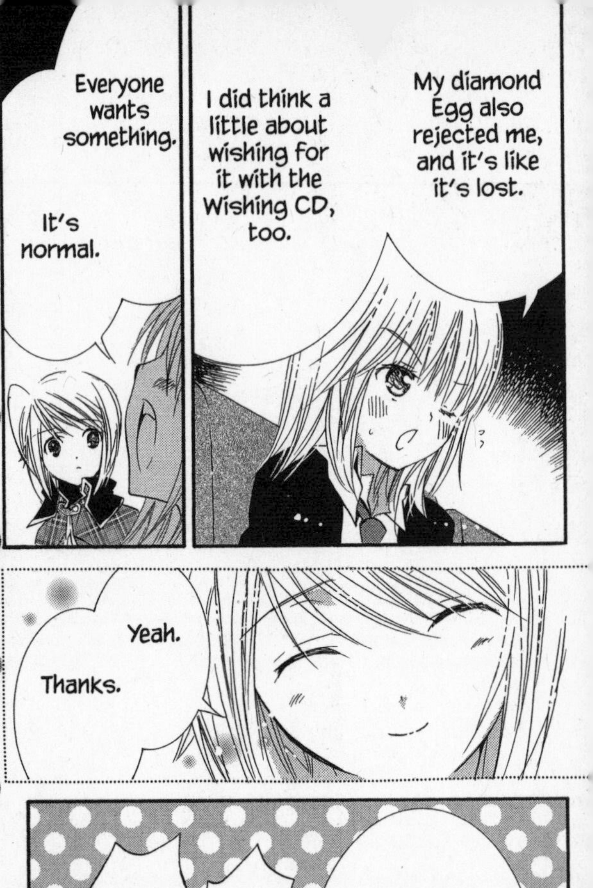
My diamond Egg also rejected me, and it's like it's lost.
I did think a little about wishing for it with the Wishing CD, too.
Everyone wants something.
It's normal.
Yeah.
Thanks.
Then if I get the CD, I'll hand it to you.
Huh?
Then I'll give it to you if I get it first.
FLINCH
She's really scared.

(Featured in 2007 "Nakayoshi," August-November issue)

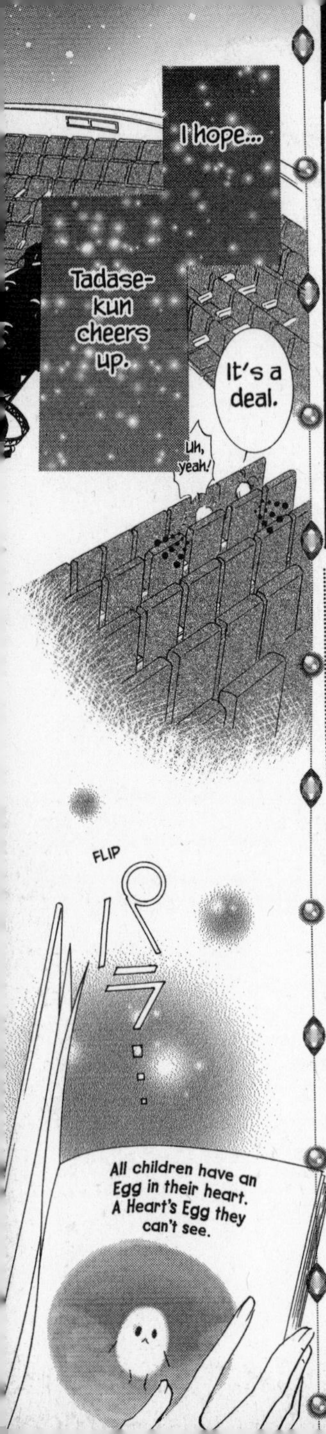
I hope...
Tadase-kun cheers up.
It's a deal.
Uh, yeah!
FLIP
All children have an Egg in their heart. A Heart's Egg they can't see.

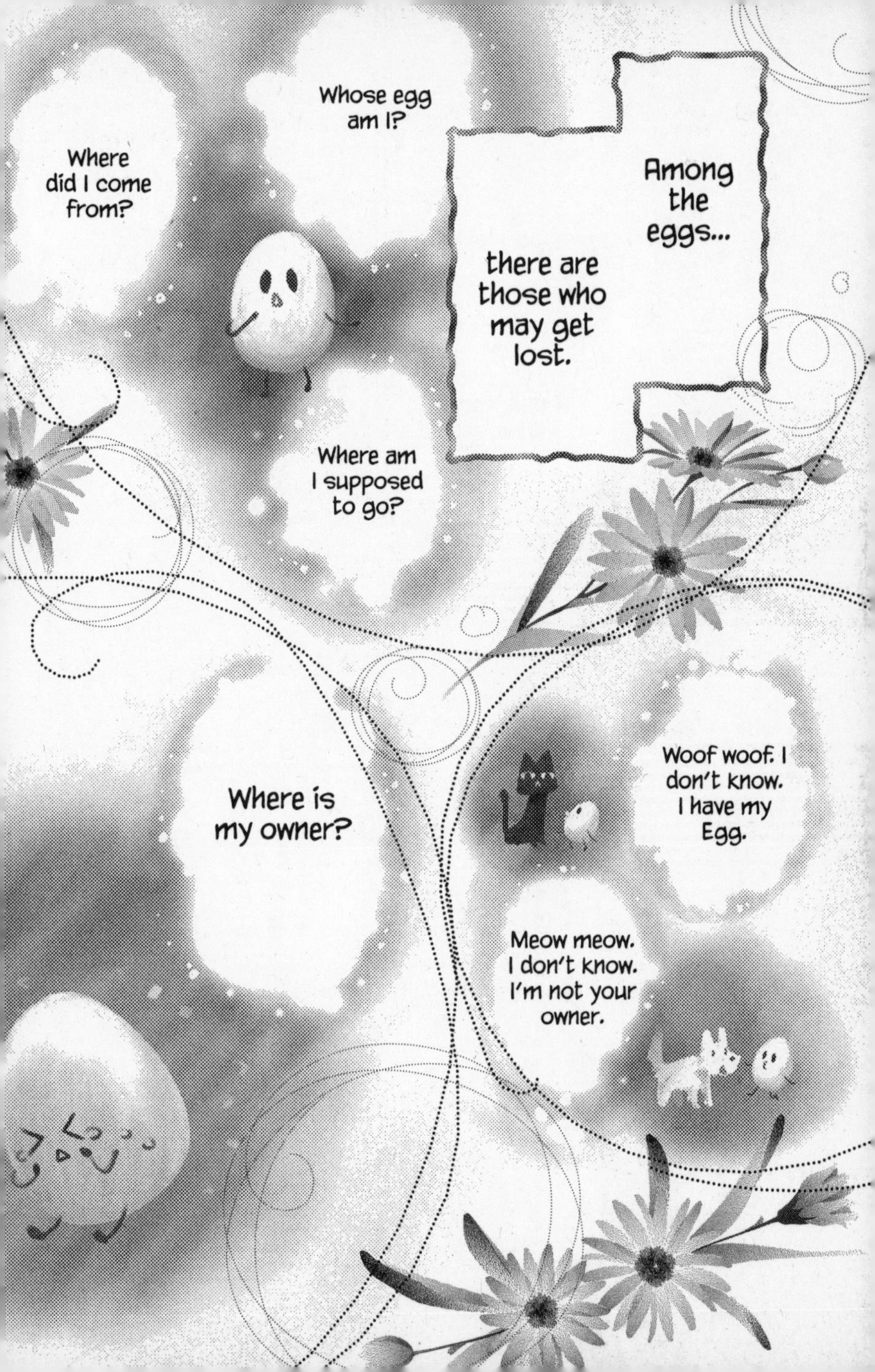
Among the eggs...
there are those who may get lost.
Whose egg am I?
Where did I come from?
Where am I supposed to go?
Where is my owner?
Woof woof. I don't know. I have my Egg.
Meow meow. I don't know. I'm not your owner.

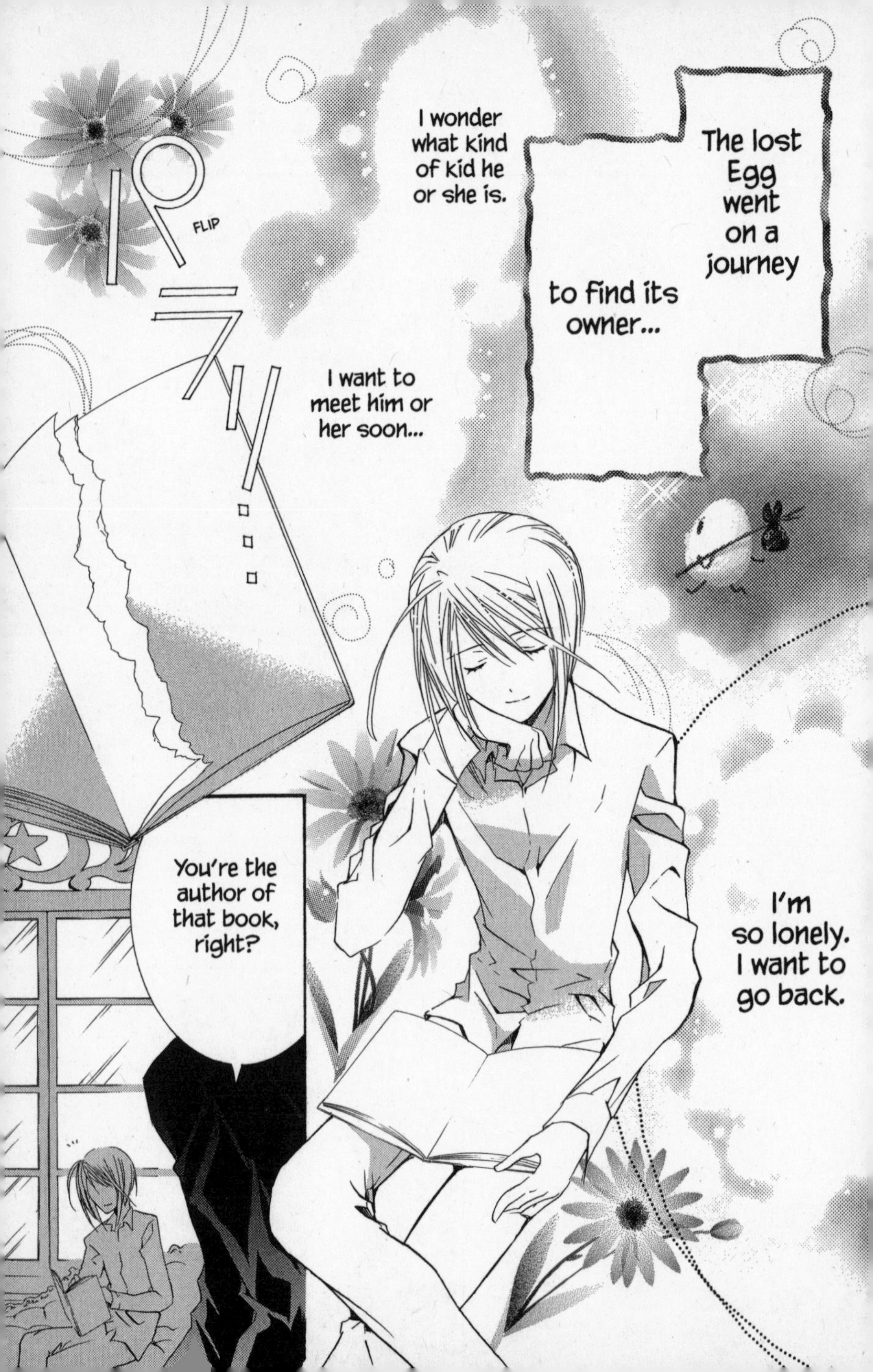
The lost Egg went on a journey
to find its owner...
I wonder what kind of kid he or she is.
I want to meet him or her soon...
I'm so lonely. I want to go back.
FLIP
You're the author of that book, right?

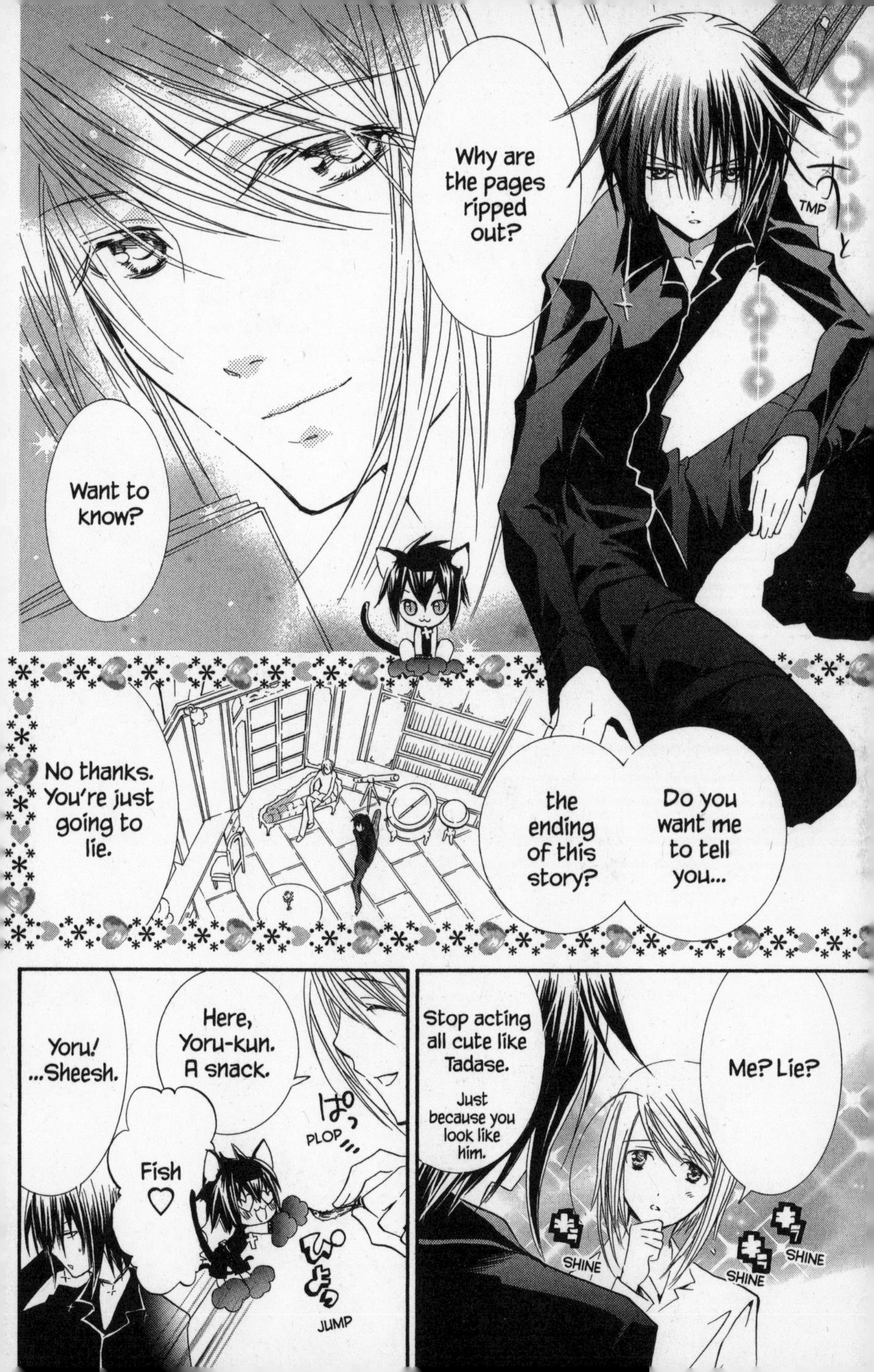

Why are the pages ripped out?
TMP
Want to know?
Do you want me to tell you...
the ending of this story?
No thanks. You're just going to lie.
Me? Lie?
SHINE
SHINE
SHINE
Stop acting all cute like Tadase.
Just because you look like him.
Here, Yoru-kun. A snack.
PLOP
Fish ♡
JUMP
Yoru! ...Sheesh.

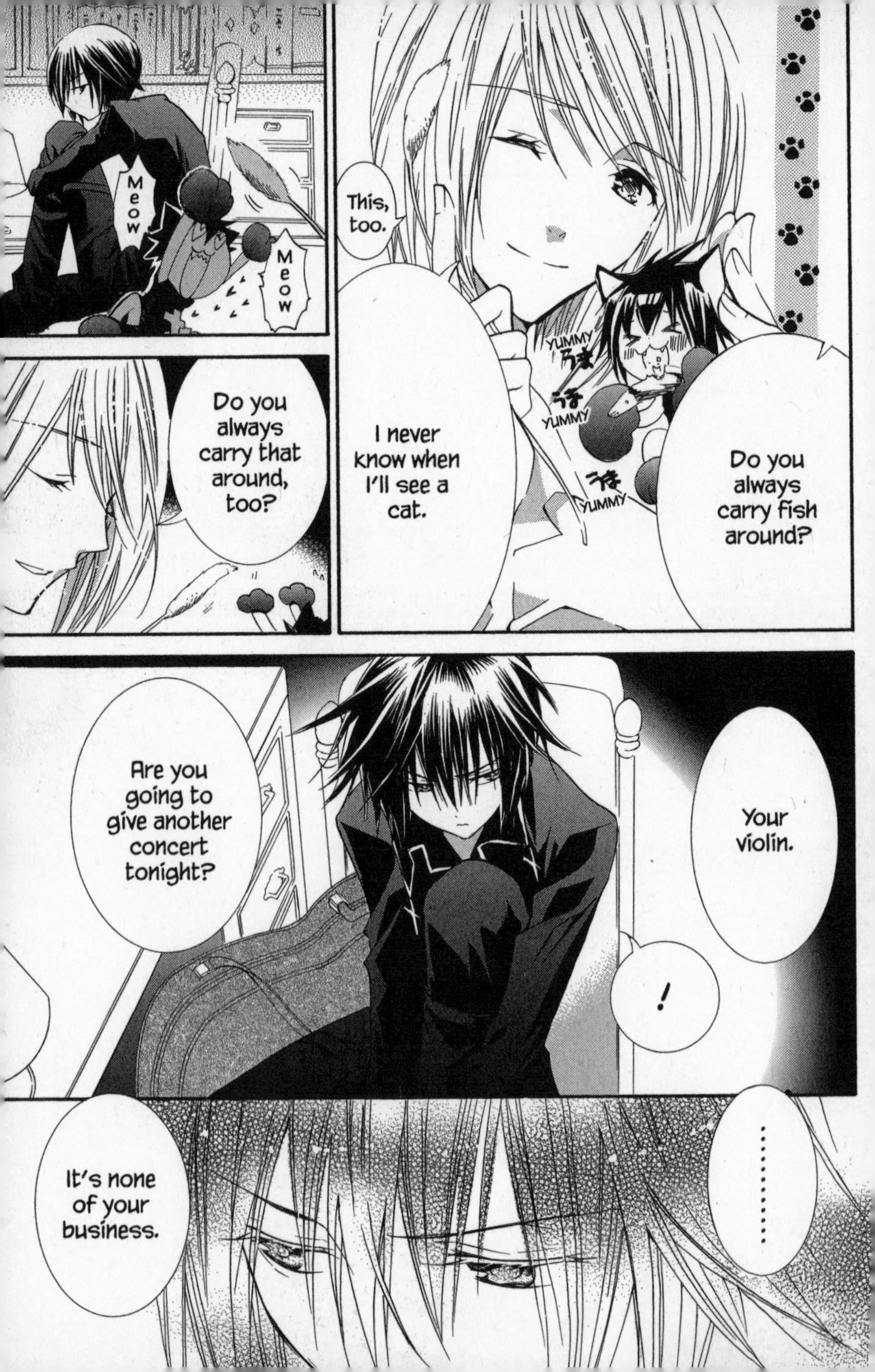
YUMMY
YUMMY
YUMMY
Do you always carry fish around?
I never know when I'll see a cat.
This, too.
Meow
Meow
Do you always carry that around, too?
Your violin.
!
Are you going to give another concert tonight?
......
It's none of your business.

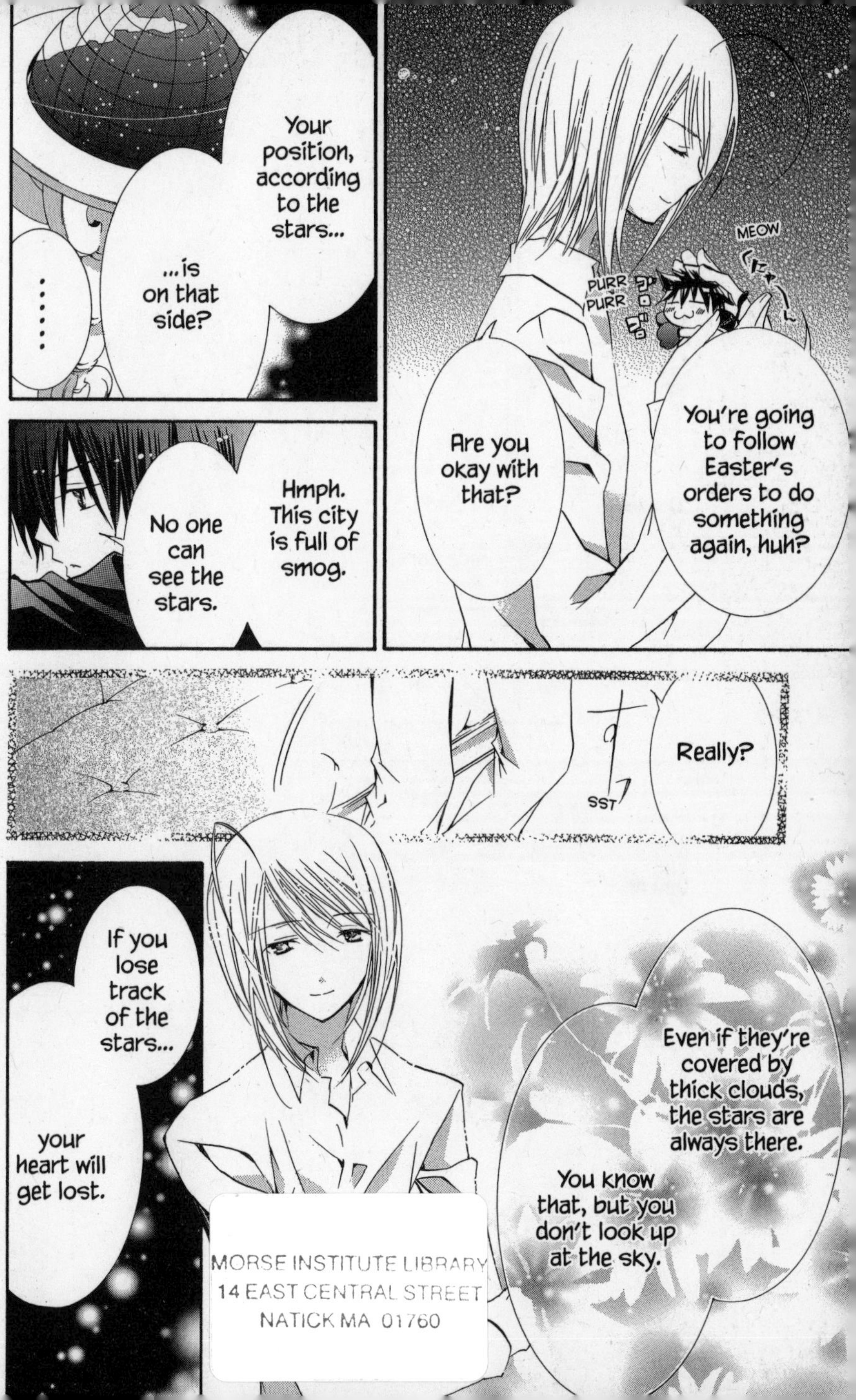
MEOW
PURR PURR
You're going to follow Easter's orders to do something again, huh?
Are you okay with that?
Your position, according to the stars...
...is on that side?
......
Hmph. This city is full of smog.
No one can see the stars.
Really?
SST
Even if they're covered by thick clouds, the stars are always there.
You know that, but you don't look up at the sky.
If you lose track of the stars...
your heart will get lost.

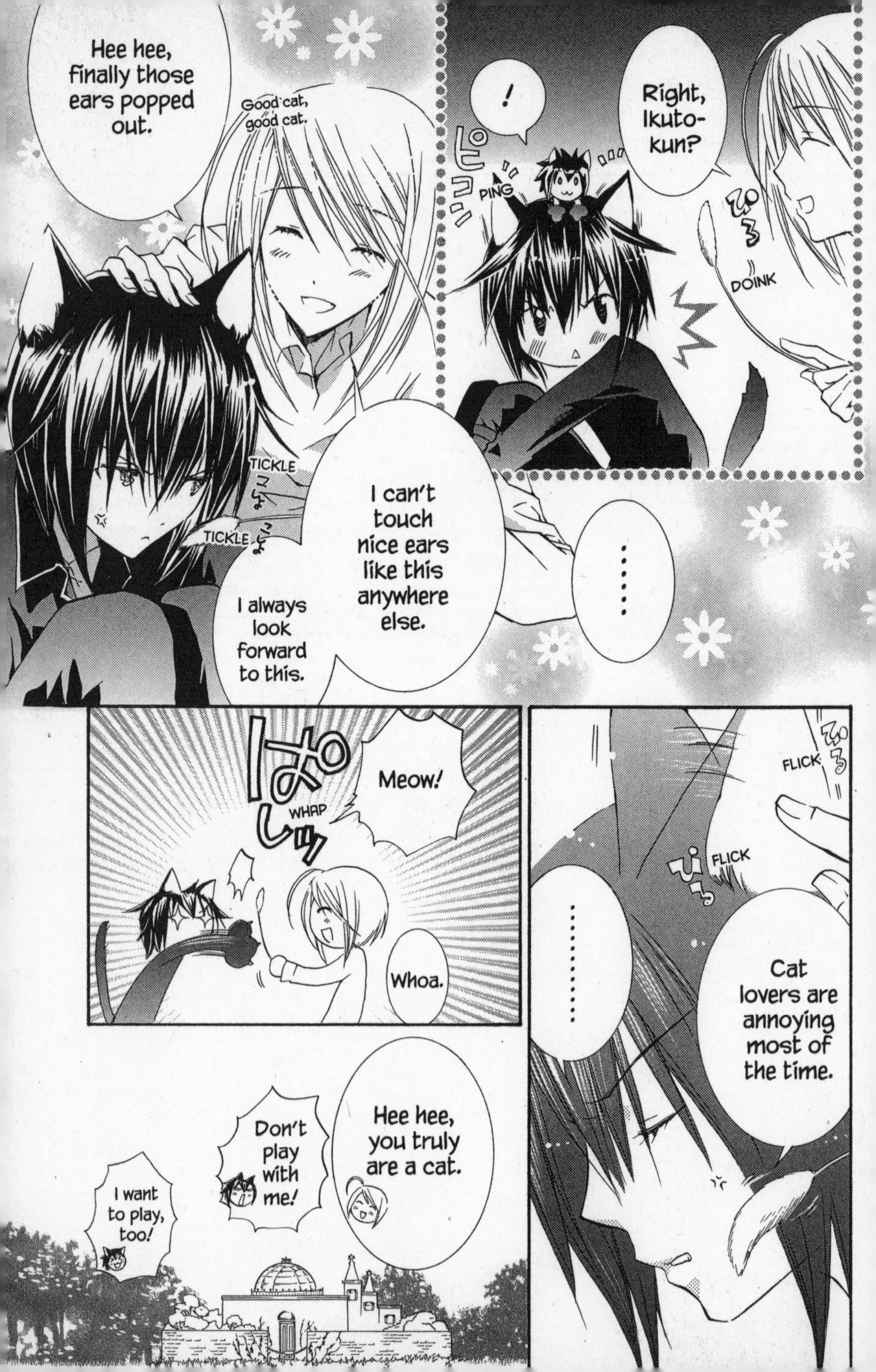
Right, Ikuto-kun?
!
PING
DOINK
Hee hee, finally those ears popped out.
Good cat, good cat.
I can't touch nice ears like this anywhere else.
I always look forward to this.
TICKLE
TICKLE
......
FLICK
FLICK
Cat lovers are annoying most of the time.
......
Meow!
WHAP
Whoa.
Hee hee, you truly are a cat.
Don't play with me!
I want to play, too!

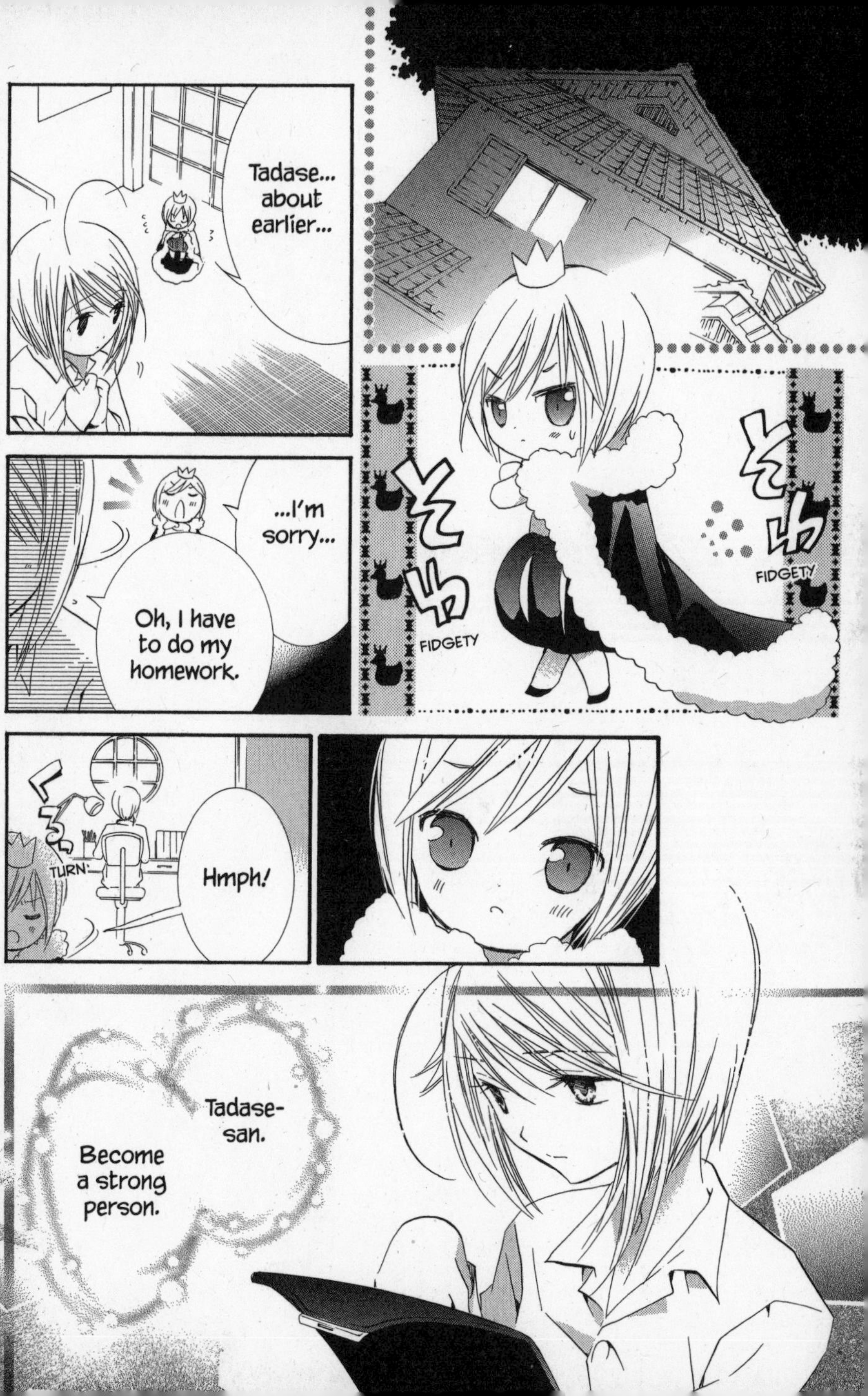
そわ
FIDGETY
そわ
FIDGETY
Tadase... about earlier...
...I'm sorry...
Oh, I have to do my homework.
TURN
Hmph!
Tadase-san.
Become a strong person.

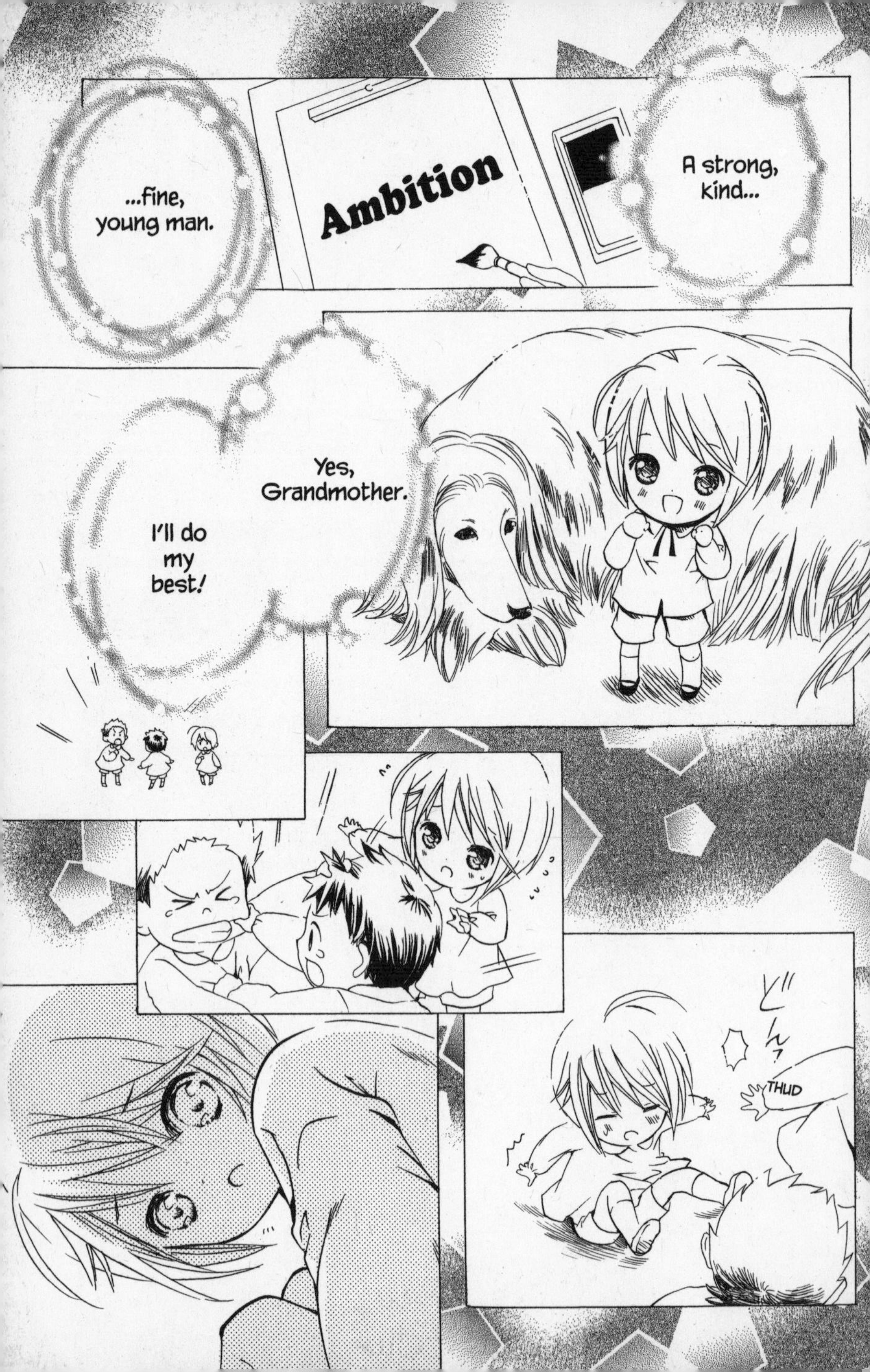
A strong, kind...
Ambition
...fine, young man.
Yes, Grandmother.
I'll do my best!
THUD

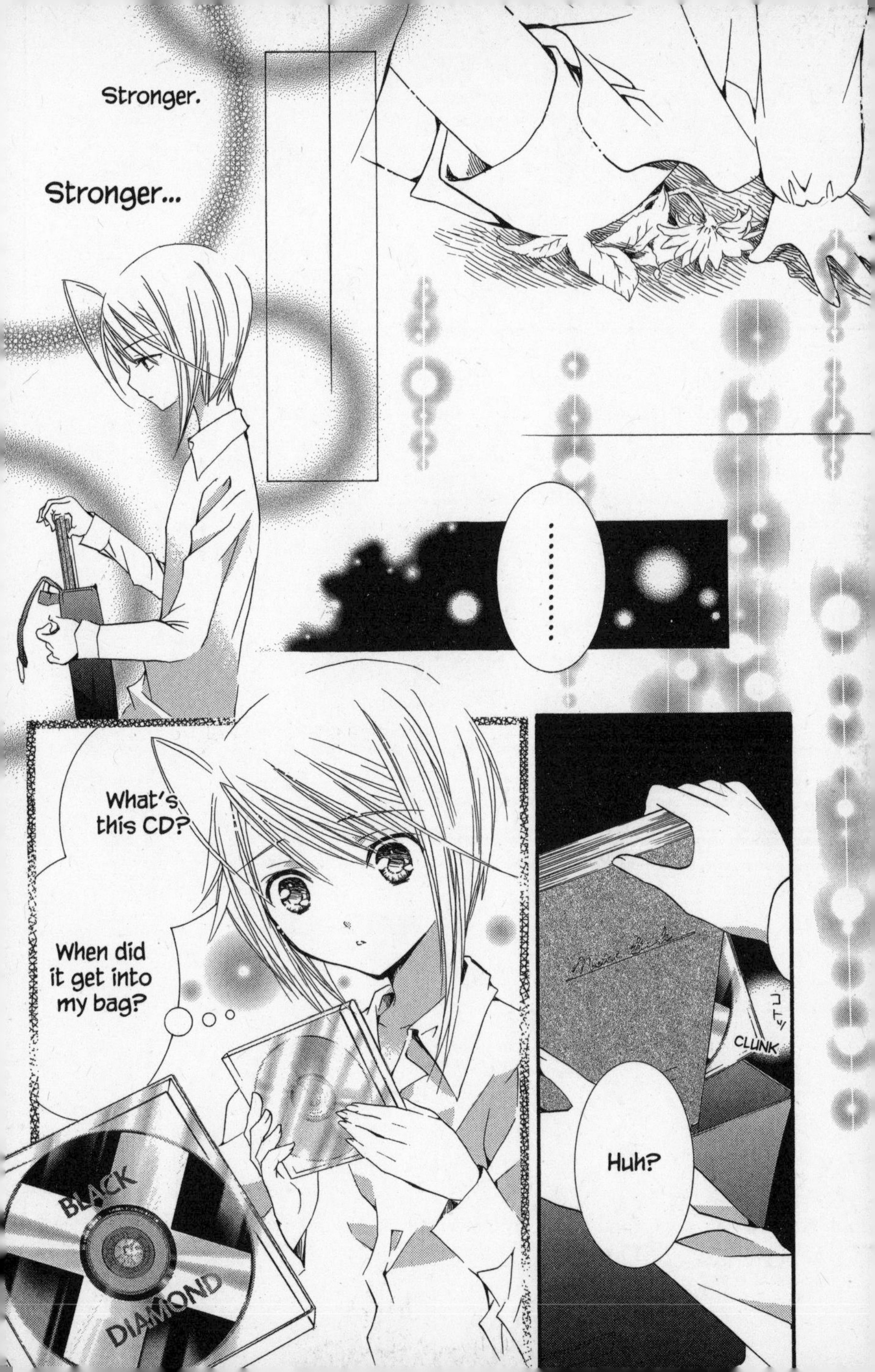
Stronger.
Stronger...
......
コトッ
CLUNK
Huh?
What's this CD?
When did it get into my bag?
BLACK DIAMOND

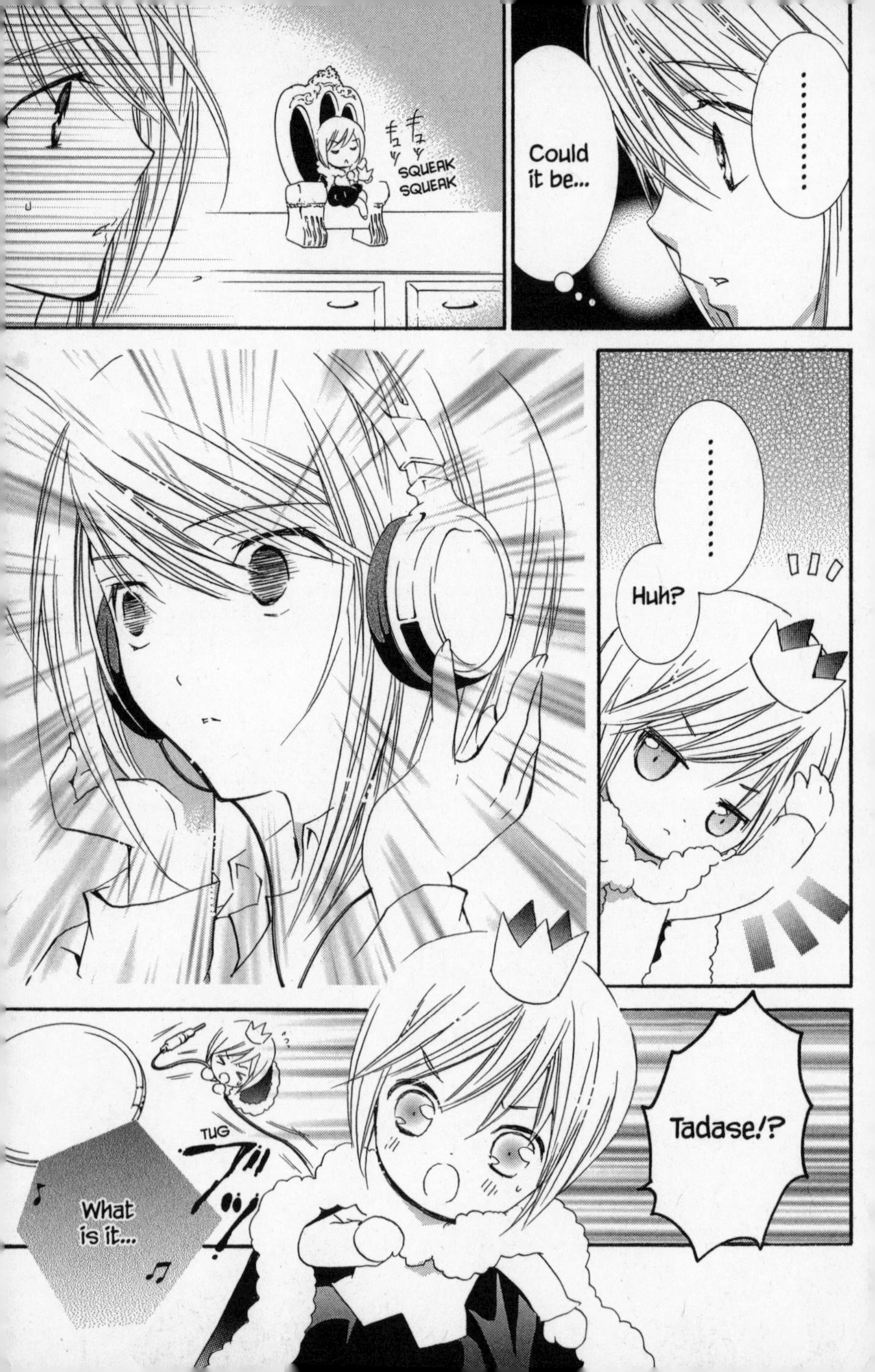
......
Could it be...
キュッ キュッ
SQUEAK SQUEAK
......
Huh?
Tadase!?
TUG
What is it...

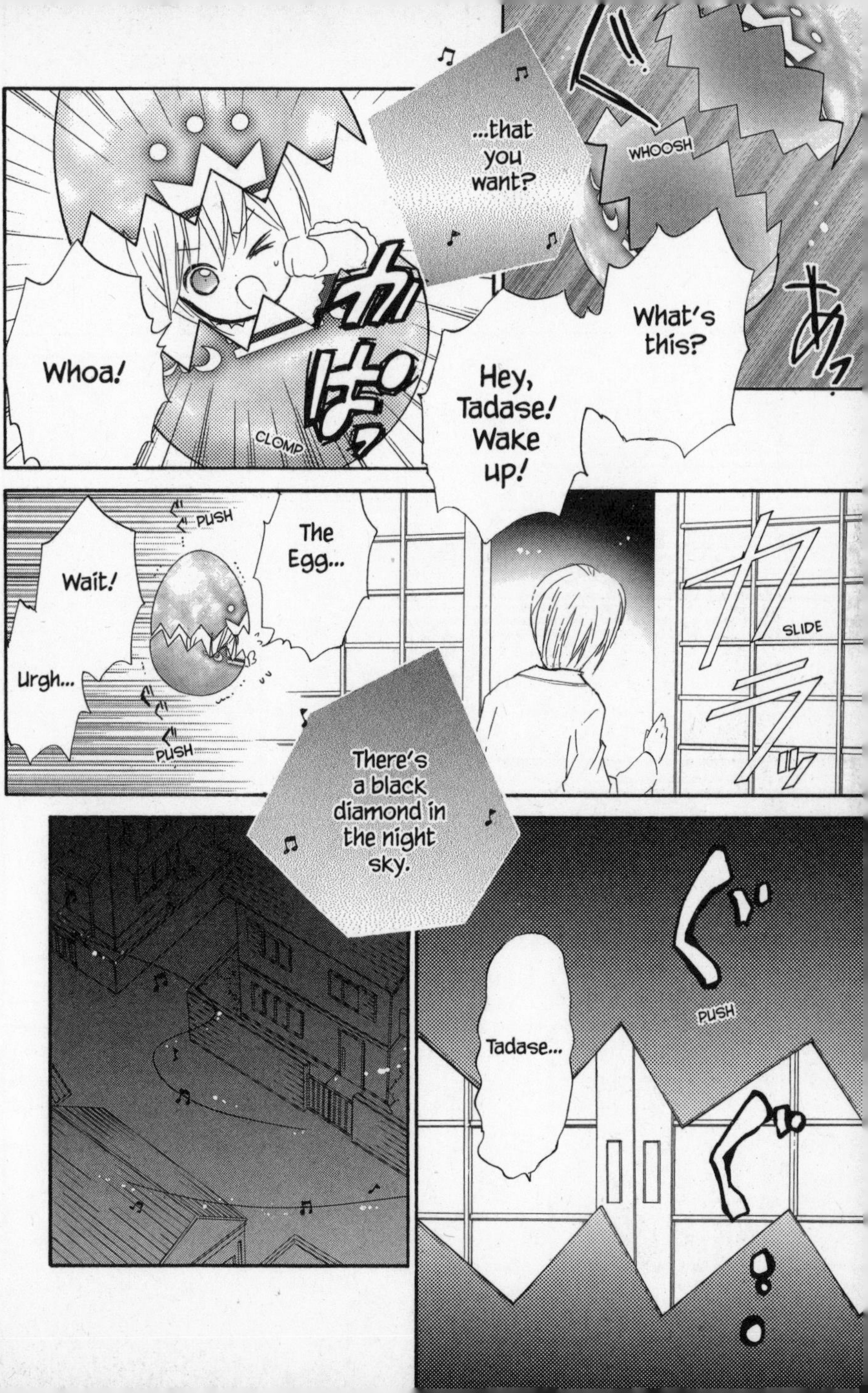
WHOOSH
What's this?
...that you want?
Hey, Tadase! Wake up!
Whoa!
CLOMP
SLIDE
There's a black diamond in the night sky.
The Egg...
PUSH
Wait!
Urgh...
PUSH
PUSH
Tadase...

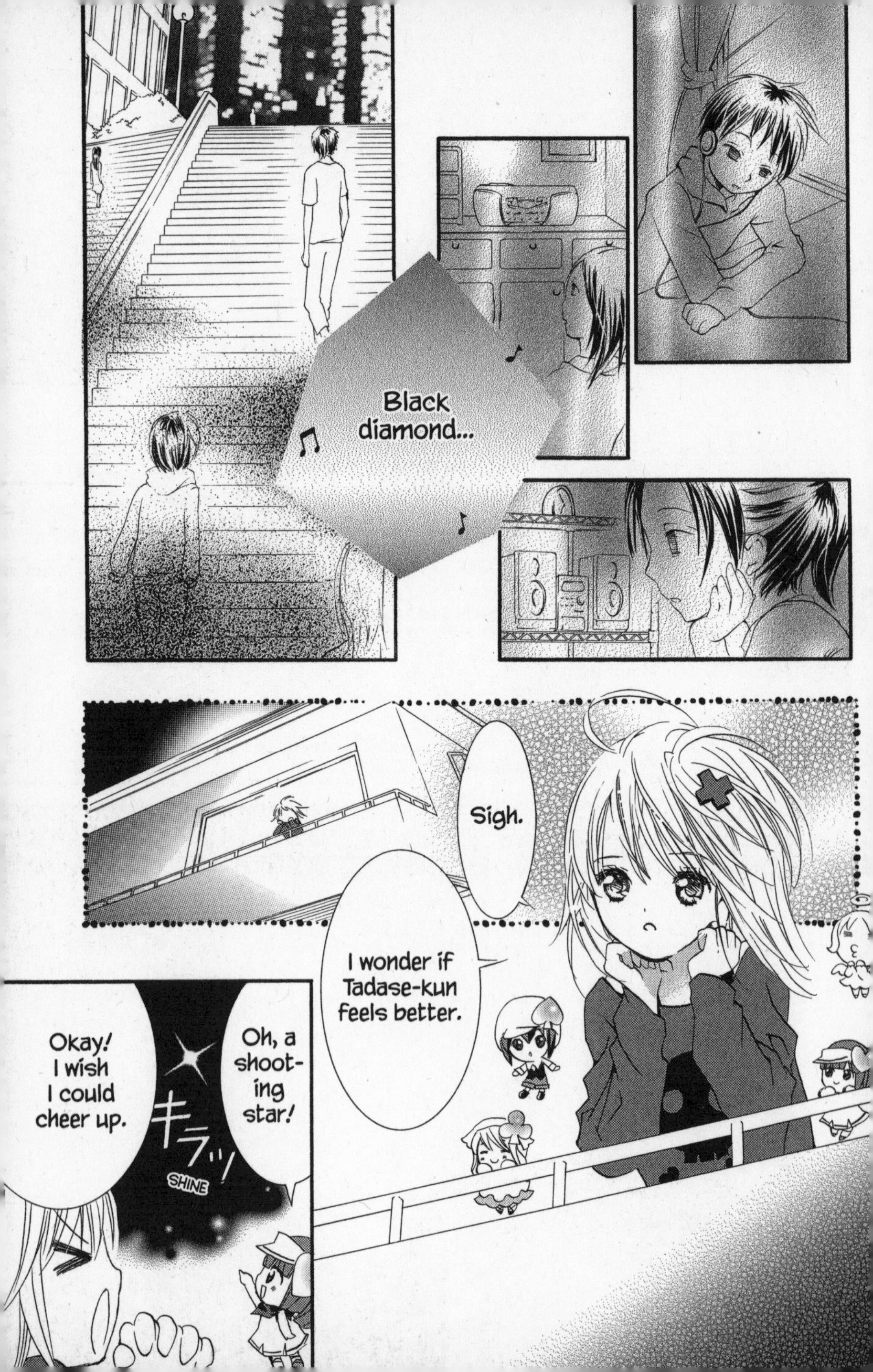
Black diamond...
Sigh.
I wonder if Tadase-kun feels better.
Oh, a shoot-ing star!
キラッ
SHINE
Okay! I wish I could cheer up.

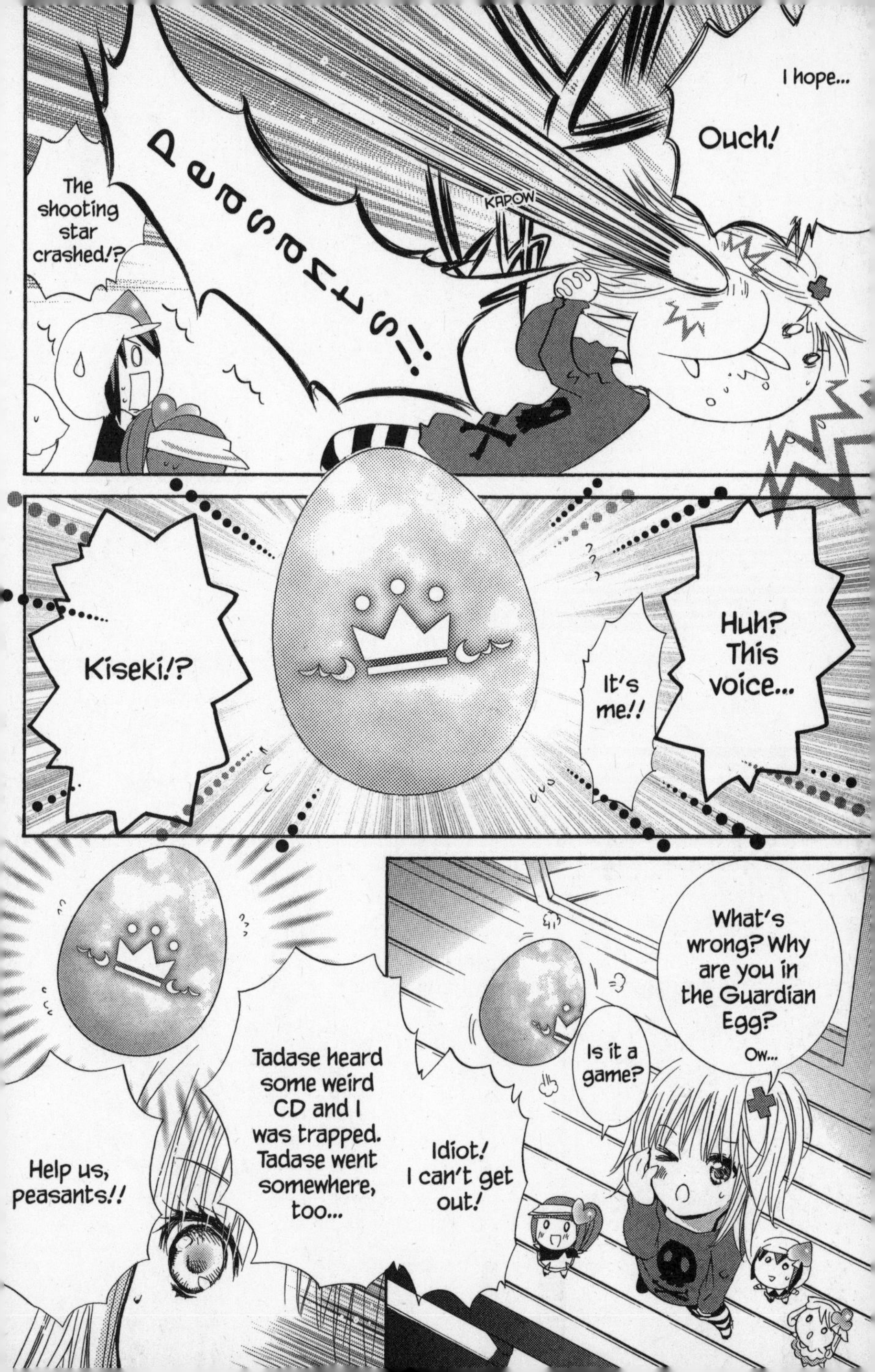
I hope...
Ouch!
KAPOW
Peasants!!
The shooting star crashed!?
Huh? This voice...
It's me!!
Kiseki!?
What's wrong? Why are you in the Guardian Egg?
Ow...
Is it a game?
Idiot! I can't get out!
Tadase heard some weird CD and I was trapped. Tadase went somewhere, too...
Help us, peasants!!

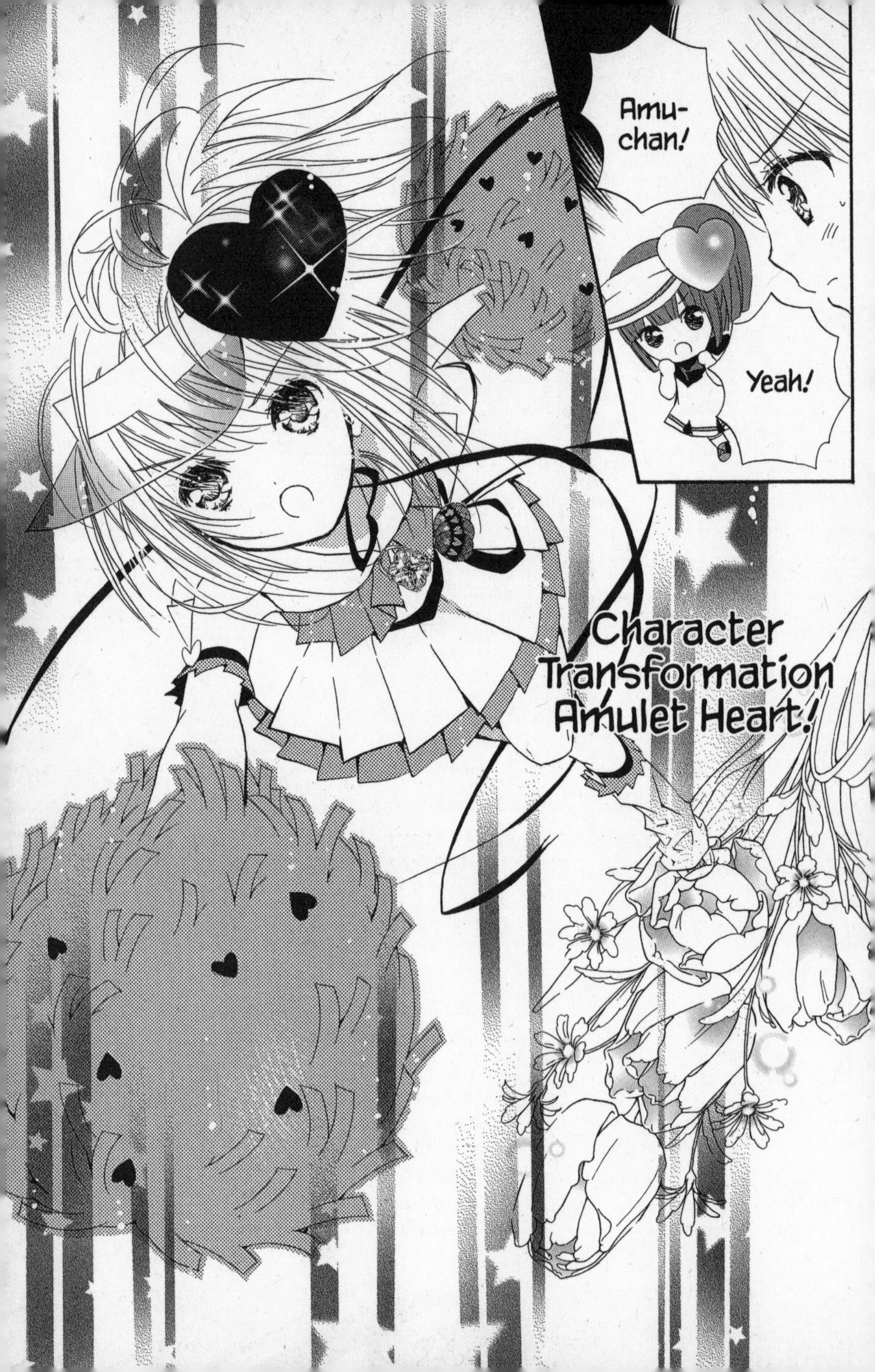
Amu-chan!
Yeah!
Character Transformation Amulet Heart!

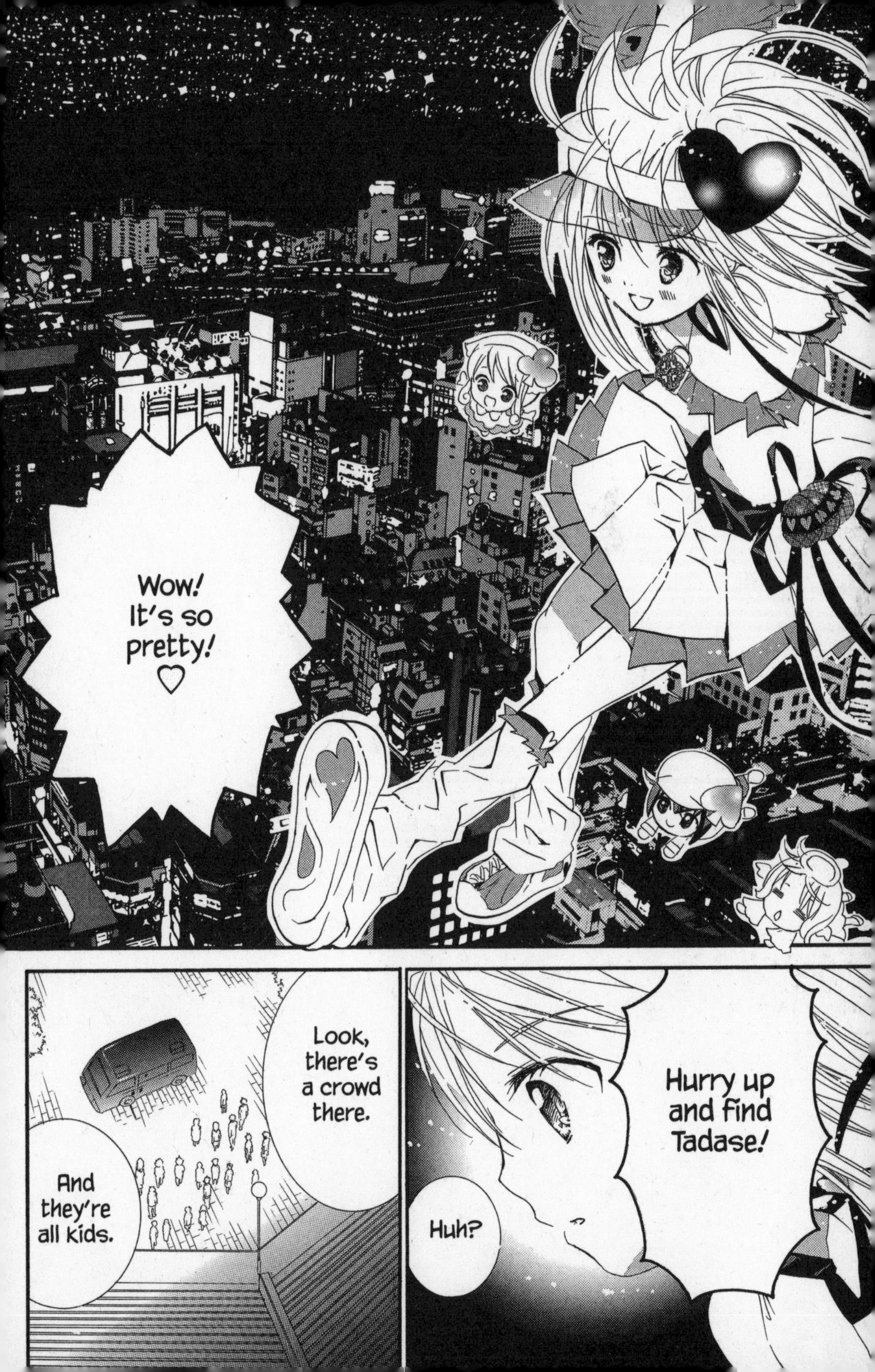
Wow! It's so pretty! ♡
Hurry up and find Tadase!
Huh?
Look, there's a crowd there.
And they're all kids.

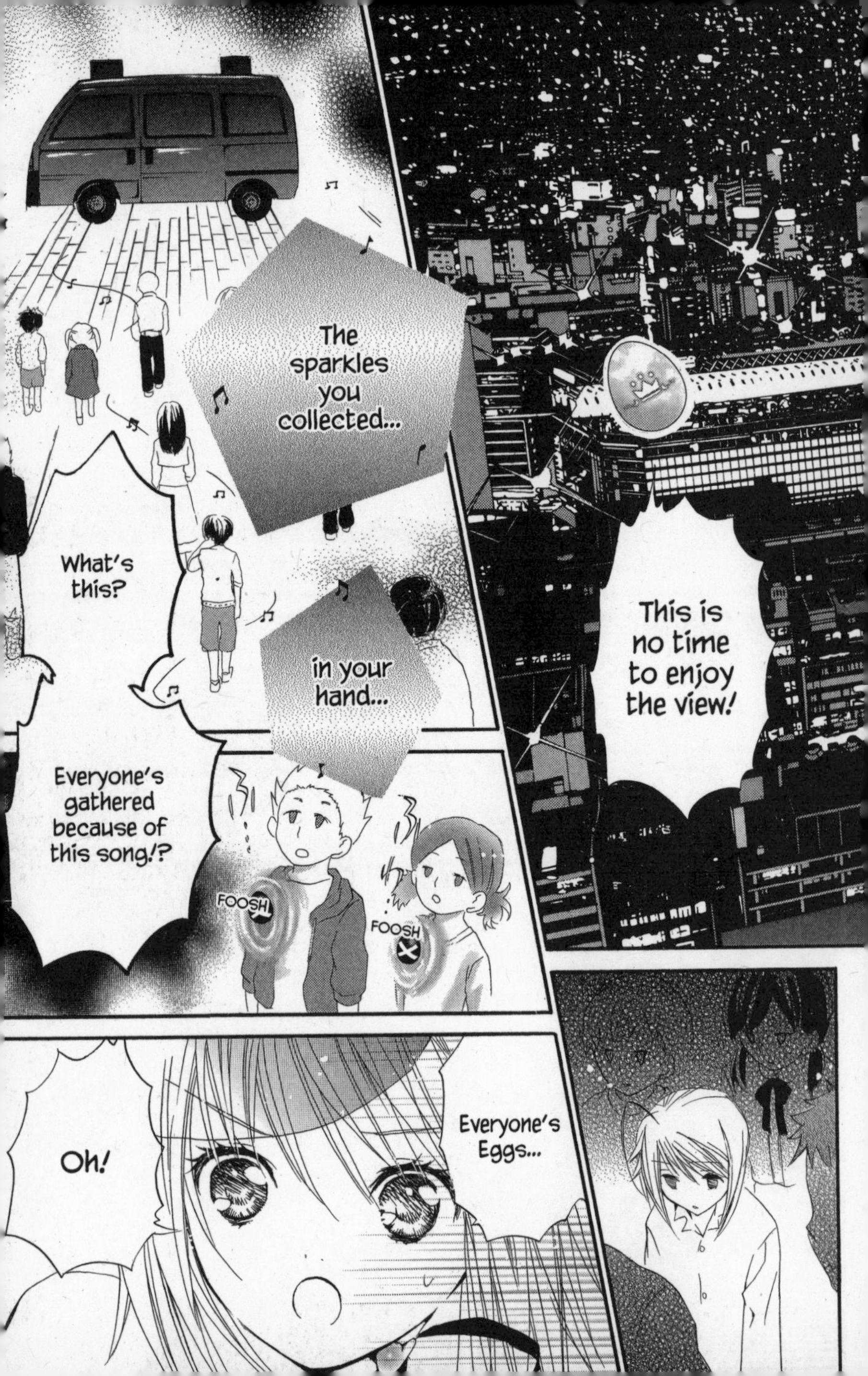
This is no time to enjoy the view!
The sparkles you collected...
What's this?
in your hand...
Everyone's gathered because of this song!?
FOOSH
FOOSH
Everyone's Eggs...
Oh!

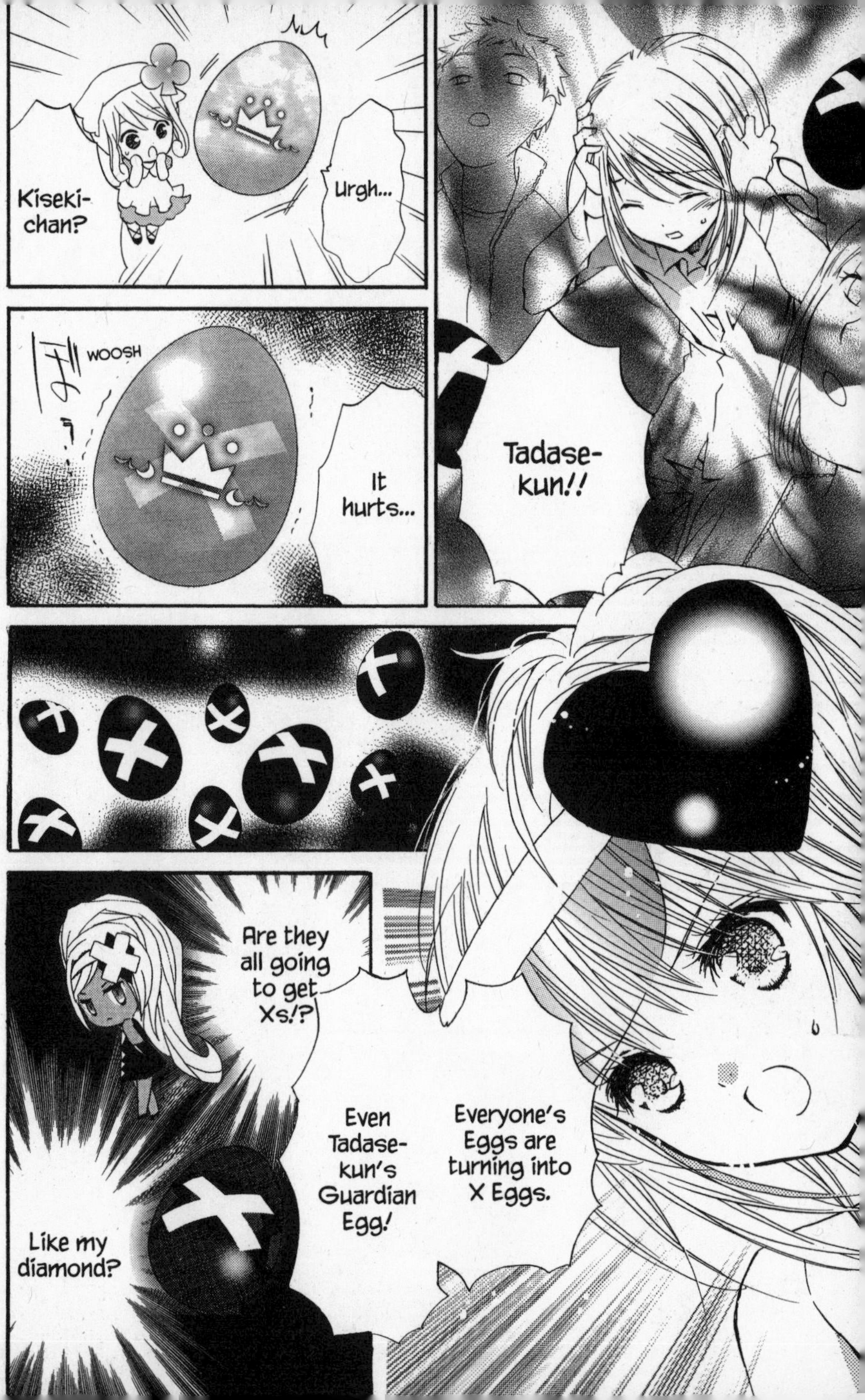
Tadase-kun!!
Urgh...
Kiseki-chan?
WOOSH
It hurts...
Are they all going to get Xs!?
Everyone's Eggs are turning into X Eggs.
Even Tadase-kun's Guardian Egg!
Like my diamond?

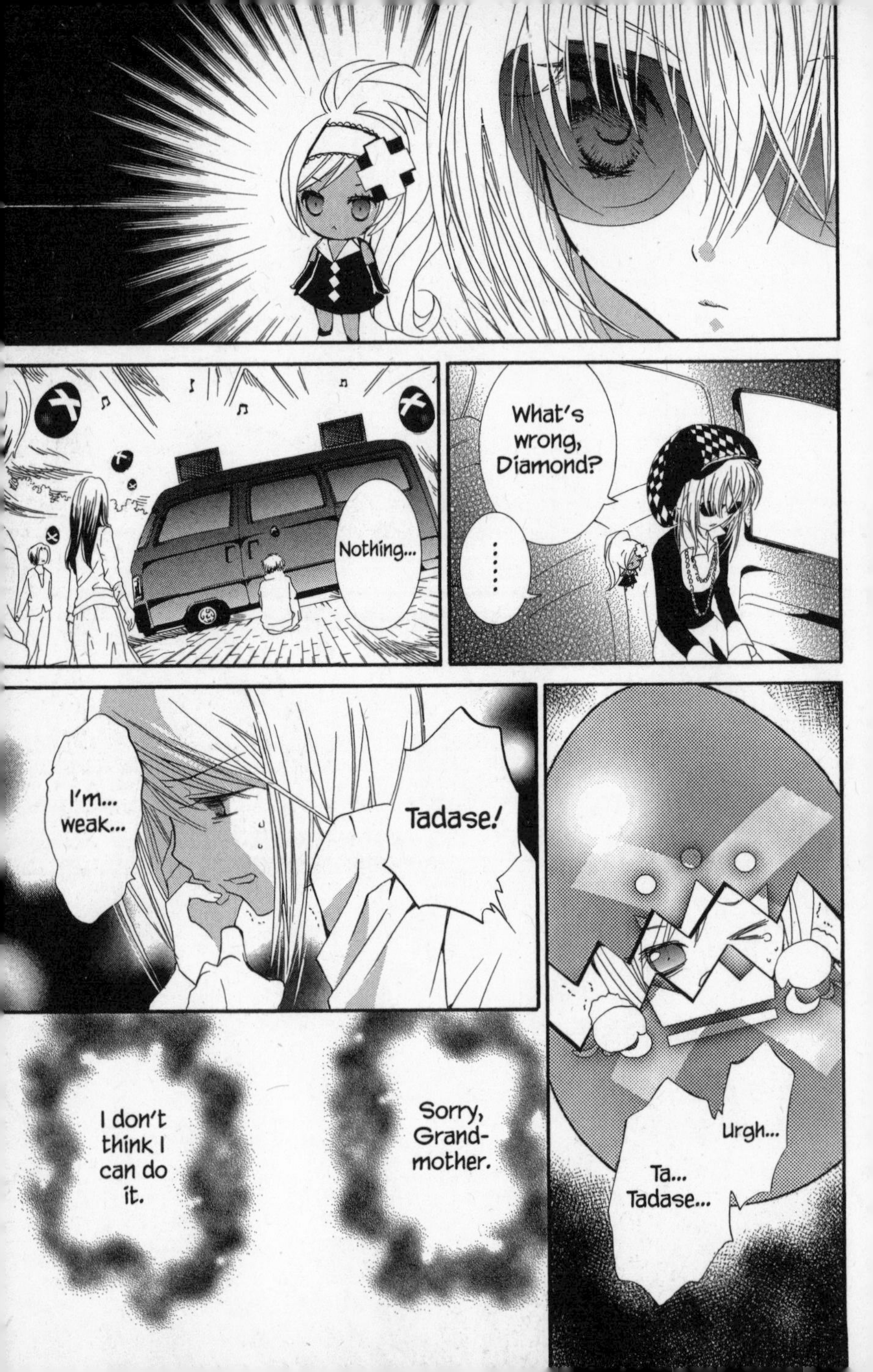
What's wrong, Diamond?
......
Nothing...
Urgh...
Ta... Tadase...
Tadase!
I'm... weak...
Sorry, Grand-mother.
I don't think I can do it.

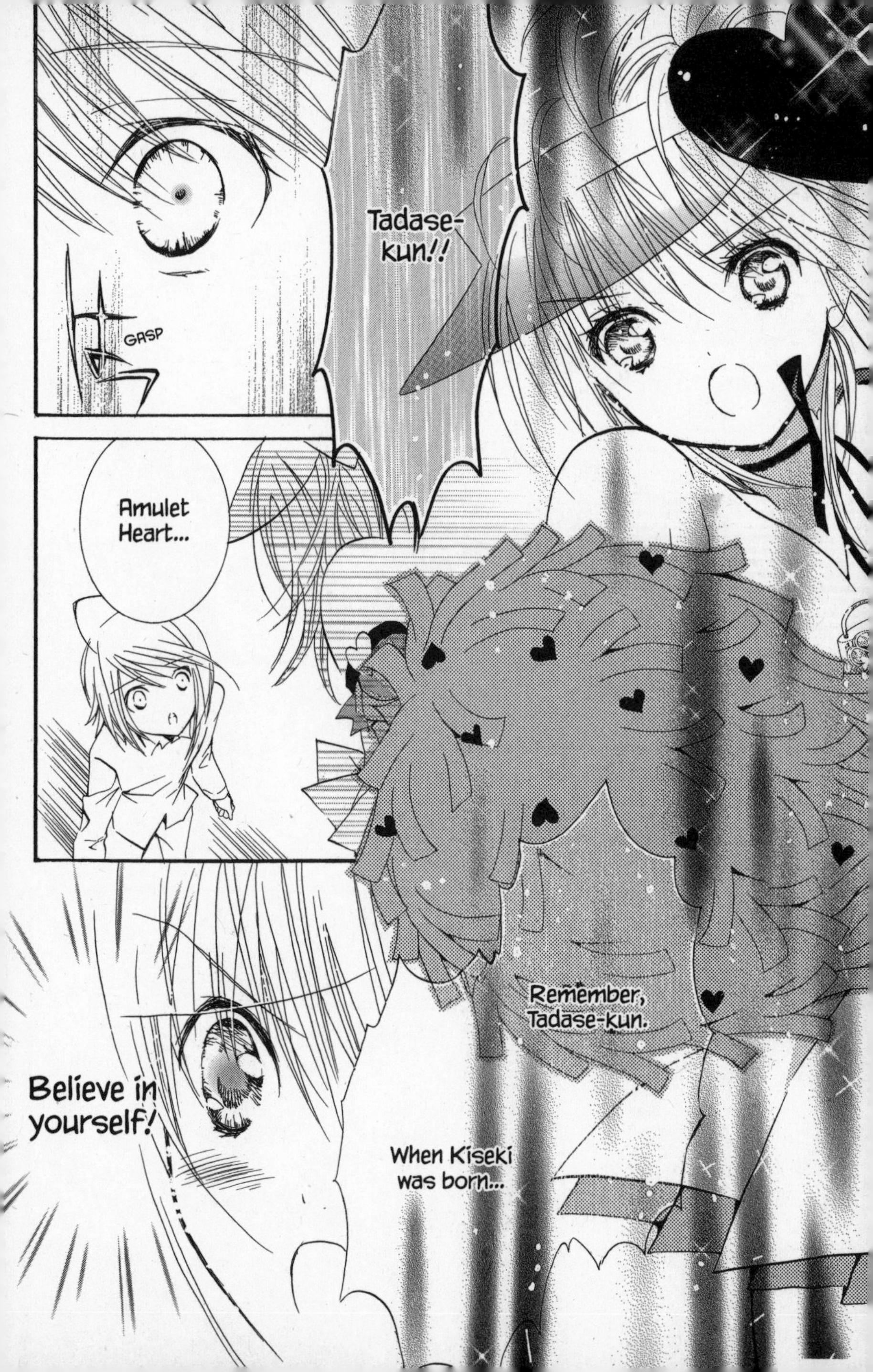
Tadase-kun!!
GASP
Amulet Heart...
Remember, Tadase-kun.
When Kiseki was born...
Believe in yourself!

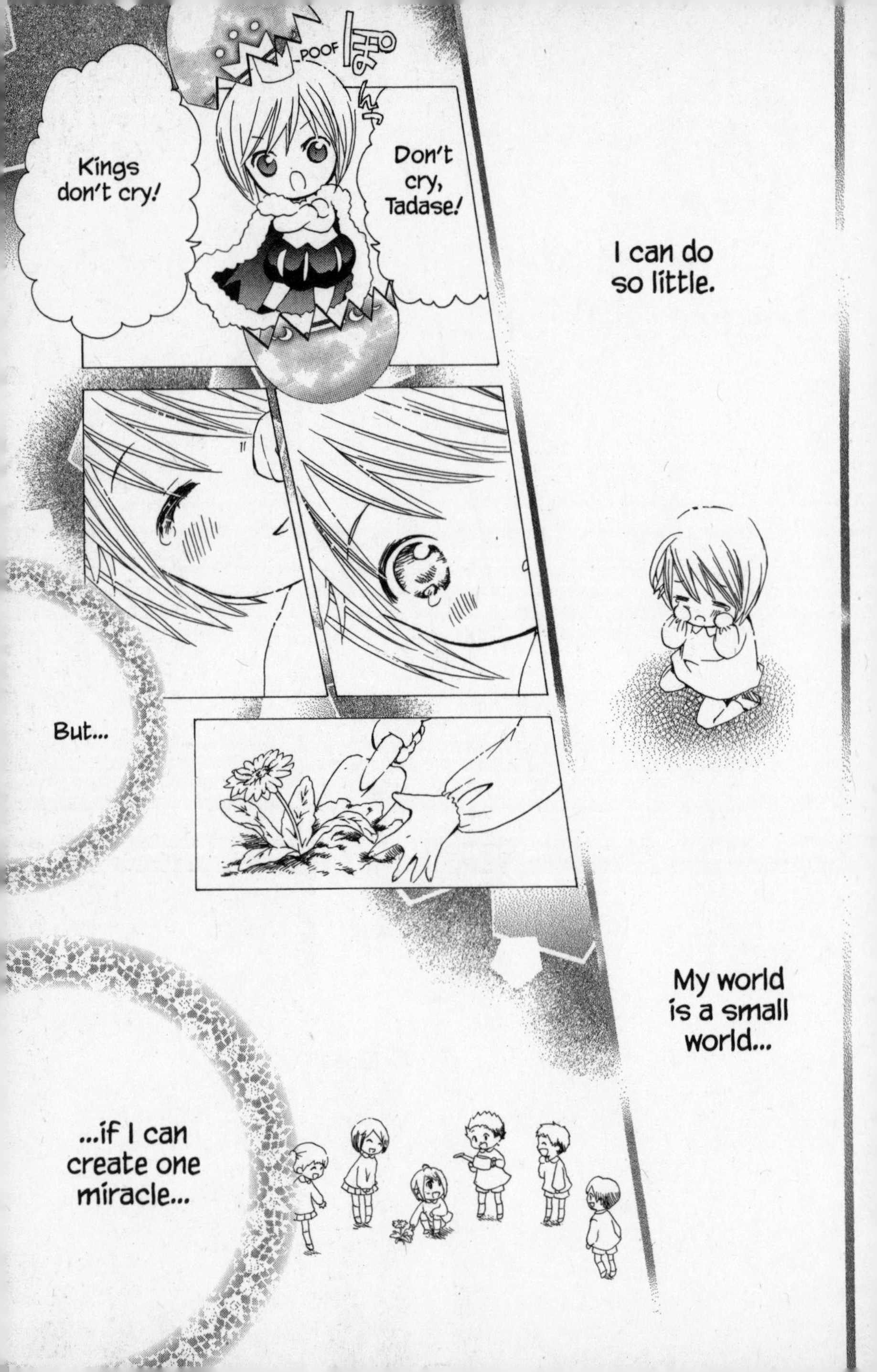
I can do so little.
My world is a small world...
POOF
ぽん
Don't cry, Tadase!
Kings don't cry!
But...
...if I can create one miracle...

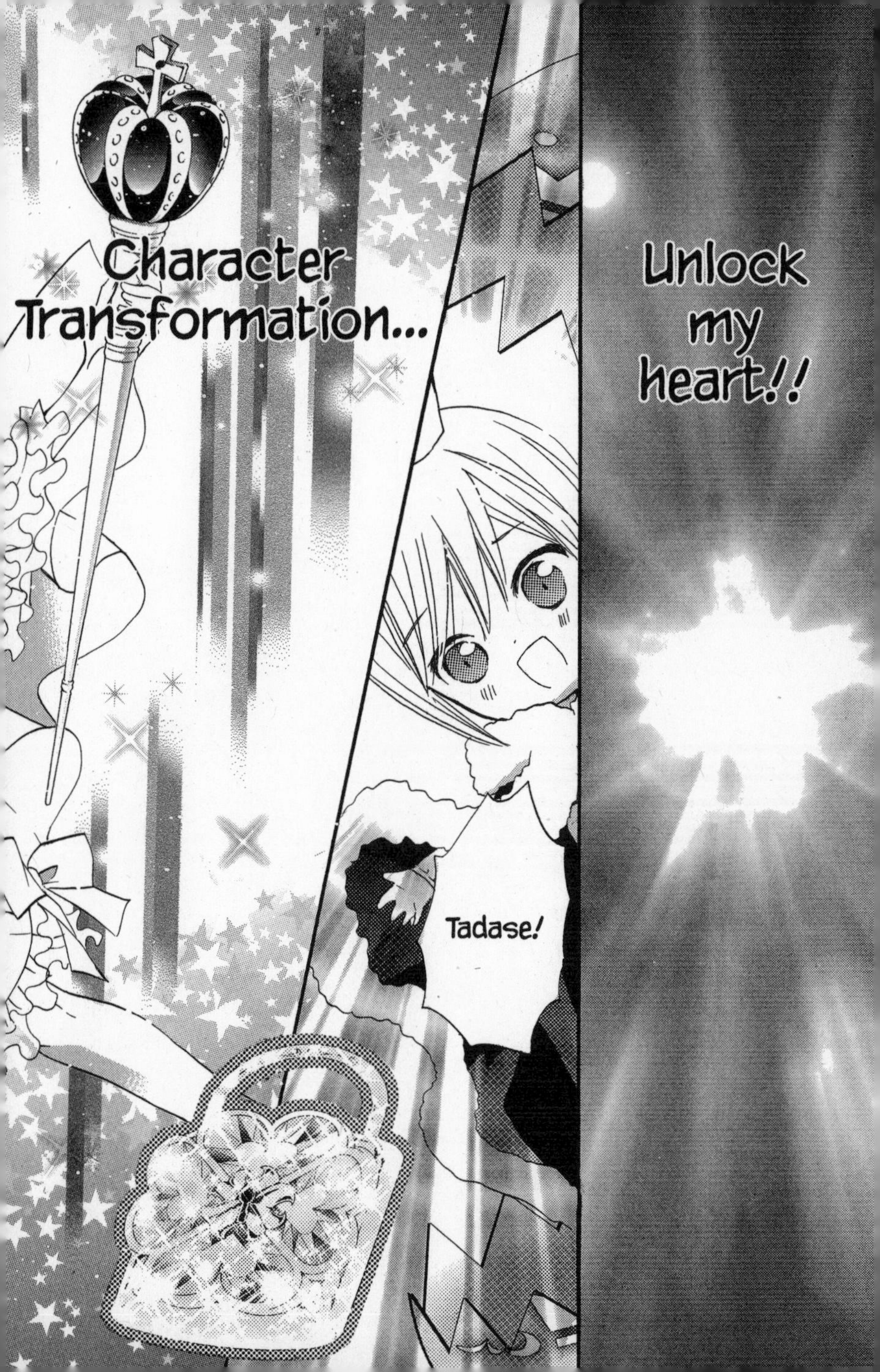
Unlock my heart!!
Tadase!
Character Transformation...

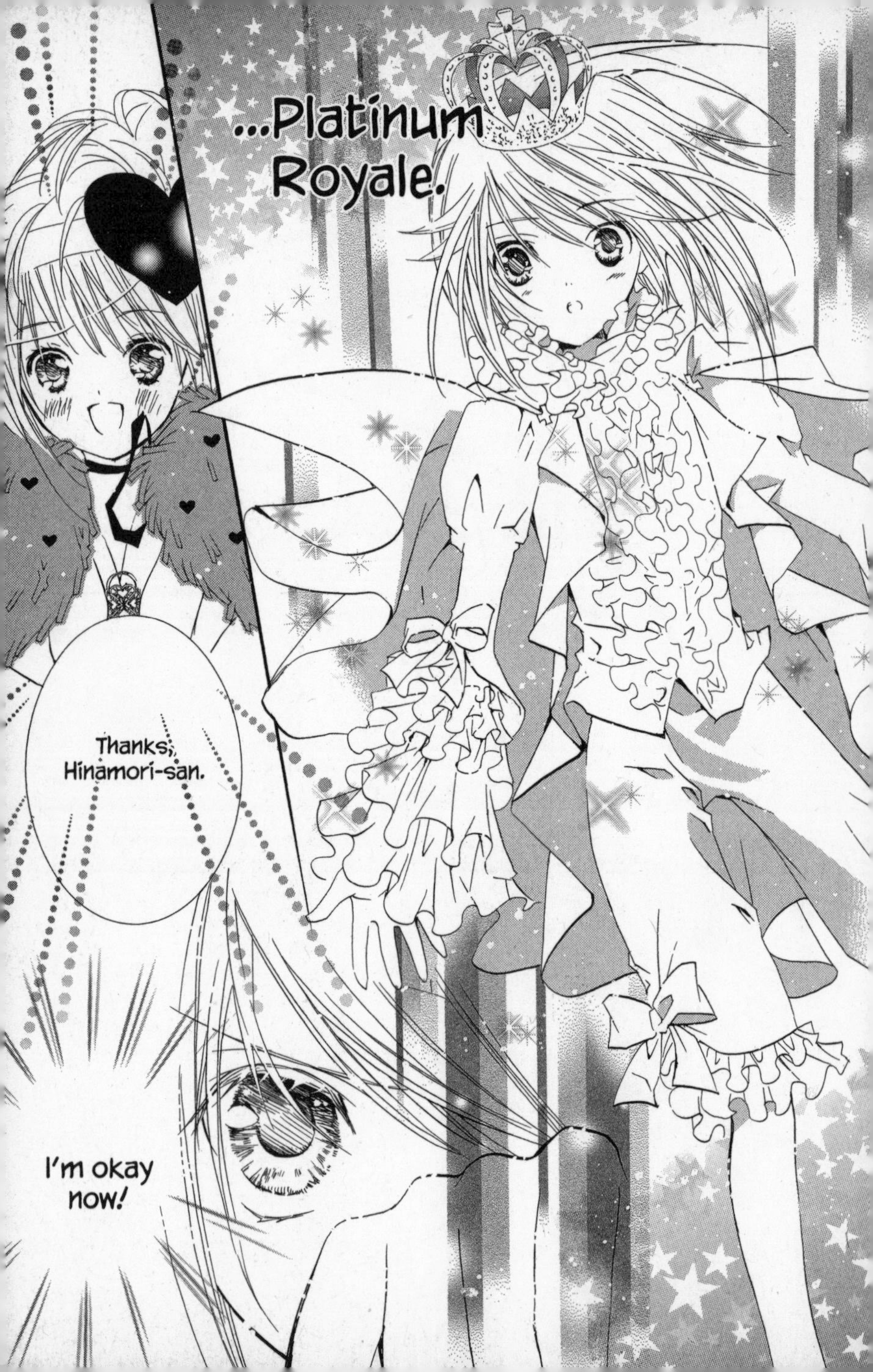
...Platinum Royale.
Thanks, Hinamori-san.
I'm okay now!

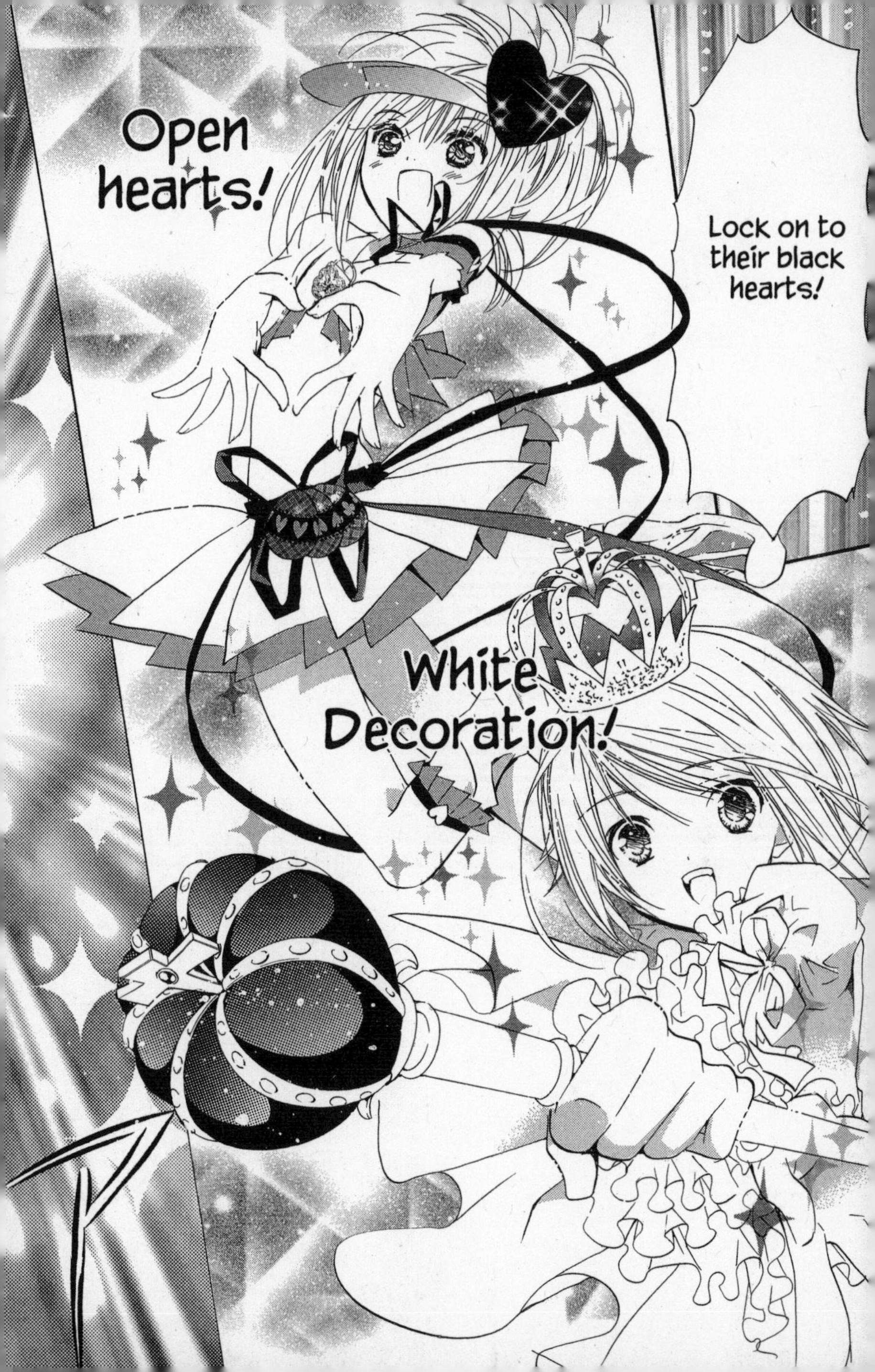
Lock on to their black hearts!
Open hearts!
White Decoration!

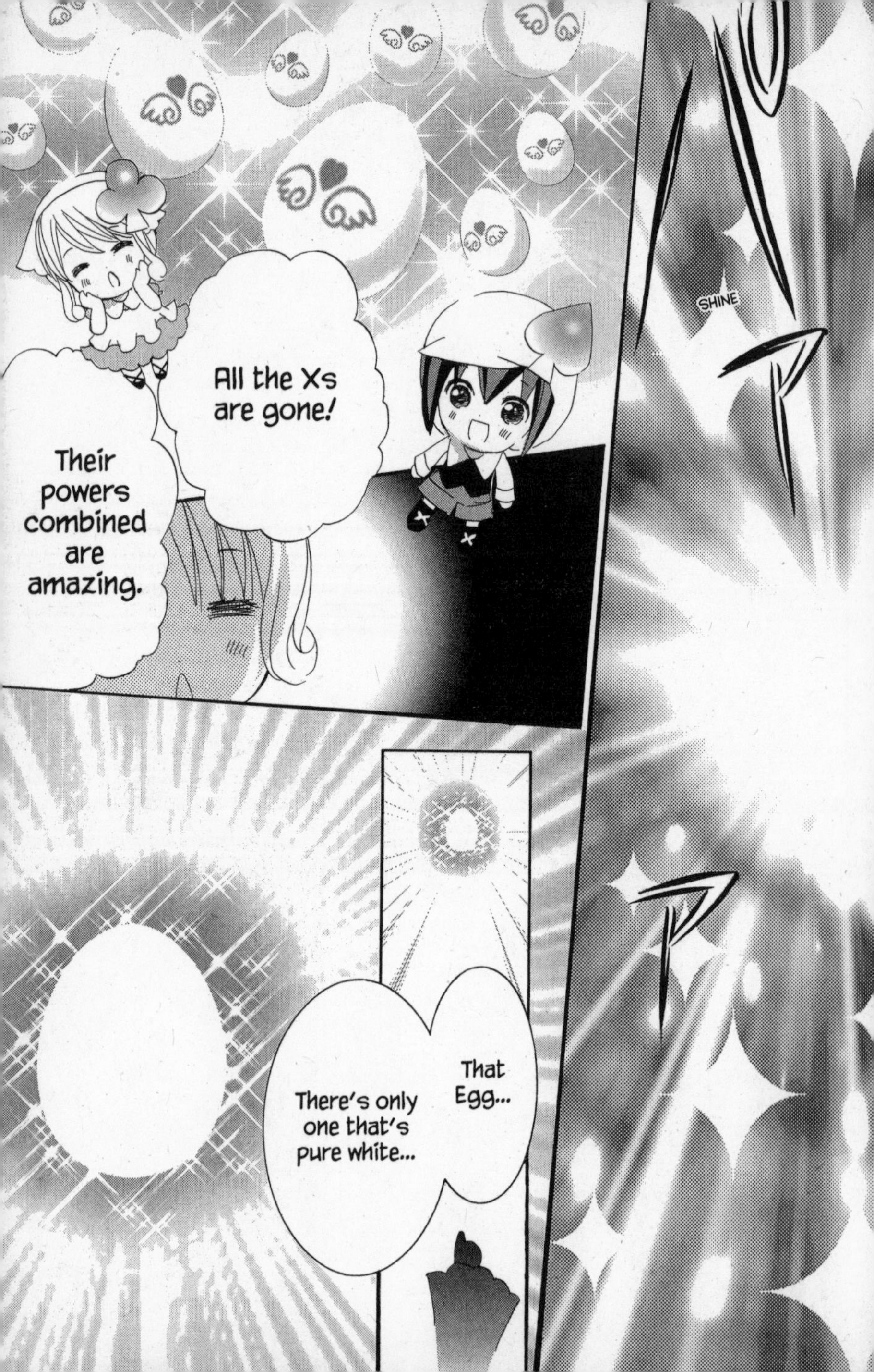
SHINE
All the Xs are gone!
Their powers combined are amazing.
That Egg...
There's only one that's pure white...

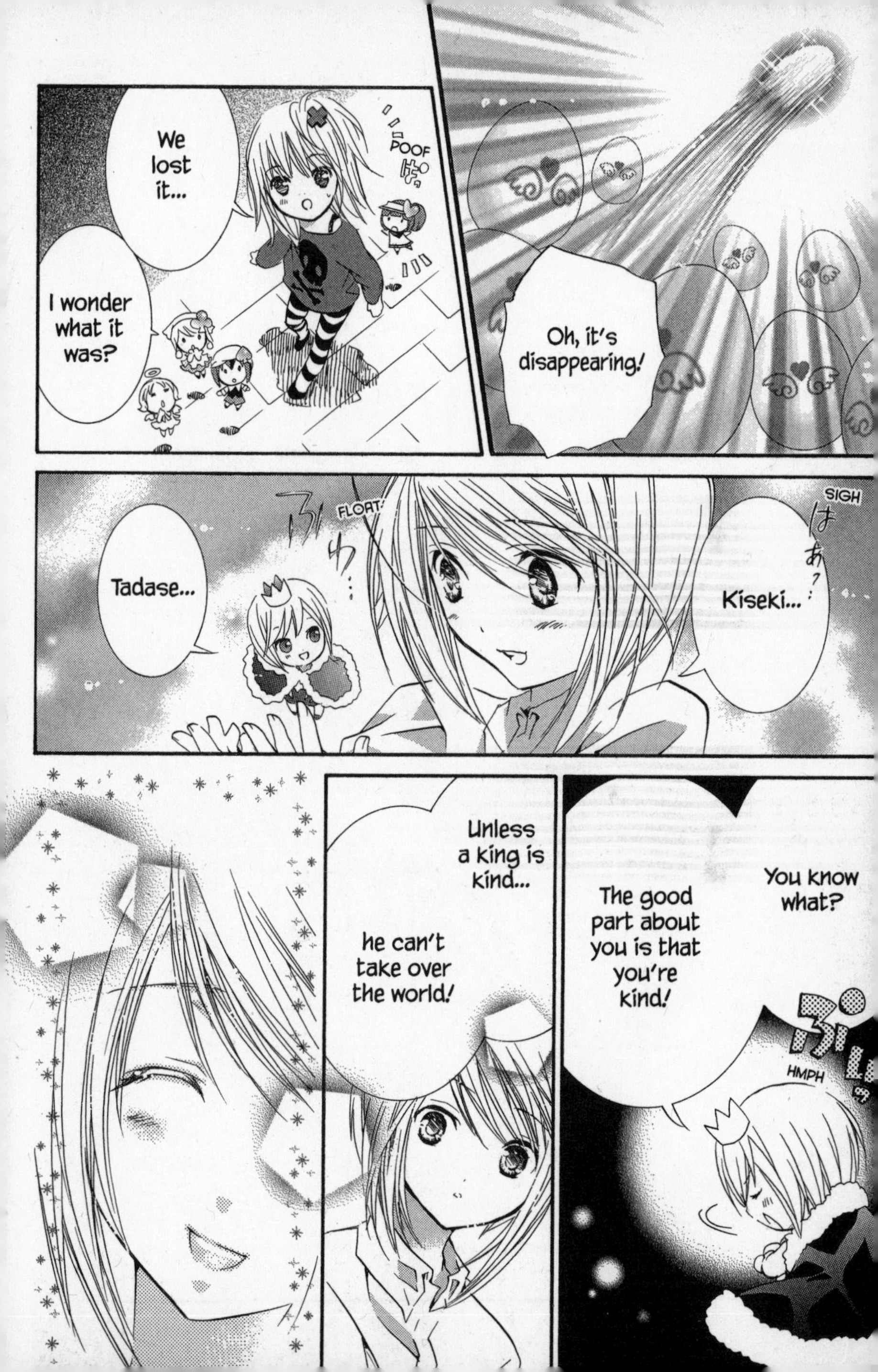
Oh, it's disappearing!
POOF
We lost it...
I wonder what it was?
SIGH
Kiseki...
FLOAT
Tadase...
You know what?
The good part about you is that you're kind!
HMPH
Unless a king is kind...
he can't take over the world!

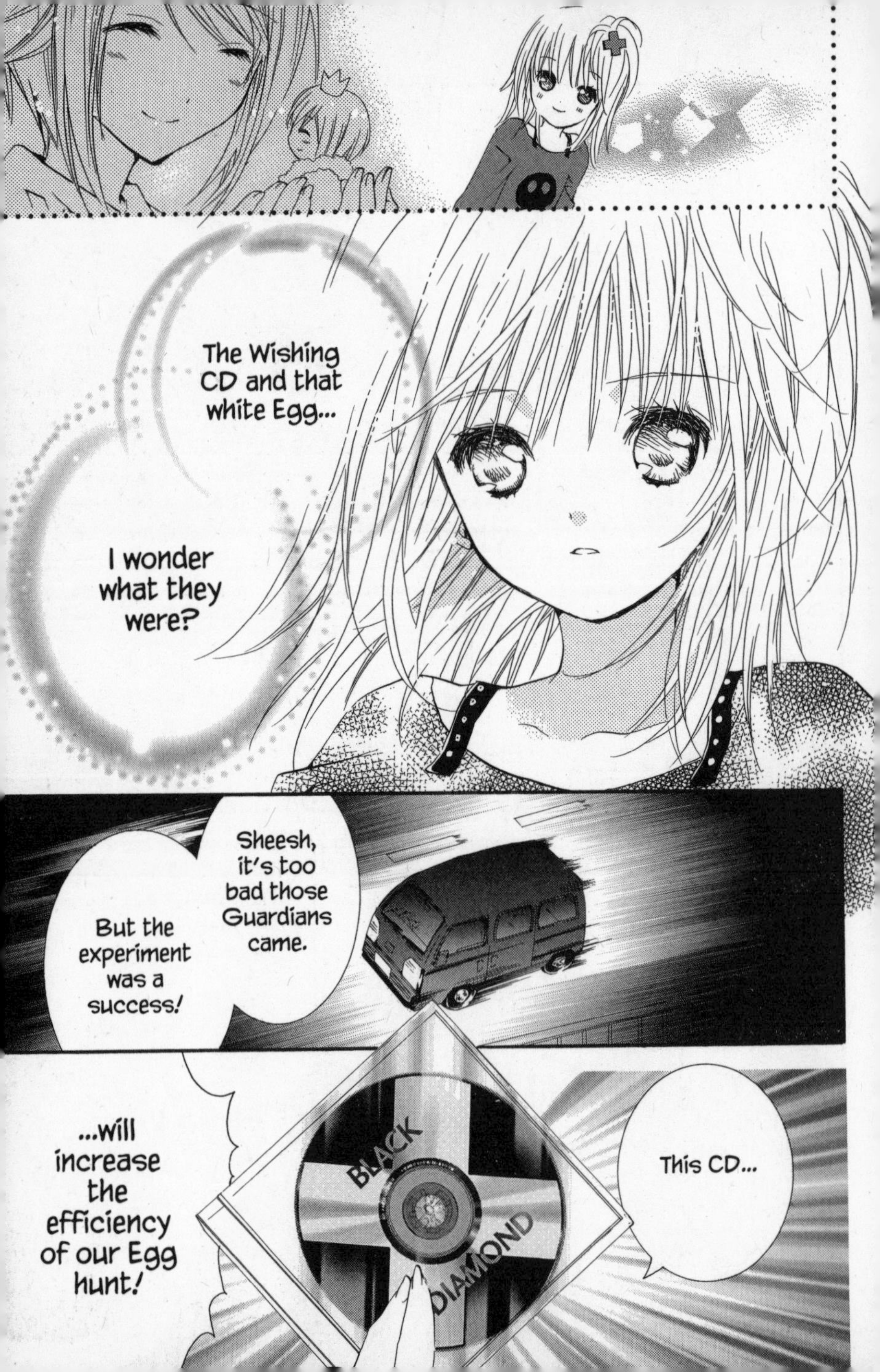
The Wishing CD and that white Egg...
I wonder what they were?
Sheesh, it's too bad those Guardians came.
But the experiment was a success!
This CD...
BLACK DIAMOND
...will increase the efficiency of our Egg hunt!

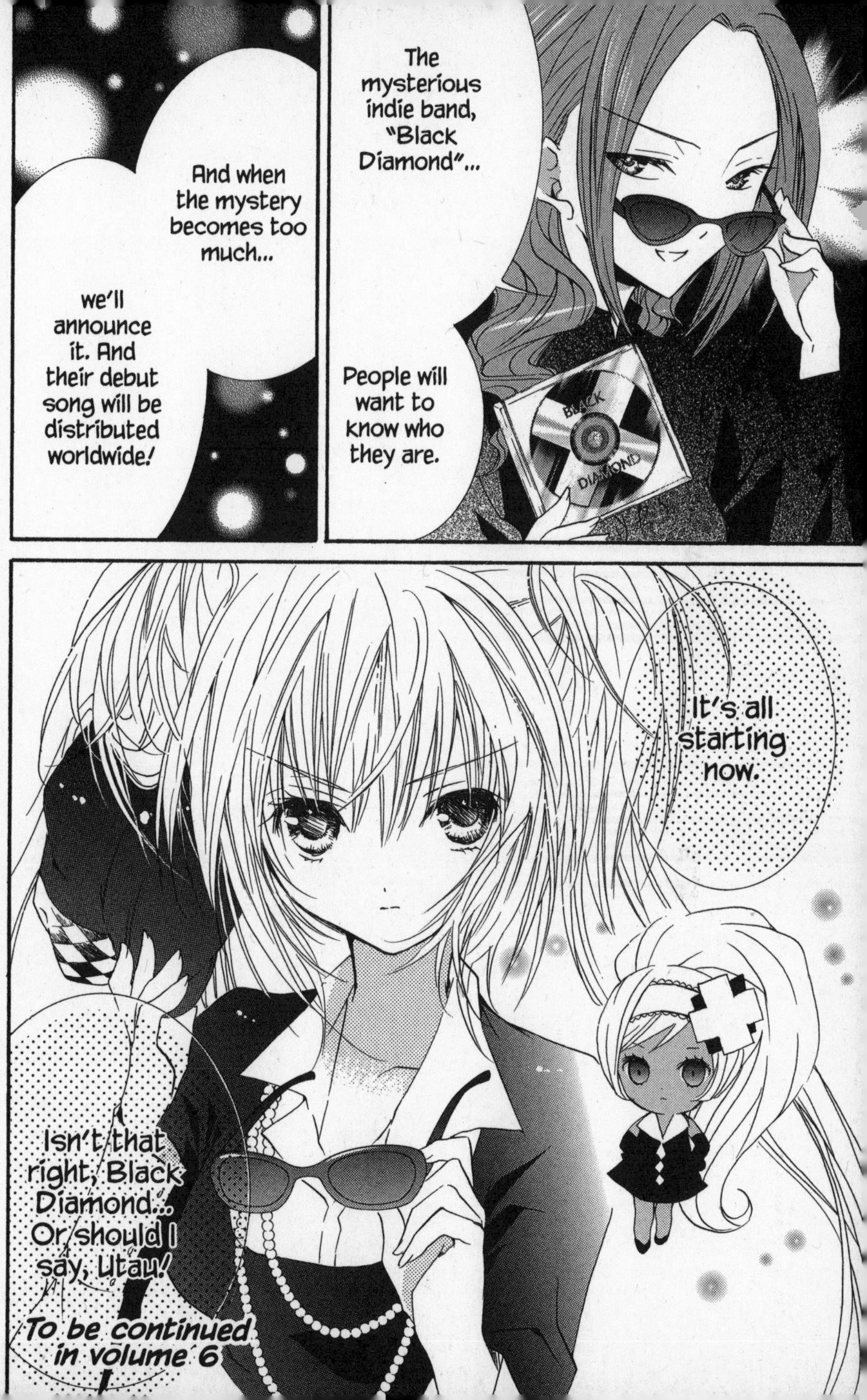
The mysterious indie band, "Black Diamond"...
People will want to know who they are.
BLACK DIAMOND
And when the mystery becomes too much...
we'll announce it. And their debut song will be distributed worldwide!
It's all starting now.
Isn't that right, Black Diamond... Or should I say, Utau!
To be continued in volume 6

Shugo
Chara!

About the Creators

PEACH-PIT:
Banri Sendo was born on June 7. Shibuko
Ebara was born on June 21. They are a
pair of Gemini manga artists who work
together. Sendo likes to eat sweets, and
Ebara likes to eat spicy stuff. Here's
something that happened recently: We
almost flushed our cell phones down the toilet...twice.

Translation Notes

Japanese is a tricky language for most Westerners, and translation is often more art than science. For your edification and reading pleasure, here are notes on some of the places where we could have gone in a different direction in our translation of the work, or where a Japanese cultural reference is used.

Mr. Class President, page 6

Yaya, and eventually everyone else, calls Kairi "Class President." This is not because he is the class president, but because he acts like one. Kairi will always respond, "Class President?"

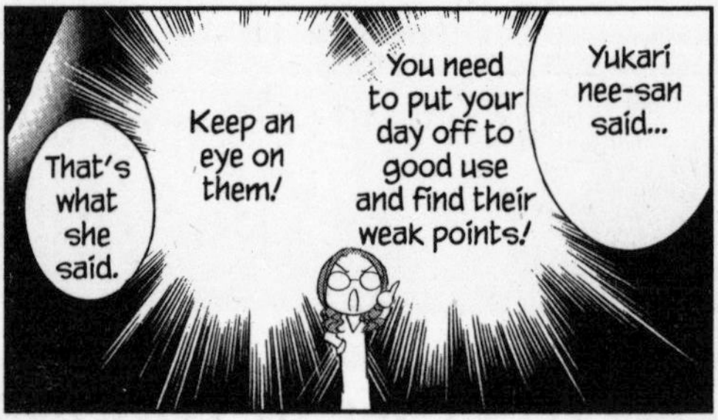

Yukari nee-san said...
You need to put your day off to good use and find their weak points!
Keep an eye on them!
That's what she said.

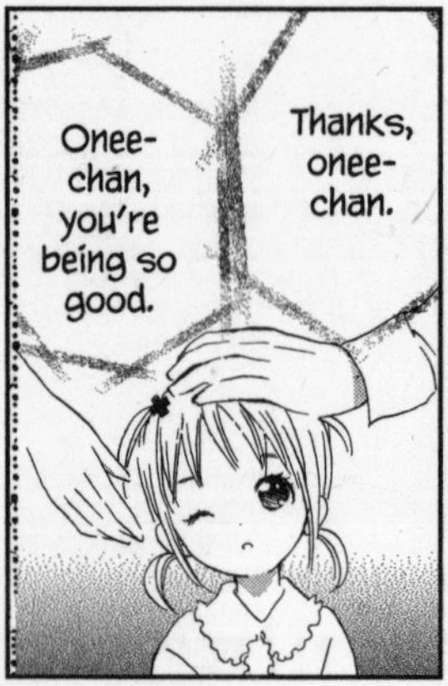

Thanks, onee-chan.
Onee-chan, you're being so good.

Onee-chan/nee-san, page 26 and page 87

Onee-chan and *nee-san* are two Japanese honorifics for a big sister.

Candies, page 43

Candies is a pop idol group that was popular in the 1970s in Japan. The three girls in the group were Ran Ito, Yoshiko Tanaka (known as Su), and Miki Fujimura. The group formed in 1973 and disbanded in 1977. They said that they wanted to "return to being normal girls," which is a phrase that is popular even today.

TOMARE!

[STOP!]

You're going the wrong way!

Manga is a completely different type of reading experience.

T… g,

That's right! Authentic manga is read the traditional Japanese way—from right to left. Exactly the *opposite* of how American books are read. It's easy to follow: Just go to the other end of the book, and read each page—and each panel—from right side to left side, starting at the top right. Now you're experiencing manga as it was meant to be!

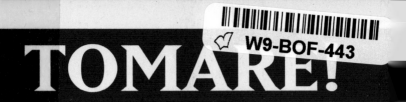